GUN LAW

GUN LAW

Fighting Britain's Deadliest Gangs: Inside an Elite Police Firearms Unit

Andy Hailwood

MILO BOOKS LTD

First published in hardback in October 2004 by Milo Books

This paperback edition published in May 2005

ISBN 1 903854 40 7

Typeset by Avon DataSet Ltd,
Bidford on Avon, Warwickshire, B50 4JH

Printed and bound in Great Britain by
Cox & Wyman, Reading

MILO BOOKS LTD
The Old Weighbridge
Station Road
Wrea Green
Lancs PR4 2PH
info@milobooks.com

Dedication

It took a long time and a lot of hard graft to arrive at the stage when I could actually state that I had written a book.

For making this possible, I want to thank my wife, Jan. Without her love, support and damned hard work, it could not have been done. She knows how much I love her and how much I appreciate her endeavours.

I would also like to thank Pete my publisher for his easy-going support and patience during this project.

My dedication goes to my mother, who unfortunately isn't here to witness my book. I know she would have been proud to read about her son and some of the episodes he was involved in.

Throughout this book I have outlined some negatives about the police service. However, there are plenty of positives. I am proud to have served as a police officer in the era that I did. I was also privileged to have served with the characters I mention and with others who unfortunately I don't (you know who you are). One or two names have necessarily been changed, for what I hope are obvious reasons.

Finally thanks to my loving family.

About the Author

Andy Hailwood served with Greater Manchester Police for almost twenty years until injuries suffered when he fell through a ceiling while searching for bank robbers forced his retirement. He now works in the private security industry and has protected celebrities, advised film companies and taught many organisations in personal safety.

Contents

Acronyms

ACC	Assistant Chief Constable
AFO	Authorised firearms officer
ARV	Armed response vehicle
ASU	Active service unit (of the IRA)
CTR	Close target reconnaissance
DA	Deliberate action (plan)
DCI	Detective Chief Inspector
DI	Detective Inspector
DPM	Disruptive pattern material (camouflage kit)
DS	Detective Sergeant
DSU	Dedicated surveillance unit
EOD	Explosive Ordnance Department
ETA	Estimated time of arrival
FAP	Final assault position
FUP	Form-up point
GMP	Greater Manchester Police
IA	Immediate action (plan)
IED	Improvised explosive device
JOP	Jump-off point
LUP	Lying-up point
MASTS	Mobile armed support to surveillance
MOE	Method of entry
NCO	Non-commissioned officer
NFT	Non-further training
NVC	Non-verbal communication
OP	Observation post
PACE	Police and Criminal Evidence Act
POE	Point of entry
PSU	Police support unit
RCS	Regional Crime Squad (now National Crime Squad)
RVP	Rendezvous point
SB	Special Branch
SCS	Serious Crime Squad
SIS	Secret Intelligence Service
SLP	Self-loading pistol
SLR	Self-loading rifle
SOP	Standard operating procedure
TAG	Tactical Aid Group
TASS	Police unit of advanced drivers trained in anti-ambush techniques
TP	Target premises

Prologue

At 04.30 on a dark and mild spring morning, I stood on a terraced street in Salford with ten other armed police officers, two covering the rear. I would be the second officer to enter a two-up-two-down terraced property in the hope of arresting an Irish gypsy believed to be in possession of a small handgun and wanted for murder: he had tortured an elderly man to death.

I was 23 years of age and my arsehole was tight enough to extract the tops of beer bottles. My stomach was in knots, but I was enjoying myself. Enjoying myself – should I even think that as a professional police officer? Through my earpiece I heard 'Strike! Strike! Strike!' This was the command to physically smash through the front door and for all teams to enter and arrest.

The strike is called three times in case it is missed over the communications network and an officer is unclear when to initiate action. The door of the property took the full force of a 14lb sledgehammer wielded by Billy 'Brass' Brains of the Tactical Aid Group. Billy made short work of the door, attacking the hinges and locks. His partner was on standby next to him carrying another sledgehammer in case Billy got tired or if it was a reinforced door. To Billy this would have been an insult, and in seconds myself and Jimmy had made an entry.

Jim located the stairs and was sprinting up them two at a time screaming, 'Armed police, armed police!' Adrenalin had kicked in and I was up Jim's backside, moving equally as fast. Jim had increased our field of vision by activating the Maglite mounted on his shotgun. He booted the first bedroom door he came across and immediately entered. I followed, conscious of keeping my distance. I had my pistol in my right hand, supported by my left and in the on-aim position.

Jim immediately made his way to a double bed in the middle of the room. I could hear booming around the rest of the property, 'Armed police, armed police!' and the heavy footsteps of officers running as they continued to storm in.

Jim had located a male occupant trying to hide amongst the mess of a bed I would normally call a duvet. Jim was screaming at him 'Armed police, show me your hands!' Everything seemed to slow down and my vision appeared to increase and focus as if I was looking through a telescope. If it was possible, the room seemed to have gone quiet, although I knew Jim was shouting. The man in the bed fitted the description of our target, but he wasn't showing hands, he was rummaging amongst the shit he slept in.

My mind had decided what he was doing. I had judged him and now I was going to sentence him. I took the first pressure up on the trigger of my revolver. I was clinically going to shoot this individual. I had decided he was looking for the small firearm which he had hidden down his Y-fronts. His hands seemed to be moving in the direction of his bollocks.

I increased the pressure on the trigger and had acquired a sight picture, when my bubble burst. Jim pulled away the bedclothes to reveal a naked man pissing himself with fright.

'Handcuff him,' said Jim.

CHAPTER ONE

Armed and Dangerous

I knew something was happening. I think we all have an uncanny knack of sensing a change in surroundings. It was 15.00 on a Friday and my team had just come on duty. Slates, the team two sergeant, and one of his lads were in the crew room and had a knowing air about them. Team two were a good team, better than others but no way near as good as us. To be fair they had some really skilled and experienced lads, some of them my good friends.

Slates grabbed me and Mick, my sergeant. 'Listen in, the Serious Crime Squad have passed on the following job. They have information that a proactive crew from Salford are going to commit a robbery next week.'

'Do we know where?' I asked.

'Possibly, but we've been given the location of a secure lockup in Irlam where they keep shotguns, ammunition and stolen vehicles.'

'What's required from us?' asked Mick.

'The squad want to plan for an arrest at the lockup.'

'Who is the team we are after?'

Slates smiled. 'Parvo Corkovic and crew.'

He had our undivided attention. Corkovic, a notorious Salford villain of Croatian descent, was wanted for a series of armed robberies across Manchester and Lancashire: in Salford, Eccles, Prestwich, Swinton and Chorley. He and his team – Lee Taberer, Anthony Erdman and James Neales – had struck at banks, casinos, B&Q stores, DIY centres and a Safeway supermarket. It was believed they had already accrued around £275,000. Corkovic hadn't been long out of prison for similar offences and had taken up where he had left off with considerable success.

Some weeks earlier I had been over at the Crime Squad's office to view a videotape from a bank's CCTV system. It showed a violent armed robbery by Corkovic's team. I was asked to identify one of the weapons being used by the gang, and was both dismayed and intrigued to see a Kalashnikov AK47 assault rifle. The AK47 is frightening to face. It fires 7.62mm calibre ammunition and this will piss through conventional police ballistic protection. We'd heard rumours that criminals had access to AK47s but although we had seen some evidence in Moss Side, we had not actually come across one until now.

Slates went on to say that Corkovic had rented a lockup garage inside a secure compound in Irlam. Inside the premises was a stolen Land Rover and the gang had constructed a homemade battering ram which they were preparing to attach to the front of it. They could then run this through the walls of their target premises. They also kept several shotguns and ammunition. The Crime Squad required options to arrest Corkovic and crew. Slates and his team were pissed off because they had to hand the job over, but it was their weekend off and we were the on-duty team.

It became obvious from the start that this wouldn't be a normal job. The information appeared good and the SCS wanted to move forward. This suited my team, as we were more proactive than the rest. A recce of the lockup was required, and liaison with the Serious Crime Squad established. However, the SCS unit informed us that the premises in Irlam would be difficult to recce. The lockup was situated in a secure compound in the middle of four other premises and surrounded by similar structures. They were single-storey, and approximately 20 feet wide by 60 feet long. The compound was surrounded by eight foot high wire fencing. Access was controlled by a security barrier and gates manned by a guard 24 hours a day.

The SCS believed that other premises owners and the security guard were less than sympathetic towards the police and might inform Corkovic and his gang if the 'filth' were seen snooping about. It was even suspected that Corkovic was paying some of them for any information about police activity – not an unusual occurrence for a career criminal.

A recce of a premises is essential if the arrest is planned for there. While conducting a recce, you are looking for lay-up points, assault positions, form-up points, rendezvous points, routes in and out, timings, cut-offs, type of premises, alarms, dogs, entry points, structural make up of windows, walls, doors and to confirm it is the right premises. This is the early stage of a job but the adrenalin starts to move. I decided to recce as soon as the light dropped.

I grabbed Bob and told him what was happening and to get into civvies. It is standard procedure to recce in pairs and Bob was my partner. He had recently joined the department, to some surprise, as he had only recently passed a basic firearms course. Most of us were initially sceptical of his appointment but he became an excellent operator and was later part of the hostage rescue team. The last I heard he was a detective sergeant and a credit to the service.

We drove out to Irlam and for the next few hours walked, sneaked and even sprinted difficult routes leading to the unit. Obviously we couldn't afford to compromise the operation and had a suitable cover story ready if questioned by suspicious members of the public. I returned to the office with many unanswered questions in my head, but I was positive we could do the job. I needed to speak to the SCS liaison. Frustratingly the weekend passed without further event but on Monday, DCI Green summoned Mick and me to Longsight Police Station.

Green was old school, a good detective and an excellent boss.

Many CID officers are loath to supply information and guard it jealously, often for the wrong reasons. However, Green always gave plenty of relevant and vital information and I knew why – he trusted me. I had worked for him on many operations and achieved the right results. Mr Green supplied us with the full facts. Corkovic was subject to intense surveillance, and intelligence indicated his team were planning an armed robbery at an Aldi supermarket somewhere in Manchester. Prior to the robbery, all the team would go to the lockup to equip themselves. It was believed they would strike in seven days' time. We had a week to plan. We knew all the gang would gather at the lockup. This would be the ideal time to arrest them. However, this was an extremely dangerous and violent team and we would have to match their mindset – in a professional sense, of course.

It was time to bring in my team, sit around the table, throw out the information and listen to suggestions, valid and ridiculous, for an operational plan. In the SAS, this is known as a Chinese parliament. It allows team members to take ownership of a plan and from the beginning feel valued (and believe me some egos needed it). Because I had inherited the job, it became mine to lead and plan.

I listened to the lads' opinions, then offered mine. We could put the full robbery team together at the target premises. A conventional containment and callout would be useless because of our lack of protection against the AK47. I suggested a full-scale assault using distraction munitions – stun grenades – and CS gas fired in 12-gauge ferrets from shotguns. A couple of the team opposed this option (wankers) but the majority supported it. All we had to do now was convince an assistant chief constable.

Malcolm George was the duty ACC and not the easiest character to deal with. This was Mick's job. Surprisingly, he got George to approve the operation. We were moving forward.

I needed another recce of the target premises and decided to do it in the early hours. I approached along a railway line, up an embankment and through some undergrowth. This led me to the wire fence, where I cut an entry. I was now at the crucial point of the recce. I had to cross 400 yards of open ground to get onto the building without being seen. My approach was from five o'clock black/red to one o'clock white/red. I managed to recce all aspects; as I've already mentioned, this is a close target reconnaissance (CTR).

There were two entry points and they were located on the white aspect: a steel shutter, approximately ten foot wide and eight foot high, and a conventional door that was controlled by a steel Judas gate. That was problem one. Problem two was that we knew Corkovic and crew would be at the lockup so we needed a safe approach. Surprise was crucial and, as I have already mentioned, one approach was controlled by security procedures, the other was across 400 yards of open ground. We needed to be on top of the team for a successful arrest.

By now I was starting to hear the usual whispers from several members of our unit and some of the training team that the job was bound to fail due to its gung ho nature. I didn't give my critics a moment's consideration. They were in the unit for all the wrong reasons: some were bone idle and others useless. As long as I was operational, keen, motivated and fit, they weren't fit to lace my boots.

Then came the answer to my problems. The SCS had managed to rent premises directly attached to the target lockup. This was excellent news. They were conducting a covert operation from that premises. Therefore people and vehicles could move freely through the security control without raising suspicion. I was allowed to recce the premises and could now start to formulate a deliberate action plan.

I needed another point of entry. I couldn't rely on the Judas gate being left open when the assault went in. I brought one of my team, Macky, to the new premises, which was now designated the holding area. Macky is a great character and a good friend.

Before joining the police he had been a builder, so I asked him to make two apertures in the dividing wall to allow access for team members. He started to probe and fuck about until he told me the dividing wall was two breeze-blocks' width from ground level to a height of four foot. Above the four-foot level it was single width. With the use of a cutting tool, he would be able to give me two apertures above the double layer, allowing for access using ladders. He would have to remove a layer of breeze block approximately seven by seven foot and then, at the time of the assault, smash through these weakened apertures using sledge hammers.

Macky guaranteed me 100 per cent access. He knew this was his job and he could not afford to cock up. Macky was a great pisstaker and knew that if he failed his life would be made unbearable. The work to weaken the breeze block would have to take place in the middle of the night when noise could not be detected. Mr Glenn OK'd this but made it quite clear that Corkovic and crew must not be suspicious; there must be no debris or dust remaining.

By now fibre-optic cameras had been inserted in the lockup and we were getting up-to-date information on the team. Their activity had increased and they were visiting the lockup regularly. We could see the Land Rover and battering ram but we did not know where the guns were. They were also bringing in large white plastic bags filled with something, but we didn't know what.

Each firearms team consisted of ten men. It was obvious ten was not enough for this job and I requested another team. I wanted team two: they were fit, hard lads, several of them rugby players and physical training instructors. They were good operators and I could trust them totally. They also took training seriously and tried to progress tactics and not sit on their arses in the crew room waiting for the end of duty.

The job was coming together. I had an assault team (who still needed briefing) but I still needed a cut-off team in case any of Corkovic's lot escaped the initial assault, either on foot or by vehicle. I would have the railway line covered with two teams of two plus a dog-handler. I requested more officers for a vehicle strike option to be deployed covertly away from the arrest scene in case any of the gang escaped in a car. This was refused because of cost – quite simply, senior management were not prepared to pay the overtime. This turned out to be an extremely poor decision, but experience had taught me to expect crap like that. At times you felt you had two adversaries: the criminal himself and certain senior managers, some of whom would run a mile at the sight of an angry man. Of course, these setbacks would never deter me; I'd just have to plan better.

I needed to infiltrate 20 men into the holding area without being seen and cater for the steel shutters of the target premises. What if our initial assault went wrong and Corkovic's crew got the Land Rover started and battered their way to freedom? Joe, one of my team and a great friend, solved the shutter problem. He decided to take one of our armoured Land Rovers to a friend who owned a garage. His friend did a fantastic job in changing the liveried spec of the Land Rover and converting it to look like a breakdown vehicle. Joe showed balls and initiative; if he had asked permission, we would be still waiting now. We moved our new breakdown vehicle into the holding area. At the strike, officers would drive the armoured Land Rover from the holding area and block the steel shutters of the target premises. We also hired a large box van to move the assault team into the holding area undetected.

The following week came and the intelligence looked good. Corkovic was still planning the supermarket robbery and I was confident all our options were covered. Macky had completed his entry points over two nights, emerging like a snowman each time. On the Tuesday evening the job was confirmed. I would be briefing a team of 25 firearms officers at 05.00 on Wednesday.

At 04.00 the lads came on duty at the armoury. There was a definite feelgood factor about this job. Twenty-five of the best lads from the department were there (well, almost). At this stage of a job there is a great deal of activity. Details are important. Coveralls are worn with overt body armour, loose bits are taped down, anything that can catch or make a noise is covered. Respirators are cleaned and filters checked. Jokers had a habit of putting cling film over your filter and if you didn't notice, you really would be breathing through your arse. Weapons, munitions, ladders, vehicles, MOE kit and trauma care packages are all prepared.

At 05.00 we made our way to the crew room for the briefing. Not only the firearms team attend these briefings, but also senior officers, CID members, the dog section, traffic, the host division and sometimes ambulance crews. The briefing officer must show no sign of nerves. You must believe in your plan and transmit confidence to the team. Failure is not an option. Each officer must believe his role is crucial to the success of the operation. Therefore it is your duty to ensure that when you brief, your psychological input will create the best team ever. I briefed confidentially and according to the IIMAC. Finally there was a radio check.

I commenced phase one – deploy. Assault and cut-off teams went to FUPs and holding areas. The CID were already manning static observation posts and the surveillance team were plotting up. The drive to Irlam in the back of the rented van took 15 minutes. This is a time when individuals act differently. Some are quiet and reflective, some chat and take the piss, others even sleep. Macky was great for taking the piss and it was usually him and Foz bickering. On this day Macky decided to bait Boothy, a giant from the TAG. Boothy had been detailed MOE duties: he was responsible for smashing through one of the weakened apertures that Macky had created.

'You may be strong but I'm like a cat,' goaded Macky.

'What the fuck are you on about?' asked Boothy, with contempt.

'I will put my window in quicker than you.' Macky was responsible for the second aperture.

Most of the lads were competitive and were soon weighing the pros and cons of Macky's challenge. Macky was the type of person you needed on a team; he was rarely down, always looking for an opportunity to take the piss and had no problems having the piss taken out of him.

'Not a chance, you fucking weed,' said Boothy. The challenge was on.

On arrival at the rented lockup the van drove into the holding area and the steel shutters closed. Our armoured breakdown vehicle was already in position. The lads debussed and made their way to a separate room and laid out their kit in team formation. It was time for rehearsals.

Inside the holding area I had chalked out the approximate interior of the stronghold next door. For the next three hours we rehearsed. Everything was done slowly and deliberately, from placing ladders into position to going through the motions of sledging the walls, to delivering stuns and CS gas.

The plan would go as follows: once Corkovic and crew were on plot and in the stronghold, the strike would be called over the air. Ten of the team would deploy out of the unit and assault from the white (front) aspect of the stronghold to black (back). From intelligence collated, we knew that when the gang were inside the stronghold they kept the Judas gate open. Ten of the team were to enter through the Judas gate. They were all numbered. Officers two and four would deploy multi-burst stun grenades and 14 bangs, 180 decibels loud, would be emitted, a bit like a machine gun. These were to be thrown to the green aspect (left) of the stronghold. Officers one to six would pair up and search to clear any contacts, who would be dealt with quickly and aggressively. Officers seven to ten would be responsible for securing the prisoners and extracting them from a CS environment.

As the assault team deployed, ladders would be placed onto the apertures created by Macky. The cover team would smash through and either prepare to assault (if the initial assault team fucked up) or deliver CS into the stronghold by firing ferrets from shotguns. Other members of the team would deploy along the railway and prepare cut-offs (seal escape routes) with the aid of more than capable dog-handlers. Two of the arrest team would jump into the armoured Land Rover and drive it to block the steel shutters of the stronghold, preventing the criminals from using their own Land Rover as an escape tool. Two other officers would drive the rental van towards the security barriers in the compound to prevent the team escaping in vehicles.

These rehearsals took most of the morning, longer than I had anticipated and something I should have planned for. We had some minor hiccups. Mick suggested throwing the stuns elsewhere rather than the green aspect. At this stage, my patience was wearing thin.

'Fucking hell Mick, if you throw them anywhere but green, I will personally shoot you,' I snapped.

Mick looked at me and replied, 'Let me remind you, I'm your sergeant. These are not Mars Bars on my arms.' He indicated where his chevrons would have been had he been wearing uniform.

Foz heard what was going on. 'Shit Mick, listen in. I don't want Andy shooting you, just throw the grenades where he said.' Foz was Mick's partner for the entry phase.

It's good to let off steam at times and humour is an ever-present tool for dealing with niggly problems. It was all tongue-in-cheek. Mick and I had a long history and had known each other since we were 16. I think he is at present serving in Kosovo as a UN inspector. He was a great supervisor but God help the United Nations.

At 14.00 the stand-down came. Corkovic had called off the robbery but rescheduled it for the following day. Generally when this happens the team becomes disheartened and lethargy creeps in. However, with this job we just knew it was going to happen, the intelligence was bang on and Mr Glenn was keeping us informed with the relevant updates. We were told to parade for duty the following morning.

At 04.00 the lads came on duty and again commenced kit and weapon preparation. At 05.00 I again briefed the team and went over what we had learned at rehearsals. The team then deployed to the holding area and the cut-offs to the LUPs. At 06.15 I received my first radio message, confirming cut-offs were at LUPs, and then established comms with the command OP. I was informed that Corkovic and team were already on the road in two vehicles. Rehearsals commenced and within half an hour I was satisfied that we were ready.

All the assault and cover teams were dressed in navy blue, fireproof, ripstop coveralls, overt body armour with ceramic plates, high-leg leather boots of their choice, gloves, hoods and respirators. The weaponry consisted of CS ferrets, multi-stun grenades, H&K assault carbines, Beretta 92P SLPs, Remington Wingmaster pump shotguns and ballistic nylon three-foot-long staves. This kit is essential, and the psychological effect it has is fantastic.

During this short period, Corkovic was seen to meet up with another known armed robbery team of four Salford lads. The meeting occurred at the rear of a barber's car park in Eccles. It was unclear what it was about but the DSU recognised some of the new crew as associates of Corkovic. At first they assumed that this team was going to join in with the rest of Corkovic's and that they were frantically modifying tactics. Fortunately the other team moved off in the opposite direction of our target team. You could possibly say it's all in a day's work for professional criminals to meet up and discuss the latest in armed robberies.

The DSU were relaying regular updates on Corkovic's progress and their direction of travel was toward us. I put the team on Condition Amber. At this point a final weapon and kit check took place. My thought process at this stage is, stay calm – don't fuck up – do what you have rehearsed. Your body starts to go through a chemical change. This is natural and, once harnessed, can assist you positively. I have seen some lads let it get the better of them and run around on a job like headless chickens with little or no recollection of what they have been involved in. I watched the team and knew they would all be going through the same or a similar mental process. The atmosphere is electric, and this is just one of many phases you can experience when the operation is going to happen.

The next radio message I heard was confirmation that static OPs had picked up two vehicles, a light blue Ford Escort with two white males on board (confirmed targets) and a red Volvo estate with two white males on board (confirmed targets), heading towards the stronghold. I placed the team on Condition Red and moved to final assault positions and waited for radio responses. The lads made their way to vehicles, hands on ignition keys, ladders picked up and held ready to run into position, weapons shoulder mounted, fingers in the D-rings on stun grenades.

The OPs were frantically calling in updates:

'Targets on plot, heading for stronghold.'

'Vehicles held, three out on foot towards stronghold.'

'Alpha [Corkovic] still in vehicle approximately twenty metres from stronghold.'

'Bravo, Charlie, Delta into stronghold. Alpha no change.'

We were completely blind to what was occurring and could only build a picture through the comms. Fortunately our SCS liaison inside the holding area picked up eyeball with the use of an installed covert camera and started to feed us up-to-date information. Then for no apparent reason he shouted 'Strike!

Strike! Strike!' over the air while Corkovic was still in his vehicle.

Once the strike command is called, there is no going back. I looked at him and was about to argue about his over-zealous call. Then I thought, fuck it, and took my place as number one in the assault team.

One of the SCS liaison team placed Wagner's 'Ride of the Valkyries' on a PA system and started to boom it all over the holding area, just like the helicopter assault in the film *Apocalypse Now*. The cover team's ladder men ran the fully prepared double span assault ladders into place above Macky's prepared apertures. The MOE men, Macky and Boothy, sprinted up the ladders and started to smash the weakened breeze block with tools and sledgehammers. I'm not sure who won the challenge but I would have put money on Boothy. By the side of the MOE men, two officers took up position ready to deliver CS ferret from shotguns.

Taberer, Erdman and Neale had entered the stronghold and were putting together a happy bag. They were putting three shotguns, rubber masks, tape, coshes, and radio scanners into a holdall, obviously for use in armed crime. All three were not particularly well-built lads, ranging between the ages of 20 and 25, and epitomised that typical scrote or scally look, synonymous with the youth of inner-city areas that have embraced crime.

Pete was at the rear of the entry team and was firing CS ferrets above our heads and into the other end of the unit. Another of the lads had formed up on the apertures that Macky and Boothy had effectively demolished and was also pumping ferrets into the unit. The CS was creating a cloud of off-white smoke and vision was starting to deteriorate. It is hard to communicate while wearing respirators unless you have a comms system, and in those days we didn't. Imagine wearing a frogman's mask – peripheral vision becomes restricted and therefore you have to make a conscious effort to move your head. I looked to my right and left, and ensured my team was with me.

At this crucial stage, one of the gang went to investigate what was causing the commotion. He actually stood under the area where the MOE men were working and started to listen, only to receive a large piece of masonry onto his swede, knocking him temporarily unconscious. Shame.

Meanwhile, my team had made an unopposed entry into the stronghold through the Judas gate. Stun grenades were erupting and we had formed up and prepared to aggressively search to contact and then clear. The plan was in full swing. Two objectives had been achieved. We had gained access from two apertures into the stronghold. One gang member was concussed and we had two to deal with.

Corkovic was still in his vehicle when the strike was called. He is not a successful criminal for nothing and all his animal instincts must have come into play. He needed to escape and that is what he did. Before the rental van from the holding area could cut him off by the central barrier, he dropped his vehicle into first, then second gear, and accelerated out of the compound and onto Liverpool Road.

The cover team started to pump CS into the stronghold. There are Home Office guidelines to follow when deploying CS into a building, but you have to be a genius to understand it – or a West Yorkshire firearms instructor. Our formula that day was to use enough until we ran out. It wasn't like we were near a school and I, for one, have no sympathy for armed criminals.

We had definitely achieved the surprise part of the plan. The next was controlled aggression. I believe you should plan in all the advantages. It's not a game of cricket, you don't give the suspect a sporting chance – you have to fuck with his thought pattern, psychologically and physically dominate him. He needs to think this nutcase dressed like Robocop and shouting obscenities at him is mad enough to pull the trigger. His only option is to hit the deck and surrender – as fast as possible. In all my time as an armed officer, this tactic never failed.

The search to contact commenced. MP5s were shoulder-mounted, surefire lights activated and we moved in a fast and aggressive formation. The unit was approximately 20 by 60 foot, poorly lit and full of CS. The floor was littered with obstacles, including vehicle parts and chassis.

My progress took me straight into two of the team who were staggering around, completely confused and incapacitated by the CS. It had taken the fight out of them. I couldn't afford to make a clinical arrest but instead needed to maintain impetus, so both suspects were dropped to the floor and immediately passed back to the arrest team.

There was little point in me shouting while wearing a respirator, as the commands would come out as muffled grunts. Wearing a respirator can give you a false sense of security. You are cocooned in a world of your own. Although this is a nice feeling, I believe it to be dangerous and I was constantly aware of this fact when working in a respirator.

We moved through the unit and discovered what the unidentified plastic bags were for: they were fertiliser bags for growing skunk, a potent variety of cannabis. At the end of the stronghold was a cultivated strip of fully grown plants.

The arrest team had now found the concussed member of the team and taken him outside to recover. Corkovic had escaped, but elements of the surveillance team had picked him up. Unfortunately they were compromised and Corkovic threatened one of them with a handgun. He then escaped again – but not for long. Corkovic was to come into loop again soon.

To my knowledge, it was the first time CS delivered from firearms and stun grenades had been used by UK police on the mainland for the arrest and procurement of evidence. We had arrested three of a four-man armed robbery team and recovered three shotguns, ammunition and enough paraphernalia to incarcerate them for at least 60 years. However, there was still an outstanding Kalashnikov assault rifle and no Corkovic. It was time to return to Bootle Street and debrief.

Debriefing is important. It is a time to be truthful and to take justifiable criticism. At times you might not like it but tough, take it on the chin and learn. Some officers cannot stand criticism and that includes senior officers – all I can say is they are not complete firearms officers and should look for another job. Important points were learned by most of us but it was noticeable that the training team stayed away. Whatever, it was a success and the team was elated. Many of the SCS liaison team attended the debrief and Mr Glenn acknowledged its impact.

If the truth doesn't come out on the debrief, then it certainly does on the piss-up afterwards. I remember being completely knackered, mentally and physically, and sat in the beer garden of the Abercrombie pub in Manchester, enjoying the camaraderie over a few pints. The night was definitely going to be a long one and we were all in for the duration. It would get more boisterous and we definitely deserved it. This was part of a team bonding and important for its successful function.

I was proud to be a member of the Firearms Department. To have planned and participated in this operation was a bonus, but what made me most appreciate its importance was when two colleagues from the Covert Ops Unit, one of whom became a good friend, joined me for a pint. Due to the nature of their job, they cannot associate with police officers. However, they joined me and thanked me for a job well done.

CHAPTER TWO

Joining Up

On July 3, 1978, at the age of 16 and fresh out of secondary school, I joined the Greater Manchester Police Cadets.

It was no surprise to my family. We had a history of service, be it in the military, fire brigade or police. My great grandfather was the regimental sergeant major for the Lancashire Fusiliers; he lost an eye in the last days of the First World War. He also served at the Crescent Police Station in Salford as an inspector. Both my grandfather and father served in the fire brigade at the Crescent, grandad making the rank of divisional officer.

I was raised in a loving, working-class family in a town a few miles from Manchester, and was the oldest of three children. My parents divorced when I was eight years old, and I lived with my grandparents for several years before my mother re-married, to a man I came to love and admire and am very grateful to. I had a standard secondary school education but only ever had one career desire: to join either the military or the police. Circumstances dictated which.

My path to the cadets began at Southmill Street, the headquarters for the city centre division. I was one of a large group attempting to pass the selection process for either Greater Manchester Police or the cadets, depending on age. My parents had bought me a three-piece suit with flares and platform shoes. I only ever wore that suit twice, but thought I looked like a combination of John Travolta and Jack Regan from *The Sweeney* – a ridiculous mix but excellent for my street cred at the time.

The selection process was in the basement of Southmill Street Police Station in a dreary, gloomy room, and consisted of tests in maths, English and spelling. Some were then asked to leave the room; I didn't realise it was because they had failed, so it was a surprise when a middle-aged, Agatha Christie type announced that only those remaining had passed. One by one we saw a medical officer who whittled out more candidates. He pronounced me fit. I would have been disappointed if he hadn't – I played sport four times a week as well as rugby for a local club.

The next part of the process was an interview with a senior police officer two weeks later. Again I passed and was told to report to Peterloo House in Manchester at 10.00 hours on July 3 – and to bring a suitcase. My stepfather took me there in our family Vauxhall, dropping me off and wishing me good luck. Again I was in my three-piece suit and felt as smart as a carrot.

In 1978, Peterloo House, a 12-floor, purpose-built office just off Peterloo Square, was the headquarters of Greater Manchester Police. Peterloo Square was infamous for the Peterloo Massacre of 1819, when cavalry, soldiers and hussars charged an open-air meeting in support of parliamentary reform, killing 11 people and wounding 500. I was instructed by a member of the corps of commissionaires to go to the tenth floor and into a room marked 'Induction Class', where I was introduced, along with about 30 other recruits, to the permanent training staff. Among the staff were instructors in law, physical training, drill, swimming and outdoor pursuits. These instructors would play a big part in my development and understanding of the police force over the next 18 months.

The class were all recent school-leavers, with a 50/50 mix of male and female. About a quarter had been to college for 12 months to study criminal law (financed by GMP) and they certainly had an advantage when it came to legal matters. Some of the class members I would never see again after the induction course, whereas I would rub shoulders with others for most of my police career. One highlight was the course sergeant handing us our first monthly pay cheque. Mine was £50 and felt like a fortune.

The first day sped along with all sorts of forms to sign and an instruction to open a bank account if you didn't already have one. The afternoon consisted of a visit to the clothing stores, where we were issued five blue Van Heusen shirts, two clip-on ties, one tunic, two pairs of pants, one peaked cap, one lanyard, an old Gamex resin coat that smelled of rubber condoms and a pair of leather boots that I still have today. We also received a pair of blue nylon shorts, a blue vest and a pair of Gola or Dunlop training shoes. After that we were instructed to make our way to the barbers and get suitable haircuts for police cadets – in those days the Bee Gees were all the rage.

The first week was a frenzy of uniform care, duties expected of a cadet, physical training, drill and swimming. After the first week, we were informed that for the next nine weeks our expected duties would be 09.00 parade at Peterloo House, 09.30 to the YMCA Peter Street, engaged in physical training, 12.00 refs (refreshments), 12.45 to Cambridge Street Drill Hall, engaged in uniform inspection and drill, 14.30 to Hathersage Road public swimming baths for swimming instruction, 16.30 retire from duty. I was the exception to the rule – I thoroughly enjoyed those nine weeks.

At first it was hard graft and at times felt physically impossible. PT at the YMCA was my favourite and at 09.30 we had to be on parade in the gymnasium. The YMCA was an imposing, early nineteenth century building, and a bit like a rabbit warren inside. As you entered from Peter Street you walked into the cafeteria area, and the first flight of stairs took you to the changing rooms. When the 'Y' was first built I don't think females had been catered for and I think the women used another changing area, originally intended for males but certainly off-bounds to us. From the changing areas you made your way to the gym area, the usual type of gym with every indoor sport catered for by way of markings on the floor. Above the gym area, running round the walls, was a suspended running track and from the running track you gained entrance to a 20-metre swimming pool. Woe betide you if you were more than one minute late for PT.

Our physical training instructors were named Hadge Bratt and Bob Loftus. Both were police constables and extremely fit. Hadge was a disciplinarian. I guess he was at least 40 and was everything a PTI should be. We found out that Hadge never expected you to do anything he couldn't. He had played for Manchester United and became a legend to us and all past and future cadets were trained by him. In later years I got to know him well. He was firm but fair and a very private man. Bob was the opposite in personality but was also an extremely fit and competent sportsman. For the next nine weeks, Hadge and Bob would beast us in the gym from 09.30 to 12.00. Women were expected to do exactly the same as the lads except for press-ups, and for any ex-cadets who read this the immortal words 'Raise . . . lower' will be ever-present in their memory.

Our drill instructor was John Haslam, who later joined the Royal Canadian Mounted Police. John was an ex-guardsman who became our 'drill pig'. He was responsible for teaching us to march from columns of three, turn about, turn to left, turn to the right, and stand perfectly still at attention. John also taught us how to wear our uniforms, iron the correct creases into them and bull our boots. 'Bullin'' boots is creating a mirror-like shine all over them, quite literally by spit and polish. It took endless time to achieve the required standard.

I was a smart cadet but crap at marching and drill. However to this day I haven't forgotten how to about turn on the march or left or right turn. Some might ask what has drill got to do with being a police officer? My answer is that it teaches you pride and self-discipline, two factors which go a long way to making a decent officer. There is little worse than a police officer who looks like a bag of shit when wearing uniform.

Swimming was interesting. Our instructor was PC George Craig and I'm sure George had a touch of the sadist about him. Swimming took place at Victoria Baths in Longsight. The baths are currently the subject of a Government and TV restoration scheme and I can tell you they need it. The baths are an old Victorian building with a 25-metre pool, with the changing cubicles situated around the edge. We would hang our uniforms in them, get changed and before getting into the water we would collectively remove the corpses of cockroaches, who had conveniently drowned the day before and were floating upside down. I don't think Victoria Baths had any heating except for the antiquated system that warmed the bath attendant's radiator.

Once we entered the water George would beast us, and we would swim length after length sprinting under and over the water. He would make us climb in and out 100 times, shouting the number each time we left the water. George's favourite trick was making you tread water in the deep end with a lead diver's belt held above your head. George would stand on the side screaming at you and God help you if your head went under the water. To be fair to George, he also never asked you to do something he couldn't, and he was also preparing us to pass the Bronze Medallion, a pretty strict life-saving qualification. For the next nine weeks we received this training. I for one was fitter, more confident and ready to move on to the next phase of cadet training.

* * *

In the late 1970s and early 1980s most UK police forces had a cadet scheme. The idea was simply to recruit younger and impressionable elements of society and prepare them for a career as a regular police officer, supplementing a dwindling police service. After the initial nine weeks, a cadet was posted to a department on a division near to their home address. This posting lasted for three months, during which you would return to Peterloo House twice a week for PT and drill.

During my 18 months in the cadets I had the misfortune to be posted to the admin on the G Division (Ashton-under-Lyne) and then the Juvenile Offenders Office. Both departments had little understanding of how a cadet was to be developed and all I can say is that I loathed every minute there. Regardless of these useless postings, I had started to gain an insight into how police officers viewed cadets and in general it was not in high regard. The more shiny-arsed the department, the more contempt a cadet suffered, shuffling paper and making brews, and I found the more operational-based an officer was, the more favourable they were to cadets.

In the winter of 1979, my luck changed, although at that time I didn't think so. I received my next posting, to the Firearms Department at Peterloo House. I knew pretty much nothing about the department in those days, but after talking with other cadets I was informed it was a shit posting and all you did was file firearm and shotgun certificates – marvellous.

I duly reported for duty. The Firearms Department was on the seventh floor. It was manned by two female admin staff and a detective chief inspector. The room was approximately 50 foot by 20 foot and wall to wall with files. The phones constantly rang – it was a busy hive of admin industry. With sinking heart I mustered up the courtesy to introduce myself and display a snide enthusiasm. One of the admin ladies pointed to my desk and started to instruct me in my admin duties. With her advice on the correct franking marks for shotgun or firearm certificates, my duties commenced. I couldn't wait until my next cadet training day.

Towards the end of the day the door burst open and seven men walked in, all with ruddy faces, wearing warm civilian clothing and wax Barbour jackets. They were quite noisy and friendly with the two admin ladies and a bit of banter and flirting took place. I then heard, 'Who's the monkey in the corner?' I looked around and realised they meant me, so I shyly introduced myself, suffixing my conversation with 'Sir'. I was told to 'stop saying fucking sir'. I kept my head down like an ostrich, hoping they would ignore me, but I could hear words like 'wire', 'Diggle' and 'monkey' and then they left.

I asked one of the admin staff who those men were. She said they were the firearms instructors and had been instructing at the shooting range.

'So where are they based?' I asked.

'Bootle Street.'

I learned that the Firearms Department consisted of a detective chief inspector (head of the department), a detective inspector (second in charge), two detective sergeants, five detective constables, three civilian admin staff and the occasional cadet. The department had three definite and independent roles. The admin, based at Peterloo House, was manned by a DCI and DI and admin staff responsible for enforcing and documenting firearm and shotgun certificates as well as registered gun dealers and firearms ranges. The Operational and Instructional teams were based at Bootle Street Police Station and manned by two detective sergeants, five detective constables and one civilian armourer. Their duties were training officers who were attached to certain departments such as the Tactical Aid Group, Manchester Airport, Special Branch and certain CID departments in the correct use of police-issue firearms. They were also responsible for planning and executing firearms operations within the Greater Manchester Police area.

I was told to bring some warm and waterproof clothing for my next day on duty. I was to parade at 08.00 at Peterloo House, where I would be collected by the instructors because they needed a 'monkey to pull the wire at Diggle'. What that meant, I hadn't a clue, but it certainly sounded better than the dread of sitting in an office, filing certificates. So the next day I eagerly waited in my dad's old British Army parka at Peterloo House. They arrived in an old personnel carrier (Transit van) and asked me if I could drive. I said yes but not police vehicles; 'In that case, sit in the back,' came the response.

I jumped in the van with two instructors, who told me to sit right at the back. The van floor was littered with leather gun cases, liners of ammunition and black metal boxes, which I later found out contained handguns. We then made our way to Diggle Range, Uppermill, Oldham. Unbeknown to me, this would be the start of a long relationship with the Firearms Department and many of its characters.

Diggle Range is outdoors in the bleak moorland between Greater Manchester and Yorkshire. It is a civilian range but GMP hired it Monday to Friday for most of the year. Diggle has four ranges and can be used for most calibres of weapon including handgun, shotgun and rifle. Being on the moors it was open to all elements of the weather, but with a couple of exceptions it was the main place of duty for a trainee firearms officer or an instructor and I thought it was ideal. The ranges were serviced by a civilian warden in the range house, a purpose-built pro-perty in the middle of the complex with a less than adequate classroom and adjacent target store. It was absolutely freezing in winter.

The ranges vary from 25m, 50m, 100m, 500m and 1,000m and are situated in an expanse of square mile surrounded by steep hills towards the north and west and a reservoir towards the east with a stream-cum-river depending on the season, running south to north. One day a historian will come along and inform us that Diggle Range has been used for a century or more – certainly by the military prior to conflicts all over the world – and I know definitely that GMP instructors have found evidence of its age: old musket balls, the rotted framework of a flintlock shotgun and an actual grenade pit. I was soon to learn what my duties entailed: I was the monkey who pulled the wire. In those early days the pistol range ('A' range) was serviced by a simple target system. The targets were 25m away from the shooters. In certain shooting disciplines they received timed exposures of the target and then the targets were 'edged' (taken away). This was achieved by a pulley system, and I was the lucky candidate (monkey) who operated the system (pulling the wire). A firearms instructor usually did the job; however, as I was to find out later, the demands of instructing were increasing and pulling the wire was tying up much needed manpower.

So this was my introduction to the Firearms Instructional Wing. For the next three months I became part of something I hadn't known existed and an aspect of policing that later became a great part of my career.

At 08.00 on each day of the working week (my cadet training days had been cancelled), I was picked up at Peterloo House by the instructors and taken to Diggle Range. I came to know the instructors, some of them quite well. Some I would work with on operations in later years. On arrival at Diggle, the van was emptied of weapons and ammunition, which had been collected from an armoury at Bootle Street Police Station in the city centre. The instructors had a separate room in the range house and would ensconce themselves within. The police officers who had come to shoot were designated the classroom with adjoining kitchen. I would have to make all the instructors a brew.

* * *

Historically, the public in England, Scotland and Wales have perceived their police service as being unarmed, and in some sense this is true. However, I remember being told by one old dinosaur that there is some ancient police legislation that states an officer has the right to carry arms while engaged on night duty. It may possibly exist, but in my 22 years of policing, I didn't ever see a uniformed officer carrying a firearm on nights, except for an authorised officer.

From the 1960s onwards, society started to see changes. The days of the local corner shopkeeper were numbered and large superstores such as Morrisons and Tesco were taking over. Salaries were starting to increase in accordance with the cost of living and we started to see large amounts of cash being transported around the country. This cash was guarded but was a huge temptation for career criminals, and therefore robberies became the *en vogue* offence. To make robberies easier, firearms were adopted – generally shotguns – making the offence one of armed robbery.

Society also started to change. Many eminent people, far more qualified than me, can explain why, but briefly narcotics started to hit the streets of Britain in a big way. The criminal element sought to control this new, illegal trade, as large amounts of money could be made. In the drug trade, as with all businesses, you have structures equivalent to rival companies with managing directors, and to control and enforce you need tools. Those tools were, once again, firearms. If into this recipe we throw extortion, terrorism, pornography and your run-of-the-mill nutcase, we start to see an increase in the use of guns for criminal purposes.

To control the ever-increasing number of criminals who use firearms, you need a counter. At that time the counter was a police officer, trained for one week in the use of a Smith & Wesson revolver with some limited tactics and strategies thrown in. The officer would then attend three or four one-day refreshers during the year and would be expected to reclassify during these periods. These officers were the force's resource when required for protection duties or to arrest armed suspects.

Authorised firearms officers, or AFOs, were recruited from the Tactical Aid Group, CID, Special Branch, Manchester

Airport, or if you had a further specialisation, such as a police rifle qualification, you could be a normal uniformed beat officer. For the next three months I mixed with those officers to see firsthand what training was required. The instructional staff included two sergeants and five PCs. The sergeants were two old-time police officers, been there and done that, friendly but strict. Roy Duckworth was a target shooter and was excellent with any handgun. His opposite, Tony Haughton, was responsible for training riflemen (snipers) and by all accounts was a tremendous shot. However, they weren't particularly dynamic and not how I envisaged operational firearms sergeants; they were both slightly overweight and unfit.

On most ranges there is a backstop. It is a physical barrier, either man-made or natural, such as the side of a hill. All targets are placed before the backstop so that once a bullet penetrates a paper target, it depletes or dumps its energy into the backstop, not allowing over-penetration. Most bullet heads are made of lead, so imagine over the years how much lead is in the earth of a backstop.

Sometimes at lunch break, Tony Haughton would send me to rummage about in the backstops and collect as much depleted lead as I could find. Being a good and obliging cadet, I set about this task with my usual enthusiasm and at times would return with vast quantities. I asked why he required this and I got the not unusual reply of, 'Don't be fuckin' nosey,' and mumblings of, 'Keep the range tidy.' I later found out why. One day I happened to walk into the target store which was adjacent to the range house. Inside I found a startled Tony Haughton bent over a fire like prehistoric man. He was melting the lead I had collected and making six-inch-long ingots. He told me it was for improving his equipment for his favourite hobby, scuba-diving, then told me to fuck off, which I did. I wouldn't be surprised if Tony couldn't swim; he didn't look like a budding Jacques Cousteau to me.

Two of the PCs were Julian Barnes and Keith Mitchell. Later both became my supervisory officers at one stage or other in my firearms career. Julian and Keith took time out with me and at lunchtimes took me onto the ranges and actually taught me the principles of aimed and sense-of-direction shooting with handguns and shotguns. This gave me an advantage in my later career. A gamekeeper's son, Julian was exceptional with a shotgun and has represented Great Britain Police in shotgun events.

The other three instructors I got to know were all ex-marines: Harry Mills, Dave Dilnut and Roger Seed. Roger was quiet, capable and at one with nature. It wasn't unusual for him to disappear at lunch breaks to climb some knoll or hill and sit quietly in the open air. Roger was a sniper and in charge of training force riflemen. There is a great tale of Roger while instructing on a rifle course. His recruits were engaged in a camouflage and concealment exercise, and he was looking for one particular student but couldn't find him. This frustrated Roger, a normally patient man. He set fire to the undergrowth and soon discovered his student. I think the title 'eccentric' should be granted to Roger. Unfortunately some years later when Roger was back in uniform at Salford, he received a severe beating from a couple of lowlifes he had discovered breaking into a property and he was forced to retire prematurely.

Dave Dilnut was a friendly enough individual and certainly knew his stuff but I don't think Dave's heart was in it. He later resigned and opened a guesthouse down south.

Harry Mills was a legend in firearms – still is to an extent, possibly of his own making – but I suppose you don't get the Queen's Police Medal for nothing. As I write this passage, I may upset some people but my experience of Harry – and it was considerable and lengthy – wasn't favourable. I was told he was a good shot and a hard man. He looked after Lord Mountbatten when he was in the marines but my first experience with Harry was either a prank or bullying. Make your own mind up. As I mentioned earlier, my only item of foul-weather gear was my dad's ex-British Army parka issued for use in the Korean war. It was apparently a sought-after item if you were in the armed forces. Harry recognised this item and constantly badgered me for it. He didn't want to swap, he just wanted it. I was only 17 and I was scared of telling someone like Harry to fuck off, so I ignored his constant barrage.

One particular day, driving back from Diggle, he cornered me in the back of the personnel carrier and demanded the parka. I said no and so he decided to spray me with confiscated CS irritant. I was later to experience all forms of CS, but that time I thought my days had come to an end – and so did the other instructors in the van. A cloud of gas enveloped us all. At least they were experienced in the use of CS. The van was stopped and they burst out into the middle of Peterloo Square. Either Julian or Keith dragged me out and told me not to rub my eyes and to face the wind. Good advice when you're not shitting yourself. I overheard comments like 'out of order' directed towards Harry. I was brushed down and sent on my way with tears streaming down my face.

All too soon my time in cadets ended. I was 18 and it was time to become a real policeman. I believe the cadet scheme was excellent and I have heard comments that you need experience of the real world before becoming a police officer. Well, some of the most respected and competent police officers I have worked with are ex-cadets. You are either a good police officer or not. In my opinion, only years of experience working with the public gears you towards becoming a good police officer; the cadets prepare your way.

And in May 1980, I was ready to become a police constable.

CHAPTER THREE

Basic Training
and First Posting

On a Monday morning in May 1980, I stood with 40 other recruits, some ex-cadets and others from all areas of society: miners, teachers, factory workers and military. We were in the theatre room of Sedgley Park, Greater Manchester Police's training headquarters in Prestwich, north Manchester. It was an old Catholic teacher training college set in its own grounds, and a rather impressive building which had recently been purchased by GMP to replace Peterloo House. We were in the theatre to swear our allegiance to the Crown in front of several magistrates and senior officers. Unless we swore this oath, our powers as police officers would be useless. I listened to some old magistrate rattle off a list of duties which we were to uphold and to repeat after him verbatim, finally sealing it by swearing our allegiance to God and the Queen.

That week we collected all our uniforms and listened to a crusty old sergeant swinging the lamp – telling us war stories regarding his time within the police service. It was interesting but not productive. The following week, all 40 of us from GMP paraded at the Home Office police training centre known as Bruche in Warrington, Cheshire.

Bruche is a pre-fabricated establishment, built in the 1950s. The size of a small housing estate, it can accommodate up to

400 students. It has a parade ground, gymnasium, swimming pool, admin block and its own licensed bar. It is designed to provide the initial training for all police recruits from the forces in the northwest region.

My intake was known as 3/80. It must have consisted of at least 200 recruits from forces such as GMP, North Wales, Derbyshire, Nottingham, Cheshire, Lancashire, Merseyside and, for some reason, Thames Valley. My two instructors were sergeants from Merseyside and GMP. The GMP sergeant was fat and useless; he was basically seeing his time out at Bruche and shouldn't have taught kindergarten kids, never mind potential PCs. The other sergeant was the complete opposite: keen, motivated, smart and ready to impart as much knowledge as possible.

For the next ten weeks we were taught law in relation to all criminal matters we could possibly encounter as uniformed officers, from badger baiting to murder. I found it boring. At 18 I wasn't ready to go back into the classroom and start learning acts, sections and stated cases verbatim. However, to qualify I would have to digest this information and take an exam every Monday morning. If I remember rightly, three failures was an automatic dismissal from the police service, and to me failure was not an option.

The cadet service certainly goes some way to prepare you for the training course. In those days discipline was a core feature of the programme. Uniforms had to be pristine and your drill abilities second to none. Cadet service had taught me these skills. I was well prepared for the punishment given out for infringements, such as an early morning run or a tough gym session. One thing I wasn't prepared for – but something I became reasonably adept at (although peers will suggest otherwise) – was the amount of alcohol I was expected to sink. In those days the police had a reputation as a hard-drinking organisation and it was expected that in your recreational time you conversed over a pint or three. Most officers who attended Bruche will tell you that after their ten weeks' initial training, they left as fit as a fiddle. I left half a stone heavier and with a massive deterioration in my fitness.

The ten weeks passed slowly as we crammed in as much law as possible. All the students were waiting for the final week, when we would be allocated the divisions we would serve on. In those days GMP was separated into 14 divisions, each prefixed by a letter from the alphabet. For example, G Division was the Tameside area in the east of the metropolitan county, including Ashton-under-Lyne, Denton, Stalybridge, Mossley, Dukinfield and Audenshaw. The division was then divided into a north and south sub-division, each having a main head-quarters and then satellite outposts.

I was hoping for an inner-city division such as D (Longsight) or E (Moss Side). I naively thought they would be really busy with a multitude of crimes, great areas to get stuck into, arrest scores of criminals and make my name as a young, keen, ambitious police officer. To me Bruche was a means to an end, and not a particularly stimulating one. One thing, however, would remain with me for the rest of my service. It was necessary for students to know and apply the law. At times the class would make their way to the roadway system on campus, where a practical session on how to report a driver for maybe a drink-drive or 'con-and-use' offence would take place. An instructor would drive towards two designated stooges from the class in a beat-up old car, minus a tax disc and contravening other traffic regulations. The two stooges, watched by the rest of the class, would force the vehicle to halt and proceed to make a complete balls-up of the scenario, usually resulting in the instructor running away, much to the mirth of the class and the instructional staff.

Certain practical points were then made about how suspicions should have been aroused: for example, the pencil in the ignition and the half-drunk bottle of whisky on the passenger seat. We would return to the classroom better prepared in a practical way. My point is that these practical sessions were as important as the theory we learned, and on most occasions more so. You should train for realism to learn how an offender reacts once confronted by an officer. His or her mind-set will be one of capitulation or escape as fast and as dynamically as possible, depending upon the offence. This process is controlled by the demeanour of the officer. At training college, officers are not taught tactical skills such as how to approach a vehicle, how to subtly or overtly put the offender in a disadvantageous position, how to work in pairs with colleagues, how to gauge an offenders' NVC (non-verbal communication), and, most importantly, how to check a suspect's hands. The list goes on – and these are basic survival skills.

The term survival skills may sound emotive, but if they were taught these right from the beginning, I'm sure more officers would be alive today. These skills should be second nature to officers, not something years of experience teach. In America they learn them at basic level, so officers start out better prepared. They are taught to respect their uniform and portray a pro-fessional image at all times, but also have a degree of under-standing of an offender's mindset. They treat all offenders the same, be it a driver or a rapist; they expect the worst and when they get the best, it's a bonus. It is about being aware of your surroundings and the people you are dealing with. No-one expects you to behave like a gunfighter on speed, but it certainly heightens your awareness and personal safety level once you start arresting or reporting people.

In certain training schools in the States, the following true scenario is related to recruits. One day a man receives instruc-tions from God to kill a police officer. He will drive his vehicle along the highway in an erratic manner and when the highway patrol stops him and approaches, he will shoot the officer dead. The offender is subsequently arrested for the murder of an officer. When searched, a traffic citation is found on him; it had been issued earlier that day by another officer. When asked why he didn't kill the first policeman that stopped his vehicle, he said that officer was professional in his manner at all times: he approached the vehicle in the correct way, kept his hands in view at all times and gave himself space to react in case of a threat. He had the edge. The offender stated it would have been extremely difficult to have killed this officer, and possibly the officer would have killed him first if he had reacted aggressively. Therefore it was prudent to seek another target. Some hours later, he was stopped again. This officer approached with his hands in his pockets, came right up to the vehicle chewing gum and looked like a bag of shit, so the offender shot him. The offender had the edge.

My point is that most of the public are law-abiding and decent; however, society has its share of crap. There are nasty, dangerous people out there who don't give a fuck about others, and if you are a pro-active policeman, you will come across them, or persons who have committed or are about to commit crime. Learning street survival in training would go a long way to preparing an officer on what to expect.

Our personal safety briefing at Bruche was a viewing of *The Blue Lamp*, a film made in 1950 about a uniformed officer who eventually gets shot after confronting an armed robber. It led to the *Dixon of Dock Green* TV series.

As you can probably tell from this chapter, I wasn't enamoured with Bruche. However, in hindsight, I wish I had paid more attention during law lectures! I was also disappointed when I received my divisional posting. I hadn't got the E or D Divisions, but G Division – and in my naive eyes it was not an exact hive of criminal industry.

* * *

It was 06.00 on a Wednesday in the middle of August 1980. I was in the parade room at Ashton-under-Lyne Police Head-quarters on the G Division, Tameside, north division. I was in full uniform and in possession of my 'appointments': a pocket notebook, a 12-inch wooden truncheon and a pair of handcuffs. To this day I don't know why they are called appointments. It was my first day as a shiny, new, out-of-the-box police constable and I was about to walk my first beat.

I was about to meet my 'scale'. A scale is a 'block' or a 'watch' – the team of personnel and supervisors you work with. I had been posted to D scale and for the next two and a half years these officers would become my friends and work colleagues. But first I would have to prove myself a competent officer. I had a two-year probationary period to pass and would be constantly assessed and reported on. At any time my services could be dispensed with.

My immediate supervisor was Bob 'Fozzie' Foster, a young sergeant with a traffic background. He would have a great influence on my early career and was someone I came to respect enormously. Under Bob's command were ten other constables, all with various degrees of service. D scale was commanded by an inspector who was an absolute miserable fucker but, to be fair, not a malicious man. I was told he was miserable because his dad had committed suicide by gassing himself and the inspector had never got over it. I would come to treat police gossip with a pinch of salt but in those days I was very impressionable.

The north sub-division was split into four scales – A, B, C and D. The scale would be based at the main headquarters and then satellite posts which included Denton and Droylsden police stations. The ten officers at the HQ would cover Ashton-under-Lyne. A sergeant and four constables were based at Denton and another sergeant and four officers were at Droylsden. So a scale consisted of one inspector, three sergeants and eighteen constables, and would be self-contained and could respond to assistance in another scale's sector. Each scale also had officers from the dog section, traffic and CID to offer 'expert' advice and assistance. Each scale would work eight-hour shifts; for example, A scale would work from 06.00 to 14.00, B scale would work 14.00 to 22.00, C scale 22.00 to 06.00 and D scale would be on rest days. In general each scale was understaffed.

Bob was a young sergeant for those days, about 30. He looked at me and told me to sit down with the rest of my colleagues around a rectangular table, with Bob at its head. Everyone had notebooks out in front of them. Some acknowledged me with grunts and nods.

'Who are you?' asked Bob.

I explained, and Bob replied, 'You're not expected until next week – and how old are you?'

'Eighteen.'

'Listen in, I will speak to you later,' replied Bob.

I wasn't enjoying this new experience. Bob went on to give out mobile and foot beats and refreshments times and related from the daily bulletin the latest in crime trends: who was wanted and information sought. What was significant was that he had ignored me. My colleagues got up, issued themselves with radios, commenced checks and left the building. I remained alone with Bob.

'Alright Andrew' – he would always call me by my full name. 'You look too young for a policeman.' That was a great start. Bob looked confused. 'I'm not sure who to put you in company with.'

For the first two weeks all new probationary constables have to accompany a seasoned constable who shows them the ropes (although this has changed in the more modern force). Bob's dilemma, as I was soon to find out, was that most of his constables were still in their probationary period, all with different degrees of service, from 18 months to 18 weeks. To further the confusion, Bob had the notion that I couldn't work unaccompanied until I was 19, which was not until October. I was now feeling really rejected.

'Well you can come out with me today. Keep quiet, watch and listen,' was Bob's decision.

For the next eight hours I drove around with Bob who introduced me to my colleagues. I would come to admire Bob and his ways. He was a competent man-manager with an unusual sense of humour. I later found out he was an ex-Cheshire cadet. At the end of the tour of duty, Bob told me for the next six weeks I could expect to accompany anyone in the scale and left me with this warning:

'I expect you to answer your radio and never drink on duty.'

It was good advice, and fair. I have always answered my radio and never drank on duty when Bob was my scale sergeant. For the next two and a half years Bob was my sergeant and tutor. He taught me how to arrest people, how to take statements, how to deal with road traffic accidents and how to negate a lot of the bullshit in the system.

The scale at Ashton consisted of six male officers and four female officers. I don't harbour strong views on the merits or demerits of policewomen. I don't judge a book by its cover. Gender, race, creed, colour or sexual orientation is of little importance to me. If you are good at your job and stand fast when the shit hits the fan, that is what counts. If an officer doesn't have the qualities of loyalty, honesty, trustworthiness, dependability and competence then I have no time for that officer or supervisor. It was something I found out to my cost at times. I'm not making a politically correct statement to impress the reader – to be honest I haven't the slightest interest in any minority within the force that demands recognition or supervisory officers sucking up to its whims. The job is tough and at times unfair, however, work with what you have – in other words, put up and shut up.

Of the ten officers at Ashton, two were a permanent van crew.

They were the most experienced officers and would be used as backup at aggressive incidents and also to transport prisoners to the police station. They were generally male. The van crew was the job with kudos, and you could wear your flat hat instead of your helmet when on the van and any probationer worth his salt aspired to the dizzy heights of the van crew. Of the rest, four were on foot patrol and were all probationers and two, Angie and Dave, were the mobile patrols. For the next two and a half years these officers would be my colleagues on and off duty.

During this period I was playing rugby union for the division and rugby league for the force. I was also playing club rugby on a Saturday when commitments allowed. Sport was then an integral part of the force and was actively encouraged. In fact, if you represented the force, every year you were allowed two weeks' team training, generally at Sedgley Park. When representing the division, you were allowed two hours' time off and four hours when representing the force. In later years these facilities were withdrawn on the pretext that the force couldn't allow all this time off.

I joined the police service in an era when most senior officers came from quite a robust background, due to the social environment of the time. Sport, in their eyes, was important, allowing officers to mix with colleagues from different divisions and forces. It also allowed the public to see another side of the police service. I have played some hard games against working-class teams in the northwest, some who couldn't wait to get a dig in on a bobby. But it was a good way to mix with the public.

Some junior and senior officers frowned on sport for various reasons: they hadn't actively been involved in a sporting environment and had no idea of its benefits; they were bloody-minded and would deter officers from playing sport because they could; they were fat and lazy and detested sport and what it stood for; they resented the occasional favouritism shown towards sporting officers. The latter point is something that, I'm quite happy to state, assisted my development within the service. If I sound biased towards sport, well it's true, I am. I find officers who train, play and keep fit are generally more efficient and motivated, though there are exceptions.

My six weeks in company soon passed. I had worked a set of nights and had witnessed plenty of arrests, from drunk and disorderly to burglary. I had reported people for summons for a variety of offences but I hadn't done it on my own. It was time to learn.

It was a Bank Holiday Sunday and Fozzie had given me a town centre beat. I was as proud as punch, it was a sunny day and I was walking regulation pace along Old Street, Ashton-under-Lyne, towards the Metro Cinema. The Walt Disney film *Dumbo* had just finished and parents with their children were exiting the cinema doors and spewing out onto the pavement. Walking among the parents, and towards me, was a crowd of about 20 young men, dressed in cut-off denim jackets adorned with motorcycle chains. Most had long, scruffy hair and days of facial growth. There were four girls dressed similarly and wearing steel-toecapped motorcycle boots.

They were in fact pseudo Hell's Angels, a motorbike gang minus their bikes on a pub crawl around Ashton-under-Lyne. They were making their way to their own adopted pub, the Spread Eagle. Many of the male members of the gang were shouting, 'Fuck off soldier boy, run home you useless twat,' to a young man dressed in full army uniform walking on the opposite side of the pavement. The abuse continued: 'Fuck off you useless wanker!'

Now I was in a dilemma. The pseudo Hell's Angels were walking towards me, parents of the children were looking at me, with that expression that says, what are you going to do about this, my children shouldn't have to hear this abuse? I had been taught never to back down. I respected my uniform, therefore I would approach the gang and tell them (not ask) to shut up. So without thought for my own safety, I went up to the gang, many of whom were out of their skulls and not just with alcohol (a radio message to control would have been beneficial at this stage), and as a fresh-faced nineteen-year-old copper, I told the gang leader, a fat 18-stone, 30-year-old piece of shit to 'shut up or someone will be arrested'.

'How are you going to do that, get your mum?' he replied.

I was stuck. He had called my extremely poor bluff. I had two options: back down or repeat my request. Now I'm not the bravest of souls but my pride wouldn't let me back down and I remembered the following bit of advice: once you have decided to arrest someone, don't let go of them at all costs. Fuck it, I thought, remember the old adage that attack is the best form of defence.

'Shut your fat mouth, be quiet and move on,' I stated firmly to the leader.

I had now forced the issue because he couldn't back down and lose face in front of his lowlife gang. The next thing I remember is being struck on the side of my head and my helmet flying. That was it. I jumped on fat bastard and we both fell to the floor. Bad move. I received one of the best beatings of my young life. Steel-toed boots knocked me around like a football. All the time I was holding on to fat bastard and screaming down my radio, 'Assistance, assistance, Old Street.'

The radio blurted back but I couldn't hear it; I was too busy defending myself. I knew this was serious because at least two of the gang had motorcycle chains and were trying to wrap them round my head. Good sense prevailed; I let go of fat bastard. I needed to survive and remember who was assaulting on me. The beating seemed to go on forever but I knew I had to defend myself at all costs – and then I saw police vehicles coming toward me (in those days only traffic vehicles had sirens) and the gang started to scatter.

One of them, who had been intent on causing me serious

damage, wore a red silk scarf and had noticeably sunken cheek-bones. In trying to escape my colleagues, he ran towards me. Fucking bingo. He ran right into my straight-arm tackle and swallowed his front teeth. He was quickly thrown into the back of a van – my first arrest.

Fozzie came over, enquired about my health and then asked where my helmet was. The fuckers had stolen it. By now the whole scale had arrived. Fozzie issued orders. He requested further patrols to the scene and told me we were going to the Spread Eagle to arrest the offenders.

'Are you up to it?'

'Of course I am, sarge.'

When we had at least 20 officers, Fozzie instructed several to create an outer cordon around the pub to seal all exits and entrances. The rest of us would enter. I would identify the offenders and they would be arrested. As we went in, a heavy metal singer, somewhat like Phil Lynott from Thin Lizzy, was performing on stage. He screamed, 'The filth are in!' Fozzie nice and calmly encouraged him over and turned off his mike.

'Right Andrew, point out the shit who assaulted you.'

We made three more arrests, including fat bastard, and all were conveyed to Ashton-under-Lyne nick. I was left with the following retort ringing in my ears from Fozzie: 'Once you have booked them in, see me in my office.'

All four offenders were booked in. While I completed the paperwork, I kept thinking, oh fuck, what does Fozzie want? I'd been on my first beat for only an hour and had caused mayhem. I made my way to Fozzie's office with trepidation.

'OK, what went wrong?' he asked.

'I fucked up, sarge. Perhaps I should have backed down.'

'You fucked up in some ways,' he said, 'but no, you couldn't back down. What could you have done better?'

I stood there dumb.

'Right, sit down.'

He then pointed out my mistakes. He explained that I had a duty to approach the gang but should have informed comms straight away and requested backup.

'Who told you to hang on to a prisoner?'

'Something I heard, sarge.'

'Well bollocks, look after yourself, he will always come again.'

Fozzie could see I was injured. I had a bloody face and motorcycle chain marks running across my back. 'Are you going sick?' he asked.

'No fucking way, sarge.'

He smiled and dismissed me with the words, 'Fuck off, keep out of trouble and think about what you have learned.'

Although I was injured, there wasn't a cat in hell's chance of me going sick. My pride wouldn't allow it. I had suffered worse in a game of rugby. Later that evening I thought about what Bob had said. What had I learned? I should have informed comms, and perhaps demanding that fat bastard shut up wasn't the best communication. During the attack adrenalin had assisted me, but more than that my physical fitness had proved a major asset. I resolved to stay fit but soften my approach. I was also happy to note that once an officer needed help, the troops came running, no matter what the consequences.

For the next year I set about my job, and apart from a few minor hiccups, kept out of trouble. I was enjoying the experience at Ashton and under the tutoring of Bob I was becoming a reasonable police officer. I also served under two other sergeants, John 'Webby' Webster and Steve 'Rocky' Wallis. John was old school, ex-Regional Crime Squad, a practical joker but a good copper who liked a drink. Rocky was another ex-traffic man but a bundle of enthusiasm and great to serve under. I felt fortunate to benefit from the experience of these three.

CHAPTER FOUR

Active Duty

In the early 1980s, England endured unprecedented civil unrest. Tensions were at an all-time high in many impoverished inner-city areas. The relationship between the police and young black males was stretched to breaking point, and on Friday July 3, 1981, it snapped. The arrest of a young black man in Toxteth, Liverpool, sparked the infamous Toxteth Riots. Over the next five nights, Liverpool saw destruction, looting and disturbances the likes of which it had never seen before. Merseyside Police tried bravely to quell the riots, but had neither the manpower nor the equipment to cope with such mass public disorder. They were forced to activate Operation Response – the title for the activation of support units from other northwest forces.

In the early hours of Saturday July 4, 1981, I was walking my beat when I heard, for the first time, the term Operation Response used over the radio network and then heard officers being called back to the station. Eventually my number was called; I was to go to Ashton HQ immediately.

The station was a hive of activity. Officers had been called in from home and from the south sub-division and other outposts. Sergeants were issuing instructions and the rumour was that we were heading for Liverpool, where several officers had already 'lost their lives' due to large-scale rioting. We were told to board a 40-seat liveried coach with GMP emblazoned on it. Once ensconced, an inspector informed us that we were going to Openshaw, a police establishment in Manchester, where we would collect packed meals and riot equipment. Packed meals weren't a surprise, but riot kit! We would then head to Toxteth, where large-scale rioting had taken place throughout the night. Many officers were injured but none were dead. On arrival we would deploy on the streets in serials of one sergeant and five constables.

We arrived at Openshaw at 04.00 and collected packed meals from canteen staff who had also been turned out, and then our riot gear was issued: a plastic visor which attached to the front of our helmets and was about as much use as a pogo stick in a swamp.

It was about 06.00 when we drove along Lodge Lane, Toxteth. The sun was up and the morning was already bright. I was horrified at what I saw. Not a window was intact, buildings were scorched and blackened from now extinguished fires, bricks and large slabs of concrete were strewn over the pavements and roads. Garden gates had been unhinged and were lying in the roadway. Officers stood, some helmetless, in groups of ten looking exhausted and bedraggled. Most were carrying dustbin lids, their only means of protection. Our job was to relieve them.

We made our way to the local 'bridewell', a Liverpudlian term for police station. Officers from most northwest forces were present. Some had just arrived but others had been involved throughout the night. Many were bandaged and had signs of blood injuries. All credit to those officers, they were prepared to continue with their duties.

For the next 16 hours, we were deployed on Upper Parliament Street, Toxteth. My serial of five included my scale colleagues Andy and Chris and we quickly obtained dustbin lids and then, more importantly, ate our packed meals. I think at some stage we tried to fit the newly supplied visors but gave up and consigned them to join the rest of the debris littered on the street.

Later that day we were issued with much more substantial protective kit: five-foot plastic shields. For the rest of the day we patrolled Upper Parliament Street. At any sign of large gatherings we would immediately form in shield formations and deploy in their direction. This usually resulted in some stone throwing before they dispersed like a starburst. It was nothing compared to the violence that had occurred the previous evening. What was noticeable was the sheer bravery of the Salvation Army. Around Upper Parliament Street they had set up little tea and coffee stops. Even in the middle of the most hostile rioting, officers could get a tea or coffee and a packet of custard creams. Bizarre I know, but admirable all the same.

Eventually we were replaced by the C Division from Grey Mare Lane in Manchester. Again we boarded the coaches and were ferried back to our headquarters. Many of my older colleagues slept most of the way home, but I couldn't, I was just too wired. The images of destruction were so vivid and in a way unreal. However, sleep eventually took hold and I was woken when we arrived at Ashton. We were informed to parade for duty later that evening and to prepare to return to Toxteth.

Copycat riots broke out all over England, including Leeds, Brixton and Manchester. Some blamed social deprivation and a lack of communication between police and local communities, but the riots were criminal, and the vast majority involved were the less savoury elements of society. Nevertheless, the Conservative government was seriously worried. Many police forces, including Greater Manchester, hadn't prepared officers for this style of policing, and therefore the only action open to senior officers was to flood the streets of most large cities with extra police officers.

For the next four months I would find myself on PSUs (police support units) between Toxteth and Manchester, either patrolling in serials of five or on mobile patrol with eight officers in the back of a police Transit or Sherpa van. The day the C Division replaced my PSU at Toxteth led to another night of violent public disorder and two officers from C Division were seriously injured. Rioters stole a JCB bulldozer and drove it into a police cordon. Two officers were struck and one suffered serious fractures to his skull and chest. At this time an order was given to disperse the crowd by use of CS irritant – not a particularly bright order, but at least proactive, as officers were in serious danger. The resulting discharge of CS made the nation's head-lines: 'Police Shoot Demonstrators'. In fact, officers fired CS into the crowd from shotguns and a capsule containing the CS – known as a 'ferret' – struck a demonstrator on the chest, causing serious harm. In the subsequent months this incident, with the assistance of the media, became the subject of public outrage.

In my pragmatic eyes it was simple: the demonstrator was in the middle of a riot. Should he have been there? What was he doing there? Were police officers' lives in danger? I believe the use of CS was justified.

At one point during this period, my PSU had completed a tour of duty in Toxteth and we were heading home when our inspector informed us that he had received an urgent radio message. The Moss Side HQ had been attacked by a mob of rioters and serious public disorder had broken out. We had to make our way there immediately. I looked at my colleagues. The older ones maintained stern attitudes, while some of the younger ones, including myself, started to smile. This can be attributed to nerves and I certainly had butterflies in my stomach.

Little was said until we reached nearby Platt Lane Police Station and debussed. We started to get our kit together. We had by now been issued with 'argos' helmets – black motorcycle helmets with visors – and also leather shin pads and riot shields. We formed up in the car park and awaited instructions. I noticed a lot of commotion and several dark green Transit personnel carriers, unmarked but with protective grilles covering the windscreens, roaring into the car park. Once stationary, ten officers and one sergeant deployed from each vehicle. They looked impressive: each wore a three-quarter-length black nylon functional anorak, and they were in possession of argos helmets. They looked fit, determined and enthusiastic. I recognised several as members of rugby teams I had played for or against. A couple of the lads I knew well came over to me and started telling me and my colleagues what had happened.

For the previous five hours, officers had been involved in running battles with rioters around the Moss Side Alex Park Estate and the Platt Lane area. Buildings had been broken into, looting had occurred and several buildings were on fire.

My rugby-playing colleagues were called away by their supervisors and I asked who they were. These lads were members of the Tactical Aid Group, a unit of 60 officers formed by GMP to supplement divisional strength in the event of serious crime. I heard a couple of comments from my colleagues, such as, 'thugs', 'animals' and 'braindead'. However, I secretly thought to myself, those lads are fit, they are in a pro-active unit and they are in the thick of it. That's what I want to do.

My day-dreaming was interrupted with orders for deployment onto Platt Lane. For the rest of the night and into the morning, we stood behind shields while members of the public threw whatever came to hand at our lines. The only time they dispersed was when the Tactical Aid Group advanced aggressively towards them. I made my mind up: get my probation out of the way and apply for the TAG. But I still had another year to complete.

Eventually the disorder in towns and cities settled down. It had not gone away, but certainly in Moss Side the level of police manpower on the streets was affecting business – that is, criminal activity. Moss Side had its fair share of West Indian families, some of whom I was to meet later in my career and who were good, law-abiding people. They became known as the older generation. Their offspring had been brought up in an environment of fewer job opportunities, and some decided that an easier way to make money was crime, particularly the drugs trade. Moss Side was becoming known as the place to buy cannabis and heroin. People were travelling to buy from dealers and business was booming.

Moss Side was to become a powder keg of rival gangs and killings which would explode five years later. Rioting and public disorder wasn't encouraged by organised gangs. It brought the police and the police affected business. Let the community leaders deal with the police and create relationships and partnerships in all sorts of drives and incentives; the gangs could get on with business.

* * *

I enjoyed my next year and a half at Ashton. I became a driver and had to attend a four-week driving course at the force's driving school, where I was taught car control. Every morning we had to parade in best uniform, bulled shoes and perfect creases, while a motorcycle sergeant in sparkling knee-high boots and jodhpurs inspected us and asked terrifying questions such as the tyre pressure of a 1,600cc Triumph Dolomite or the principles of corners and bends. In my eyes he was a prat, but a prat I was glad to come across and I believe the job is sadder for not having that type of character anymore. He was a disciplinarian and his eccentric ways made you learn a boring subject.

After my driving course, Bob had me in his office. 'OK Andrew, now you can drive I don't want you hurtling around and having an accident. Watch what you are doing.' He wanted to avoid the tons of paperwork necessary if I had an accident in a police vehicle.

During this period two events stay with me that really started to mould me into the type of policeman I was to become. Bob had caught me rip-shitting about in a marked police Vauxhall Chevette and for a punishment had given me five beat for a set of nights. Five beat was a walk from the police station through the town centre and out towards Tameside General Hospital. It was a reasonably quiet area but had its share of burglaries. So for the next seven nights I would patrol on foot using my best techniques to catch burglars. Needless to say, by Sunday evening I was empty-handed.

At 22.15 Sunday, I left Ashton Police Station, wrapped up in my full-length greatcoat and, contrary to regulations, wearing a scarf – it was freezing. I completed a radio check and made my way onto Old Street, Ashton. I would walk through the town and out to the hospital at regulation pace, that would take a good hour, walk around my beat for two hours, walk back to the nick, another hour, have my refs, repeat the process and then, end of duty.

I was almost at the end of Old Street, near to the Highland Laddie public house and to be honest, daydreaming, when I noticed three lads in their early twenties come out of the Angel pub at the top of Old Street and walk towards me. They couldn't have seen me because the next thing they did was to jump onto the bonnet of a black MG parked in the street. The three of them then ran up and down the vehicle. Fucking hell, I thought, I don't need this, I'll go over to them, bollock them if there's no damage and send them on their way. Can't be fairer than that – it's just a stupid prank because they're pissed. So over I went.

As soon as they saw me, I heard, 'Don't let him get to his fuckin' radio' – and as a unit they attacked.

I wasn't prepared. They were extremely violent and I struggled to call into my radio for help. My movements were hindered by my thick greatcoat, it was three against one and I'm no street fighter. My only hope was to match their aggression and try to use my truncheon. No luck, they overpowered me and started to kick at my head. I finally managed to radio for assistance and now all I had to do was survive. Two of them were brothers called Cotrill and I managed to grab one and bring him to the floor. The pair of us fought while the other two were intent on kicking me all over Old Street.

I was thinking assistance was taking its time when I saw, from the corner of my eye, a short man in his mid-thirties, dressed in a red suit in the style of a teddy boy, come out of the Angel pub. Yes, a teddy boy – Ashton had its fair share of idiots. He walked over to me fighting with Cotrill and family as cool as a cucumber. I thought, he's not the most capable-looking but at least he's going to help. Instead he lashed out with his right leg and kicked me in the head. He was wearing black cowboy boots with pointed steel toecaps. I was incensed at this and all I could think of was smashing his face all over the tarmac. That was if I could get at him. He then went back into the Angel pub.

Help finally arrived after what seemed like half an hour but was in fact minutes. Two new policewomen on the shift had actually tried to commandeer a bus to reach me but had only caused it to crash. What could I say but thanks, and hard luck – they had a lot of explaining and writing coming their way.

Rocky Wallis was one of the first on the scene, with Andy. Two of the offenders had run off but I had managed to hold onto Cotrill senior. Taffy Williams, an old but brilliant dog-handler, had arrived and his dog was already tracking. Cotrill was thrown into the back of a police van. I stood there, blood dripping from my face and angry as fuck. I was outraged this had happened. I had only been going to bollock them!

Rocky enquired about my health but I was in no mood to listen. 'Just back me up sarge, I'm going into the Angel,' and off I stormed, straight into the pub. It was past last orders but 30 customers at least were still drinking up. The Angel attracted its fair amount of crap and in those days the landlord wasn't any friend of the police. These people must have seen what was going on outside but not one came to my aid. Nonetheless, I was after the teddy boy. He obviously wasn't gifted with intelligence; the idiot was sat drinking his pint. Now the rules of evidence said I should warn this fucker I was going to arrest him for assault and caution him. I obviously did this as he was flying through the exit, covered in his beverage, and was unceremoniously dumped in the back of a police van.

Taffy's dog tracked the other two and all four were charged with various degrees of assault and criminal damage to the car. I again had received a wake-up call. One, don't rely on the public to assist you. Why had the teddy boy attacked me? A combination of alcohol and a dislike for police officers. Two, stay aware at all times. I had dictated the outcome before even talking to the offenders. Nothing is what it seems, keep your guard up at all times, don't concede your advantage (in this case reactionary distance), radio for backup, and only concede when it is safe to do so and you can communicate on an equal level.

The public are a fickle lot and have little understanding of the bigger picture of policing. The following example stays with me. A bogus official had been stealing from areas of sheltered accommodation and warden-controlled flats for pensioners. The offender, described as a 14-year-old white male, would knock on the doors of the elderly, purporting to sell raffle tickets for a local charity. Once inside, he would aggressively search the flat for valuables, giving no consideration to the occupier. The youth had committed many serious offences. On this particular day he had been active in the Hurst Cross area of Ashton and a good description of what he was wearing had been obtained and circulated.

On the off-chance, I decided to go to the town centre fish and chip shop because certain days of the week in the afternoon they gave reductions to pensioners. I thought I'd visit the shop in case the offender had decided to ply his trade there. Sure enough, among the pensioners in the queue was a youth fitting the exact description of the offender.

I went into the shop in full uniform and approached him. As soon as he saw me, he displayed all the signs of the fight-or-flight syndrome: in his case flight, as he was looking for a way out and acting agitated. I knew this was the offender and, reaching into his pockets, found a book of raffle tickets. I took the tickets off him and gently clipped him on the head with the book.

Now this had been watched by at least 15 pensioners, all of them my gran's age. As soon as they saw me touch him with the tickets they were outraged. At least four tried to physically snatch the young boy back.

'Police brutality,' they shouted.

'What's your collar number? We'll complain.'

I was quite bemused. In hindsight, of course, they didn't realise I was arresting someone who was actually preying on them, but it showed me that people are prepared to believe the worst of a police officer. Why? Maybe media misrepresentation, rotten apples in the barrel – or is it human nature? In national newspapers we very rarely see what good deeds police officers do, but more the failures and fuck ups, perhaps it makes more interesting reading and therefore we become conditioned to expect the worst.

In August 1982 I completed my two-year probation and received a slip of paper acknowledging my continuing role as a police constable. My superintendent also wanted to see me. A glimmer started to glow in my mind: this would be a good time to request a transfer to the Tactical Aid Group. I had completed my two years and, according to force regulations, I was entitled to request a transfer. Fozzie said he would endorse my report but didn't think I stood a chance due to my short service and youth. What did Bob know?

Off I went to see my new divisional super, Colin Rankin. He had recently been in charge of the TAG. I knew him because in his younger days he was a competent rugby player. As he had got older he had become involved in the administration of the force rugby union team and had often watched matches. This was the ace up my sleeve; maybe a bit of favouritism would get me at least an interview for TAG.

So after Colin had congratulated me on my appointment as a qualified police constable, I gave him my request for a transfer to TAG. Colin looked at me from behind his desk, smiled and informed me that he respected my request, however I would have to complete another 12 months on uniform patrol duties and then he would endorse my request.

'Oh fuck.'

Colin was fair, I respected what he said, and I would wait another 12 months. In fact, I would wait only six months before I received a summons to see Mr Rankin again.

I wasn't that disappointed – I was still enjoying my time at Ashton. I suppose I had developed confidence and a certain arrogance during my probationary period. I was confident in my skills and felt competent to deal with most policing situations. How foolish I was.

* * *

It was a summer Sunday evening, I was unaccompanied on mobile patrol when my radio blurted out, 'Control to 6076.'

'Go ahead.'

'Can you attend The Gates of India? Trouble with customers.'

'Will do.'

I altered my route to The Gates of India restaurant on Stamford Street. It was about 23.00 and it had been quiet. I knew other patrols would attend because a call of that nature generally meant customers the worse for drink and volatile. Also the Indian restaurants were good to us; you could always get a free coffee and an onion bhaji on a cold night.

I was the first to arrive. I parked my van outside the restaurant and went up a steep flight of stairs that opened into the restaurant area. It was packed, with at least 80 people inside. The manager, Mr Patel, an elderly and distinguished Indian gent, pointed out two obviously blind men, both with white sticks, aged between

25 and 30, of slim build and scruffily dressed. They were together at a table near the stairwell. Mr Patel explained they had refused to pay and were shouting, swearing and being obnoxious, upsetting other customers. Shouldn't be a problem, I thought, so I called off the other patrols.

'Right Mister Patel, come with me. You ask them to leave, I'll do the rest.'

We went over. I noticed that both men were definitely visually impaired. One had an empty eye socket and an eye that didn't fix or focus. The other had eyes that were completely clouded over. Mr Patel politely informed them that he wanted them to leave and would forfeit the bill. A decent thing to do, I thought; whereupon one of them told him to 'stick' his meal. I sat down and explained who I was.

'How the fuck do we know you are who you say you are?'

I let them hold my police helmet, which they threw to the floor. This wasn't going as planned.

'Now listen lads, the manager has been good enough to forfeit the bill, will you please leave the restaurant.'

'Fuck off, ape.'

'There's no need for that language. Should I get you a taxi?'

'Fuck off.'

My sympathy was diminishing. 'Listen, I am a police officer, please leave.'

They had thrown my helmet onto the floor and I had embarrassedly retrieved it, hoping no-one had seen. Fat chance. OK, I thought, I'll give myself some credibility.

'I will prove to you I am a police officer.' I would let them touch my radio, which was on a harness around my neck.

'Listen lads, I'm serious, I am a police officer – feel this radio.'

Stupid move. As soon as one of them got hold of it he started to swing me to and fro on my seat. I tried to act as if nothing was happening but by now I had the full attention of the restaurant. I extricated myself as coolly as possible.

'OK lads, you give me no option but to escort you from the premises.'

I stood up, took hold of the first one and led him to the top of the stairs. This was going to be difficult because he was shouting and struggling and I would have to assist him down the stairs. After an arduous struggle, we made it to the bottom. I told him where we were and to be careful as the main road was just outside the doors.

'Fuck off twat,' was his reply. Not 'thanks' as I had expected. Oh well, I would go and get number two.

Number one had now started to attack the front door and was kicking and hitting it with his white stick. When I arrived upstairs, number two was howling like a wolf and waving his stick about. This was going from bad to worse. I ducked under his stick, got hold of him underneath his armpits and lifted him from his seat. I then had the same problem escorting him downstairs. I eventually arrived in the small foyer downstairs, where number one had gone berserk, kicking and lashing out. I tried shouting, 'Come on, behave, I will get you a taxi.' They both homed in on this noise and started hitting me with their white sticks. This was becoming highly embarrassing and I couldn't radio for assistance. I would be the laughing stock at the nick.

All three of us found ourselves outside on the pavement. Blind one and two were still behaving violently but I was more concerned they would wander onto the main road and get knocked down. By now I had the inkling of a plan. I wouldn't arrest them but I would force them into the back of my van; hopefully they would calm down. I was also aware that the majority of the customers were watching from the windows above.

I grabbed number one and manhandled him to the back of the van. I was talking to him all the time telling him to calm down, he wasn't in trouble, I was trying to help him. As I opened the back doors, I felt an almighty crack to my head and started to see stars. I turned and saw number two about to hit me again with his stick. To this day I'm still ashamed but I had no option, he could have seriously wounded me. I struck him straight in the face and he fell over. I immediately picked him up and threw him into the back of the van. Number one now attacked and struck me at least twice with his stick. Blood trickled into my eyes as I pushed him into the van as well and shut the doors, as if I was preventing a cat escaping.

I then thought, oh fuck, what have I done? I heard loud tapping noises on glass. I looked up and saw all the customers who were looking out of the windows applauding me. I couldn't have done that badly then. I took the blind pair to Ashton-under-Lyne. Subsequent checks revealed they had plenty of form for police assault and similar offences. However, I managed to bypass the system. My pride wouldn't allow me to charge them, contrary to the advice of my superior officers. I actually took them to number one's home address, where I met his mother, who had several other children, all blind. She was a lovely lady who deserved better than her son's behaviour.

I had been taught another valuable lesson: don't judge a book by its cover.

CHAPTER FIVE

The Tactical Aid Group

In late February 1983, I was summoned to the superintendent's office.

'Sit down,' Colin Rankin instructed me. 'Have you got a pair of hiking boots?'

'No sir.'

'Well get a pair, you start on TAG next month. Don't let me down, they need a good centre.' TAG's rugby team was short of a half-decent player for the back three-quarters.

Chief Inspector Phil Sunderland knew me and knew I wanted to go on TAG. He was its commander and a good friend of Mr Rankin's. I left Rankin's office thanking him and with the following warning in my ears: 'Don't let me down.'

Six weeks later I paraded at Longsight Police Station, the headquarters of the D Division. I had received my transfer orders and been posted to Four Group, Longsight Tactical Aid Group.

In the mid-1970s, Greater Manchester Police had decided that the force needed a unit of men who could deploy and supplement divisional officers in the event of a major incident. The idea of the Tactical Aid Group was born. In the beginning, TAG was a part-time placement, but as demand grew it became full-time. The then-Chief Constable, James Anderton, knew how effective the unit had been during the Moss Side riots and also noted that the force had been seriously disadvantaged when TAG had been deployed to Toxteth. He issued instructions that the unit was not to be used on Operation Response, but was to be kept in force at all times. He also instructed Chief Inspector Sunderland to define and clarify TAG's duties and specialisation.

By 1983, TAG had clear terms of reference. Each officer would be trained to the highest standard in public order tactics. TAG would be deployed to deal with violent disorder and the term of the day was 'early resolution'. TAG would assist the CID with major incidents such as rape, murder, abduction and bombings. Officers would specialise in firearms and supplement the Firearms Department if required. They would be used for protection duties such as movements of Category A prisoners or of high-value loads, and for minding highly prized informants – this was the beginning of the 'supergrass' era. TAG units would also be present at most football matches.

Each TAG officer would have the opportunity to attend a range of courses: bomb scene management, basic surveillance, shotgun, rifle, pistol, public order instructor, advanced driving, heavy goods vehicle and public service vehicle. All officers would be sent to Bailey Head in the Kielder Forest near Carlisle for a five-day duties familiarisation course.

When I joined, one chief inspector was in overall command, with an inspector, a sergeant and a police constable stationed at Fiddis House in charge of administration and operational deployment. Another inspector, two sergeants and twenty PCs were based at Stretford and split into two groups, known predictably enough as One Group and Two Group. Longsight had Three Group and Four Group and Heywood had Five Group and Six Group. The TAG was part of X Department, GMP's uniformed operations command structure.

I was full of trepidation when I arrived at TAG's headquarters at Fiddis House, an old detached property near GMP's main base at Chester House in Old Trafford. I was leaving the comfort zone of G Division, where I felt confident and at ease with my duties, to join what was already a notorious unit. As I walked in

I saw some of the TAG lads dressed in civilian clothing and all at least ten years older than me. One or two faces I recognised from rugby but they just grunted and barely acknowledged me. I would later find out why, but at the time it worried me. What had I let myself in for?

I walked in in my best uniform and introduced myself to the admin PC, who looked up from his desk and coolly appraised me with a look he usually reserved for some piece of shit on the street.

'Go upstairs,' he said. 'Forrester and Robins will see you.'

Who are they, I thought? This was meant to be a formality; Colin Rankin never mentioned an interview.

I went up to an open-plan office, which was empty. I looked around and, as no-one was about, I sat down and picked up a daily crime bulletin from the desk, thinking I would read this until Forrester and Robins appeared. I was so engrossed that I didn't notice the appearance of a uniformed sergeant and inspector.

'Who the fuck said you could read items from my desk?'

I jumped, looked around with my heart in my mouth and saw a uniformed inspector, approximately 5ft 9ins, sporty build with short grey hair and somewhat like an Action Man, glaring at me. Now a crime bulletin is for everyone to read, so naively I tried to explain.

'Stand up when you address a senior officer.'

Oh fuck, I was off to a bad start. I was instructed to put the bulletin down by a grizzly old sergeant who was 6ft 2ins, of large build, with an amused twinkle in his eyes.

'Sit down, son,' he said. 'Tell us why you want to join the Tactical Aid Group.'

For the next half hour I answered the stock questions that everyone gets in the quest for a job. Forrester asked most of them with Robins glaring on.

'Would you carry a firearm?' Robins asked.

'Of course sir.' The stock answer.

'Bit young aren't you?'

Not this again I thought. I was about to answer when a larger-than-life character walked in. He was in full uniform with three pips on his shoulder.

'I've told you Gordon, we need a good centre, that's why Hailwood is here,' he boomed across the office. Phil Sunderland had joined the interview.

'Going OK?' he asked.

'Not sure sir.'

'Well fuck off, see you next Monday.'

When I joined TAG in 1983, interviews meant as little as in most specialised departments within GMP. It was an informal process. First a recommendation, then fact-finding. Did an existing member of the unit know the individual? Did he have bottle? Could he be trusted? Could he work in a team and did he have a sense of humour? Once this was established, an official order was issued and a transfer arranged, which was when the real proving took place. To start with you were treated with contempt by your peers, you bought the brews, you drove, you did the menial tasks and more importantly, you kept your mouth shut. It didn't matter who you were or how good you had been in your division, you had to prove yourself again, and a chance to do that would never be far away.

In an arrest, a large-scale fight, a violent football match or if a colleague needed assistance, your response would be judged by your operational group. This might take months and your future would be discussed over a pint or during downtime among the nine officers who made up your group. If you couldn't handle the piss-taking or menial tasks, or your bottle was in question, then they would approach the group sergeant and tell him – if he didn't already know – that you weren't up to it. It seemed a primitive selection system but over the four and a half years I served proudly with TAG, it was a system that proved itself time and again. TAG had no time for malingerers or wankers and the lads soon got rid of them. Primitive but efficient.

So one cold Monday morning I found myself on the fourth floor of Longsight HQ, outside the room that would serve as my operational office for the next four and a half years. I had a pair of hiking boots and warm clothing. I was 22 years of age and the youngest member of TAG. How long would I last?

★ ★ ★

I knocked on the door and walked into an atmosphere of raucous inter-group rivalry. The office was about 40 by 40 foot, crowded with enough lockers for 23 officers. In the centre were two tables with a phone on each, and at the back behind the lockers was a single table adorned with files and a phone. A whiteboard covered one of the walls. The office was full to capacity and hot from the body heat of 20 adult males, arguing, laughing and taking the piss. As I stepped over the threshold I felt like a cowboy walking into a hostile saloon. The place went deathly quiet.

'Who invited you in?' boomed a voice. 'Get out and wait till you're told to come in.'

I found out later that all new boys go through a similar introduction but I wasn't about to argue, so outside I went. Five minutes later, as I was running through the options of how to introduce myself, the door opened and out stepped a smartly dressed (for hiking kit), bald-headed male, approximately 6ft tall and slim, who introduced himself as Phil, the sergeant of Four Group. He was cool with me and told me that every Monday the full TAG got together for a training day. On this occasion we would be going on a 15-mile walk across the Derbyshire moors. He went on to tell me that at times we might have to assist mountain rescue teams, so a bit of familiarisation with the moorland wouldn't do us any harm. Also, a training day was a time for 60 TAG officers to get to know each other better and to introduce their new boys. I wondered what he meant by the last statement, but kept my mouth shut.

Phil enquired if I was fit.

'Reasonably.'

He smiled. 'A few of the lads say you are OK, but we'll see. Get to know the lads and remember you are now a member of Group Four.'

Introduction to my colleagues took place in the back of a personnel carrier. Each group had a three-litre navy blue Ford Transit or riot van, with enough seats for 12 men in full riot complement. All the vans had attachments so that protective grilles could be fitted and were equipped with a PA system, klaxons and blue lights. They were the latest in riot technology and six vans in convoy looked extremely impressive. I was to find out that they were superbly effective in large-scale public disorder situations.

En route to our start point somewhere in Derbyshire, I introduced myself to the lads. Some would later become solid friends, but not until I had proved myself. GMP had its fair share of characters within its ranks and TAG was no different. Some of them scared me senseless.

Steve, or 'Jabba' (for his likeness to Jabba the Hutt in *Star Wars*), was one of the main characters and at times the bane of my life. He was 6ft 2ins, 34 years old and easily 18 stone, with a massive beer belly. His face was the colour of a strawberry and he had a voice like a foghorn. Jabba had the best sense of humour and was extremely intelligent and quick-witted. Before joining he had his own team of doormen working in Blackpool. He was respected by all the TAG lads and mixed easily with each group. Although he was 18 stone, I would later see him run a half-marathon, and his bulk never hindered him. It took time but I would come to respect Steve and his qualities as a policeman. He would also get me into a lot of shit, but he is someone I am still proud to call a friend. Jabba was also an exponent of the extremely skilled art of van fighting. He weighed me up and must have rubbed his hands, because for the next couple of months I would be his main sport.

Joe was Mr TAG – he lived and breathed it. He had joined young and was now senior PC and one of the lads who had recommended me. He was five ten and solid, of Italian extraction, and had played rugby league to an extremely high standard until the job and injury forced him to quit. Joe kept me at arm's length for a while, but he was to become my mentor at TAG, responsible for my improved fitness and another firm and reliable friend.

Joe was in charge of the riot equipment store and he made sure I was issued with the appropriate kit: flame-proof coveralls, protective shin pads, a groin protector, a NATO helmet, protective gloves and anorak. The anorak was an excellent bit of kit which only TAG lads were allowed and it was worn with pride. Joe warned me to keep an eye on it all because Three Group were 'thieving bastards' and Robins had a habit of turning the unit out at all hours for kit inspection.

Steve had come from the G Division and had relinquished the role of new boy to Tony. He had the ability to make you laugh in any situation and was an honest and likeable character, never stuck for words. He had at least twelve years in the job and was highly experienced. He was one of the main characters in the group and would give Jab a run for his money. Steve was the spit of the character Gomez from the black-and-white TV series *The Addams Family*. He was also a fantastic singer, so the van was never short of a tune or two. He again was a man I would come to respect and rely on, another great friend.

Tony had been the new boy until I arrived. Nothing fazed Tony, he was a former Marine with a real laid-back attitude. He was extremely competent and would have gone places within GMP if it wasn't for an ex-Marine pal of his to whom he displayed absolute loyalty. Tony was sacked from GMP but this didn't appear to bother him; he got his head down in the law books and is now a solicitor earning twice as much money.

Sanders was an ex-squaddie and there was nothing he couldn't drive, from HGVs to tanks. He wasn't the most dynamic lad and if Jabba wasn't on my back, he was on Sanders'. This didn't seem to bother Sanders as long as he had a fag in his mouth. He was never the first out of the van but when assistance was needed Sanders was never far away.

Paul was a monster of a lad and again an experienced policeman. He was a good six foot two, of solid build and a great sportsman when he put his mind to it. He was a proper Mancunian with no airs or graces, though patience was not his strong point. Paul was a genuine lad and would always give you his friendship without question.

I mention these officers for a reason. TAG would teach me about teamwork and how important and effective a close-knit team can be. I would forge friendships and camaraderie that I have found hard to equal, formed through difficult and exciting operations we would encounter while serving together.

The walk was a usual TAG training day. Each group stuck together and constantly took the piss out of the other units. Competition and rivalry were a big part of the TAG spirit. During the day I came across quite a few faces I knew from rugby. A couple of the lads acknowledged me but not warmly, though I was told to be at Stretford for midday Thursday – we were playing F Division (Salford) and I had a place on the team.

Eventually we came back to the car park we had started from. I was about to get into the van when I was shouted back.

'Where are you going?'

I thought the day had been going too well.

'What about a song from the new boy?' came the shouts and jeers from the other units.

Jab introduced me as Four Group's new boy and said I would

sing a rendition of 'You Can't Kick Nelly in the Barn'. As I sang, all sorts of bits of crap were thrown at me. I was then grabbed, stripped naked and made to run through the car park before getting back into the van. The rest of the lads jumped in and the comment 'fuckin' useless' was made.

I needed toughening up and Jabba set about teaching me the art of van fighting. For the next hour on the journey back he wrestled me around the van. The purpose of his attack was to 'blurt' my nose – pinch the tip – so I would end up like a clown from Billy Smart's Circus. For half an hour I kept Jabba at bay, but eventually his bulk wore me out. He bundled me under a seat where I remained for the rest of the journey. As the van pulled up at Longsight, the rest of the lads grabbed me and held me down while Jabba finished his dirty deed. For the rest of the week I walked around with a nose blazing like a Belisha beacon. So finished my first day on TAG.

This event could be classed as humiliating, conduct unbecoming of a police officer, childish, even bullying. However, the exercise had its purpose: first, to teach the individual he starts from base level no matter what his background and how competent an operator he has been, and second to test his response. If an individual can't handle this type of abuse, how would he react when faced with a hostile crowd intent on assaulting him, throwing urine, excrement or even used sanitary towels at him? If an officer couldn't take the shit the TAG lads dished out, what use would he be in a cordon facing 500 football fans full of alcohol and intent on committing violence? He would be a liability and a weakness in the ranks.

This initiation served TAG well for many years. PCs, sergeants and inspectors all went through it. It was later banned by senior officers who had never served on the operational side of TAG and would not have been good enough if given the chance. I suppose in this age of political correctness it had to go, but since then I have seen a fair few wankers who have had the front to call themselves TAG officers, and I think this is due to the 'correct and formal' selection criteria.

Training days were usually held at Hough End in Whalley Range, where the Mounted Section is based. Hough End is also the force's recreational complex and has a large weight room and gymnasium surrounded by rugby, football and cricket pitches. A training day usually consisted of a five- or eight-mile run. Once the unit had finished we would complete a series of physical exercises such as press-ups, sit-ups and squat thrusts. The training day would then finish with a game of murder ball.

Murder ball is played on any type of pitch and has few rules. Two teams oppose each other and numbers don't matter. A medicine ball is thrown in the centre and the object of the game is to pick up the ball and pass it to a team-mate or run towards the opposition's goal line. The tricky part is that the opposition can stop you scoring by any means apart from punching or kicking. Murder ball was the only time each group would play as a unit, with One and Two groups representing Stretford, Three and Four Longsight, and Five and Six Groups Heywood. Stretford would play, say, Longsight, with the losers playing Heywood. These games were tough and physically demanding, but fun and a great way to create *esprit de corps*.

* * *

In February 1984 I was given joining instructions for a ten-day basic firearms course at Diggle Range. No longer the new boy, I was looking forward to it and both Jabba and Tony were on my course. It had been delayed due to bad weather and didn't commence until the middle of March. There were 14 students and six instructors, and among the students was Chief Inspector Young, who had recently taken over command of TAG.

It was a Monday morning and the weather was bitterly cold. The range house had limited heating and the wind whistled through. The instructors' room, situated at the rear, was like a furnace and they would only wander out to deliver lessons or when it was time to go on the ranges. The range house would serve as our classroom, drying room, weapon cleaning room and dining room. It was multi-functional, though nowadays the Health and Safety Executive would have a heart attack.

We were split into two details of seven. One detail would partake in range duties in the morning while the other would learn theory, then we'd swap over in the afternoon. Mike Antrobus, the firearms sergeant in charge of the course and someone who still makes me chuckle, made it quite clear this was a pass or fail course. In those days instructors didn't need a clinical excuse to get rid of a student – gut feeling alone could be enough and you were knackered if your face didn't fit.

The range suffered from poor drainage and little shelter. Goretex was in its infancy so you either wore heavy-duty nylon or the traditional wax-coated jacket, as weather conditions were often terrible. The sand and grit surface was covered with wooden duck boards which were soon covered themselves when it pissed down or snowed. They were also treacherous if you ran along them.

In the early 1980s the standard issue firearm for police officers in most forces was the Model 10, four-inch Smith & Wesson revolver, holding six rounds of .38 calibre ammunition. Incidents such as that involving Barry Prudom, who shot dead three police officers in North Yorkshire, the Cherry Groce and Stephen Waldorf shootings in London, and Michael Ryan's massacre in Hungerford, had made senior police officers sit up and take notice, though some had to be pushed screaming and kicking into this new, unstable era.

Firearms attracts more than its fair share of incompetents. One of the sad facts of being an AFO is that it can be a great earner in overtime. Don't get me wrong, I enjoyed the money and believe you should be recompensed for working unsociable and difficult times, but it shouldn't be the motivation to be an AFO. I actually wanted to arrest armed criminals, something that would later become almost an addiction. Yet I was to find it was only a small minority of officers who actually strove to arrest armed criminals, and these officers could be ostracised and treated unfairly by other members of the force.

The Model 10 revolver is accurate to 150 feet in the hands of a good shot, though most officers are competent to only 75. I had an advantage with my shooting skills as I had been taught to shoot as a cadet. I was also familiar with the instructional staff, so I felt that if I didn't fuck up or get on the wrong side of an instructor, I should pass the course. The only problem was Harry, the senior instructor, and it wouldn't be long before he noticed me.

We were taught to shoot from standing, kneeling, sitting and prone and to reload or tactical reload (part reload) under pressure conditions. The Model 10 revolver's six-round cylinder revolves anti-clockwise and you have to understand the mechanics of the weapon to keep it operational, something which is hammered into you and rightly so. Harry was excellent at this, he would only have to walk on to the range and officers immediately put themselves under pressure. He would start bawling instructions and orders, reduce the exposure timings of the targets and some officers would go to pieces. In a way this made sense but I argued that this pressure should be applied once you have learned the basics, not while learning.

Extra rounds were kept in your right pocket if you were right-handed or your left pocket if you were left-handed, then loaded individually into the chamber while the other hand rotated the cylinder anti-clockwise. In the freezing weather, with your hands numb and inflexible, bullets often ended up on the floor, and Harry's logic was to kick them down the range or stand on your hands when you attempted to pick them up. This was not altogether helpful when you had to maintain constant shooting averages. Most of us learned to put up with this and get on with passing the course.

On the fifth day I was in the classroom with Tony, Jab and Chief Inspector Young, catching up on how we were doing over a brew, when Young was summoned to the phone. After five minutes he returned and spoke to Jab.

'Did you entertain members of the Parachute Regiment about a year ago?' he asked.

Jab replied that the Paras had been invited over for a tour of TAG and the dog section. Senior members of TAG had accompanied them and then gone massively on the piss with them. It was then that TAG had been invited to join the Paras on an exercise called March Hare.

We could tell Chief Inspector Young was not happy. He addressed the three of us.

'So while on the piss you thought it was a good idea to invite yourselves on this Para exercise?'

He looked at Jab. Jab explained it wasn't just him, shrugged his shoulders, smiled and in his usual charismatic way asked Youngy why he appeared to be displeased. Youngy explained that the phone call he had just received had been from a chief superintendent from Oldham requiring the names of the officers attending March Hare. Four were required and when the chief superintendent had asked TAG admin for names, he had, not surprisingly, drawn a blank.

I could see where this was heading and tried to excuse myself, with Tony nearly falling over himself to come with me. Youngy called us back and explained that though it wasn't an order it would be in our best interest to comply with his request. He went on to explain that because we were part of Four Group and Jab had organised the invitation, and in order not to let GMP and, in particular, TAG down, Jab, Tony, Phil (our sergeant) and I would be at the Paras' HQ in Oldham that evening at 18.00 to take part in the exercise.

I tried to present a defence but Youngy quickly talked over me. Tony smiled and took it on the chin. When I tried to take my anger out on Jabba he told me to fuck off or he would splat me – a useful tactic he'd developed over the years.

I was meant to be playing rugby on Saturday followed by a good drink, and I hadn't had a pint for a couple of weeks. Also, I needed to recharge my batteries for the next five days, but all that was out the window. I approached Jab moodily and asked him what we could expect. He had no idea and told me to go and ask Tony, an ex-Marine who should know. Tony explained it would be shit and not to expect much sleep. Apart from that, he knew nothing.

CHAPTER SIX

Operation March Hare

Operation March Hare was to take place in the Kielder Forest. A unit from the Parachute Regiment Territorial Army would attempt to infiltrate an exercise area within the forest, plant specialised demolitions and remain undetected for 30 hours while 'enemy' forces would try to discover them. The infiltration would be attempted by three operational groups. Group One, led by a young captain, would parachute to an area nearby, Group Two would attempt infiltration by tactical patrolling, and Group Three would take care of logistics – basically a food party.

At 18.00 I met up with Phil, Tony and Jab outside the barracks in Oldham. I was in scruffy training kit and had a warm jumper and waterproof jacket. The rest of the lads were dressed similarly. The four of us made our way through the barrack gates unchallenged and into a large drill hall, whereupon a squat, bandy-legged male in his late 40s shouted, 'Who the fuck are you?'

Phil informed him and asked him who he was.

'Sarn't Major Gee,' was the reply. 'Fuck off in there and get kitted out.'

Gee pointed to a room that was a hive of activity. Soldiers were entering, and leaving carrying bundles of equipment. We made our way in and were immediately equipped with full DPM (camo) kit, including boots, Bergen (rucksack), waterproof jacket and ground sheet. Tony enquired about sleeping bags and was told politely to fuck off.

We were directed to an operations room and each found a

71

seat. A young, capable-looking paratroop officer introduced himself to us and said we were expected. He informed us that shortly he would conduct a full operational briefing and implementation and detail us to relevant duties. Up to this stage I was under the impression that we were to act as observers. It was becoming quite clear that we were more than observers and were expected to partake in the exercise.

To be honest I took no notice of the officer's briefing, it was beyond my understanding. I had little knowledge of military jargon and his terminology went right over my head. The only time my ears pricked up was when our duties were detailed. Tony and I were selected to join Sgt Major Gee's group, tasked with patrolling into the area. Phil was to join the captain's group and Jabba was posted, not surprisingly, to the food party. After an hour the briefing finished. We were told to get a few pints in the local pub and be on the coach for midnight. Phil and Jabba joined their respective groups – I wouldn't see them again until Sunday afternoon.

Prior to boarding the coach, Sgt Major Gee introduced us to his lads and informed Tony and me that our unit would be responsible for transporting and deploying the special munitions. For the purpose of the exercise, the special munitions were two brown ammunition liners filled with concrete. I good-naturedly volunteered myself and Tony to carry the ammo liners, which were approximately 1ft by 1ft. Without any hesitation, Gee's men passed over the ammo liners, much to Tony's annoyance.

'What the fuck are you doing?' he asked.

With some embarrassment I explained I was only being helpful.

'Well don't be,' said Tony.

We put the special munitions into our Bergens and climbed aboard the coach.

'Listen to me,' said Tony, 'stick to me like glue. If we get bumped we fight like fuck to escape, do you understand?'

'Yes,' I said, wondering what there was to worry about.

The drive to Kielder was extremely boring and most of the unit fell asleep. After about four hours, Gee started shouting along the bus.

'Start preparing for the drop-off point.'

Lights were switched on, kit was checked and camouflage cream passed about. Tony cammed up my face, then his own. This Gee is a joker, he informed me. 'Start switching on,' was his next remark. After a few more miles the coach stopped and 20 paratroopers and two civilian police officers deployed into the dark.

'Go tactical,' someone shouted, and the paratroopers deployed in all-round defence, pointing their self-loading rifles (SLRs) and Sterling sub-machine guns towards their area of responsibility. As my eyes adjusted to the dim light, I began to see more. We were on a country road in the middle of a pine forest. Both sides of the road were dense with undergrowth. The sky was black but for the bright glow of thousands of stars. It was freezing.

The coach drove off and Gee whispered that we would tactical patrol for a mile or so and then find somewhere to get our heads down until first light. We moved off along the road, myself, Tony and Sgt Major Gee in the centre of the moving formation. After about 45 minutes we pulled off the road. The squaddies started to unroll sleeping bags and get inside them, boots and all, and immediately fell asleep. I put on my spare jumper and placed my ground sheet on the floor. I was feeling really sorry for myself when I heard Tony whisper.

'Andy, come over here. Don't take this the wrong way, but we are going to have to cuddle up together and throw my ground sheet over us or we will freeze to death.' I didn't have a problem with this and the pair of us shared a freezing couple of hours huddled together.

Eventually I heard birds start to sing, then weak sunlight

filtered through the branches of the trees we were sheltering beneath. The Paras packed their Bergens and deployed again in tactical formation. Sgt Major Gee appeared to be having trouble confirming where exactly we were located. He was consulting another soldier and referring to a map when Tony strolled over and after a few minutes confirmed where we were and gave Gee a grid reference. This impressed Gee and he asked Tony where he had acquired his skills. Modestly Tony informed Gee he had served in the Marines for seven years and that Gee himself was nothing but a 'Para wanker'. Gee laughed and invited Tony to look after part of the map, which had been split in two for security reasons.

Gee told his Paras to start patrolling and pointed in the direction of the road. I'm no tactical genius but even I didn't think this was too smart. Within ten minutes, two military medics came running down the road towards us. The advance patrols stopped them and questioned them, finding out that the enemy was up ahead and coming our way. They also threw in an extra bit of information: the enemy had dogs.

The two medics took off as if the dogs were after them, leaving Sgt Major Gee somewhat bemused. He seemed to be struggling with his decision-making before finally settling for something basic.

'It's the Jocks, peg it.'

I had a problem with this command: surely we could do something more constructive, like hide or fight a tactical withdrawal, but no. The next few minutes were bedlam, with Paras running from one side of the road to another, trying to force their way through dense vegetation. Tony grabbed me.

'Come on mate, we're bugging out,' and legged it in the opposite direction to the Jocks with me not far behind. As we were sprinting away I could hear shouts and then the barking of dogs. Oh fuck I thought, I hope they don't release the dogs. I have seen police dogs in action and they are extremely effective but I have always been on the same side. I was about to find out what it was like to be on the receiving end. I was crapping myself and increased the pace.

I shouted at Tony, 'Keep running mate, they've released the dogs.'

Tony didn't reply but veered left into the undergrowth and started forcing his way through with me almost up his backside. We were running in a blind panic. I noticed that we were alone and the sound of the dogs seemed to be further away. Tony called a halt and hastily told me to hide. He pointed at a large tree that had been felled years earlier and was lying on the forest floor covered in moss and bracken.

'Get right under it.'

I didn't need telling twice. I started digging like a mole, pulling loose foliage over me in a blur of fright and panic. Police dogs scare me to death.

I lay still not daring to move. The forest had gone quiet and Tony was obviously doing the same as me. I strained my hearing but all I could hear was the thumping of blood circulating through my ears. I held my breath, scared in case my breathing was heard, and then I had to exhale and suck in oxygen as quick as I could because I had nearly asphyxiated. It was then I heard a dreaded noise, the patter of four legs on the forest floor, followed by a growling and sniffing. At least one dog had picked up our scent and was tracking us. I must have been giving off enough pheromones to put a skunk out of business.

The growling increased and my Bergen, which was still on my back, started to shake. The dog had found me and was shaking it furiously with clenched jaws.

'Tony, Tony, can you hear me?' I whispered. 'The fuckin' dog has got me.'

'Keep still, I'll sort it,' replied Tony.

What did he mean, sort it? Tony appeared from his hiding place armed with a two-inch penknife. He was going to stab the dog. I hope he does a good job, I thought, or he'll really piss the dog off.

'Put your hands up, shithead!'

It was a Scottish accent. I looked up from my hovel and saw our area had been surrounded by at least 15 squaddies in camouflage kit pointing weapons at Tony. A couple of them grabbed Tony, threw him to the floor and tied him up. The police dog was still tearing away at my Bergen, which was now in bits, though that was the least of my worries. Eventually a handler arrived and brought the dog under control. I was thrown to the deck, my arms pinned behind me and tied up.

'Where are your weapons?' the same Scottish voice asked.

'Fuck off,' shouted Tony. He had obviously resorted to being a Marine. Smash, I was kicked in the back.

'Where is your weapon?'

'I haven't got one.'

'Search the area,' shouted the Scot.

Both of us were sat up and again asked the whereabouts of our weapons. Tony didn't help matters by again telling them to 'fuck off, Para wanks'. A corporal came over to us and explained he was part of the hunter force and that we had been captured by members of the Scottish Paratroop TA Regiment and members of GMP Dog Section.

Fucking marvellous, how do I get out of this, I thought. I explained to the corporal that we were civilian police officers from GMP acting as observers, which was why we didn't have weapons. The corporal was reasonable and requested some evidence. Tony and I produced police warrant cards.

'Untie them,' he instructed.

The corporal soon became chatty and told us our unit had all been captured. As we retraced our steps back to the road we saw paratroopers lying prone, blindfolded and tethered amongst the verges. They were being guarded by the Scots Paras and dog-handlers. One of the dog-handlers walked over to us, had a good laugh to himself and returned to his colleagues telling them how two TAG 'empty heads' had been captured. The corporal told us that he was considering joining the police and asked us about the job. He even made us a brew and for half an hour we chatted over the merits of joining the force. I asked him what would happen to the captured soldiers, to which he replied some would be interrogated.

At that moment, a contingent of 15 Scots with dog-handlers, led by a senior NCO, came into view. The NCO took in the scene straight away and in a loud and arrogant manner asked the corporal who we were and why we weren't tied up with the others. Tony assessed the situation and immediately came up with a plan.

'Run!' he screamed at me.

Tony bolted like a bat out of hell in the opposite direction to the new arrivals. I didn't need asking twice, having decided the NCO was not good news, and set off after him.

Our escape attempt lasted all of 60 seconds as we ran straight into another team from the hunter force. Tony's intention was to run through them, creating as much damage and mayhem as possible. I followed, using all my skills to batter a way, but it was a lost cause. Sheer weight of numbers and physical force was against us.

We were quickly bound and blindfolded and thrown down with the rest of the unit. Tony had resorted to form and was again calling them 'Para wankers'. I was made to kneel with my hands behind my head. Not being the most supple of people, this stressful position took its toll. Eventually I heard someone approach me and ask if I was OK.

'Not really, I'm a bit uncomfortable like this, can I go back to lying down?'

This was not the right reply, and I was kicked in the back and thrown into the prone position. My damaged Bergen must have attracted my attacker's attention because he started searching it.

'What the fuck's this?' he asked.

'What the fuck's what?' I replied, with more than a little anger.

'This, you twat,' and he removed my blindfold and showed me the brown ammo liner.

'Special weapons,' was my naive reply.

'Search the other one.'

On Tony they found the same. I was picked up and thrown around like a rag doll and then someone decided to tap dance on my back. I twisted away, jumped up and pulled away my blindfold, quickly taking in the scene. There were four of them, with one little fucker wearing green gaiters. I tried to swing at him with my hands bound and managed to connect with the back of his head. It wasn't a particularly hard strike; I had wanted to knock him senseless, but it was just enough to annoy him.

I was forced back onto the floor and made to lie on my belly with my arms stretched above my head and re-tied. My outburst hadn't served any good purpose except to get me noticed and also gain me a serial tormentor. I had upset the little fucker, who I was later to find out didn't like police and was a midget with a real nasty streak. I was made to lie with the rest of the captives. All this took place in silence except when I was visited by the midget, who would whisper nasty things in my ear and then give me a kick in the side.

Eventually we were told to stand up, get in single file and hold on with both hands to the Bergen of the person in front. We were all still blindfolded and must have looked a sorry sight as we were made to walk along the road. The midget tripped me by kicking at my heels and calves whenever he could. This was really pissing me off and the next time he tried that I planned to jump him. Fuck the consequences, I thought.

Sure enough, soon after he returned and lashed out at my legs. I dived towards where I thought he was while trying to rip my blindfold off. Within seconds my captors were all over me like a rash and I heard the midget's voice.

'You dumb fuck, you will never be a Para.'

After another hour the terrain changed; we were no longer walking on tarmac but grass and dirt tracks. I now had to endure the midget's new trick of walking me into trees when the command to halt was shouted.

We were forced to lie down again in the prone position on what appeared to be a well-kept lawn. No further instructions were given and I just lay there listening to the sounds of vehicle engines and men with Scots accents shouting orders. Any time I tried to pull down my blindfold I received a swift kick in the ribs. The sound of snoring filtered through; obviously some of my captured colleagues had managed to sleep. It wasn't a bad idea but I was too annoyed. I hadn't expected to be captured and picked on by a midget and there didn't seem any way of explaining my way out of this nightmare. Obviously I wasn't helping myself by struggling – my best course of action was to keep quiet and not react.

I had noticed that the sun was starting to set and I was bloody freezing and shivering badly. I had heard of things like this going wrong and people dying of exposure; after all it was March and I wasn't dressed for winter weather. I had also been sweating considerably and my clothing was soaked. As I was considering my latest predicament, a voice said in my ear.

'Are you OK?'

I answered honestly, 'Not really, I'm freezing.'

'What? Freezing? You fucking wimp.'

All hell then broke loose. People were shouting at me, I was picked up bodily by at least four soldiers who started to run with me, headfirst.

'You will never make a Para!' they screamed at me.

Then I was flying through the air. I landed face first in an icy-cold swamp. I quickly started to struggle and fight for oxygen. I had been winded as I landed but the icy water shocked my system into defensively closing down. Then the midget was on me, forcing me under by jumping on my back. Instinctively I lashed out at him, trying to orientate myself by pulling down my blindfold. I noticed we were in the grounds of a large country mansion and I had been thrown into what was once a duck pond. Military Land Rovers were scattered about and the place was lit up with arc lighting. I was surrounded by four soldiers who quickly pulled me out and re-bound me. I was struggling quite violently when I heard a voice in my ear.

'Calm down or it will get worse.'

This was bad, I didn't want it any worse, so I tried to relax and take in my surroundings.

For the next few hours I was left alone and lay there shivering and feeling sorry for myself. The cold was really bothering me. I was soaked through and feeling miserable when I heard a shout.

'All senior NCOs and civvy police to be interrogated.'

This obviously applied to me and I felt relieved that I should now get a chance to explain my whole sorry situation. About half an hour later I was forced to my feet, my blindfold was removed and I was marched over to an open-back Land Rover where I joined seven other soldiers and Tony.

'Are you OK mate?' Tony enquired.

'Shut your face,' one of the MPs told him.

Tony laughed and winked at me. 'Dickhead,' he directed at the MP.

No, I thought, this is not going to plan. We were loaded up onto bench seats in a Land Rover. The MP struck the side of the vehicle and it lurched forward causing us to bunch together. The driver then accelerated away as if he was Michael Schumacher. We grabbed for anything that would prevent us bouncing about the vehicle. For the next 15 minutes we were driven at the speed of sound by an absolute lunatic along badly lit country roads. I'm not generally a poor passenger, but this drive was terrifying and by the look on everyone else's faces it wasn't just me who was crapping it. Without warning, the vehicle skidded to a halt, forcing us all to concertina again. I was grabbed by a huge individual wearing a red beret. He lifted me out of the Land Rover and planted me on the deck. I was completely shocked. I tried to get up, whereupon another red cap descended on me, forcing me back down. Then, expertly and proficiently, the pair of them stripped me of my clothing and left me naked except for a black hessian sack which one of them placed over my head and loosely bound around my neck.

Both captors then picked me up and forced me to run towards the fields. Fortunately the ground was frozen so it was easy going, but unfortunately for me I went over on my ankle and felt it crack immediately. I've had enough injuries in rugby to realise this was going to be painful. I was brought to a halt and forced into a wire cage. The boxed enclosure I had seen from the roadside had now become my accommodation. To get comfortable I was forced to sit with my knees crunched up and my head bowed. Back at the mansion I had felt miserable, cold and depressed. Now I felt fear, vulnerability and confusion. What had I done to end up this deep in shit? I then heard some female voices.

'Look, how big is that?' They were obviously referring to my old man. It seemed humiliation was the next ingredient to be added. I then heard someone screaming not to be thrown in, followed by a huge splash. They were now chucking people into the ponds. It will be my turn next, I thought.

Probably two hours later, I heard my cage open and a pair of hands pulled me out roughly. I was made to stand up and the sack was taken from my head. I blinked a couple of times and because it was dark didn't take long to orientate myself. I was standing completely naked in front of two MPs. A large olive green tent was some quarter of a mile ahead of me. Several of the captured Paras were in similar enclosures and looked as thoroughly miserable as I was. My ankle had ballooned to twice normal size and I could hardly stand. Here we go I thought, time for a ducking in the pond, but to my surprise I was made to limp towards the tent. I was pushed through the flaps and confronted by three senior military officers who were sitting at a makeshift wooden table. The interior was well lit and extremely warm. On the table in front of the officers was all my kit including the special weapon (the ammo liner) and my police warrant card.

'Name, rank, number?' I was asked.

'PC 6076 Hailwood,' I confirmed.

'Where is your weapon?'

I attempted to explain who I was and why I was here. Typically of most senior officers, they didn't digest half of what I said.

'What is the strength of your unit? What were your specific orders?'

'Fuck knows,' I replied. 'I wasn't listening.'

For the next 45 minutes I stood bollock naked in front of these men trying to explain my predicament.

'Take him away,' one of them finally shouted.

I was grabbed by the two MPs and returned to my cage. This time they threw in my clothing. I dressed the best I could in the confined space and left my boot loose on the swollen ankle. Some time later a regular Para major came to my cage.

'Are you really a civvy cop?'

'Yes.'

'Well, endex [end of exercise],' he replied.

He opened the cage and sent me to another tent in the field where there were obviously medical facilities, because it had a large red cross emblazoned on it. I saw a doctor who treated my ankle and told me to jump into a sleeping bag and get some sleep. I soon dropped off and was awoken by Tony and a regular sergeant major, who explained what had happened. The process of being left in the cold and sensory deprivation, which adds to fear and confusion, is the army's standard operating procedure when questioning the enemy. It is a weakening process, but something that I shouldn't have been subjected to without proper preparation and appropriate training. Tony's marine training had worked for him.

The enemy had been confused by my story and thought I was a plant to test their interrogation skills. When it became clear who we were, they couldn't get us out quick enough. The sergeant major apologised in typical blunt fashion and said what we had suffered was against the Geneva Convention. How true this was, I'm not sure. Then he drove me and Tony to a nearby army camp and ordered us a massive plate of bacon and eggs. It was Sunday morning. This whole process had taken almost 28 hours.

Later that day Phil and Jabba showed up. Phil had a large gash above his right eye. He explained his unit had been ambushed but he had escaped, and during the escape had been struck with the barrel of a rifle. He was in a good mood and had enjoyed the experience. Jabba explained that he'd had nothing to do on the food party. None of the designated units had rendezvoused with them during the last 30 hours and he was sick of eating and ready to go home.

'Before we go,' I explained to Jabba, 'come and help me look for a sadistic Scots midget wearing green gaiters.'

I filled in Phil and Jabba about our 28-hour ordeal. We then scoured the camp looking for my tormentor and had given up when I saw him looking out of the window of a departing coach. He was giving me the 'V' sign.

There was nothing I could do. Jabba, as usual, cheered me up.

'Fuck him,' he said. 'Now let's get on the coach and get back. I can't wait to tell the TAG lads what you've been through.'

CHAPTER SEVEN

Gun Cop

Monday morning came around all too fast. It was 08.30 and Jab was holding court with the rest of the course in the classroom at Diggle. It was another freezing and miserable day, the rain was lashing down and smashing into the windows of the range house. Jab had them hanging on every word as he described the weekend's events and how I had 'turned turtle' and squealed for all I was worth when caught by a bunch of inbred Jocks.

I limped over to defend myself – too late. Jab had already delivered the verdict and the lads had convicted me. Never let it be said that Jab let the truth get in the way of a good story. Oh well, I could live with it; I had more pressing worries. My ankle was in a bad way and I didn't want to get binned from the course. I wasn't about to complain to the instructors. I would have to hope the course didn't get too physical. By the look of the instructors, that shouldn't be too much of a concern. I had my ankle heavily strapped and had to hope that was enough.

The next four days passed with shooting and tactical skills. We learned the characteristics of the Model 10, how to shoot it in various positions, from standing supported to kneeling, sitting and prone. Our sense of direction skills developed. We were able to shoot 12 rounds in 25 seconds at 20 feet at multiple targets and expect 12 out of 12. We learned to draw the weapon from the holster safely and immediately engage targets to our left, right and rear. Shooting a handgun is not an easy skill to acquire. Television and cinema misrepresent the actual skills of hitting a static, never mind moving, target.

If a member of the public with no firearms skills at all was randomly chosen, and that person was given a revolver or self-loading pistol and asked to shoot a barn door 50 feet in front of them, I would put money on them missing. To shoot and hit a moving target is extremely difficult. Certain skills must be mastered, such as a firm and well-balanced stance. The weapon should be held correctly – the second and third fingers are the major support in the grip. If you hold the pistol too tight or too loose you can over- or under-compensate the shot. The target has to be acquired correctly through the sights of the weapon. This is known as sight picture.

The actual target should be a blur, the foresight of the weapon should be crystal clear and framed equally in the back sight. The forefinger should pull the trigger, rolling it in a constant motion allowing for follow through. The pad of the finger rests on the trigger. You should never snatch the trigger or, again, you will miss the target.

The margin for error is minimal and breathing is important. You either hold your breath prior to the shot and exhale immediately or constantly exhale throughout the shot. If you are employing SD (sense of direction – combat style), the target is acquired by bringing your weapon to eye level and keeping both your eyes open unless you are cheating on the range. Cheating by closing one eye makes sense, but in a live situation you would lose half your peripheral vision. Then you fire two quick rounds into the target. This is infamous and known as the 'double-tap'. The double-tap creates maximum trauma and in theory neutralises the threat more effectively.

Contrary to popular belief, a police officer is not taught to shoot to kill or wound. He is taught to shoot in the upper chest area, the actual life support system. It is believed if this area is hit then the threat will be incapacitated. The officer is taught to stop or neutralise the threat. During training you are taught to adhere to three priorities while engaged in firearms duties: number one is the safety of the public, number two is the safety of the police and number three the offender.

How to arrest an armed criminal on foot or in a vehicle is included in the course, followed by practical exercises. It is important to find appropriate cover, identify a backstop and, when practicable, announce your presence as an 'armed police officer'. The offender is meant to put his hands in the air and follow a series of complicated commands. If the offender is in a vehicle he would actually have to pass an exam before he could surrender properly.

I listened to these lessons and practical exercises with a keen ear and a willingness to digest everything I was taught, but at the back of my mind was a slight doubt of its practicability. Would this all work while engaged on an operation? Only time would tell. I would revisit these lessons many times in my career as an operational firearms officer and some, but not many, would be of value. The majority proved to be nonsense, but only experience would determine this.

On the Wednesday, all the students were taught the effects of CS irritant. It is believed that the only way to understand how CS affects a person is to experience it for yourself. Personally I agree with this but in this age of 'know-nothings', some senior person would argue to the contrary.

As I have already explained, Diggle Range covers a large area of moorland. Around this area are many derelict sheep and shepherd huts, ideal locations to stuff ten students into, all wearing aged S6 military respirators. So we were all made to spread out into a shepherd's hut which was approximately 10 by four. An instructor joined us and explained that he would fill the hut with CS. Once he was satisfied, he would make us walk over to him one by one, remove our respirators and calmly tell him our collar numbers, warrant numbers and place of duty. We were then to leave the hut in an orderly manner.

Now I had experienced this before as a cadet, and knew this wasn't exactly what would happen. The instructor told us before we were to experience our first dose of CS that we had to leave the hut. We left the hut and were immediately met by two other instructors, Roger and Harry. They started barking orders: we were to run up the nearest incline five times and then go through a series of press-ups, squat thrusts and burpees. The next 20 minutes were spent running up and down hills, press-upping and squatting to the commands of Harry and Roger. This procedure was designed to make us sweat and also increase our breathing speed. We were quickly ordered back into the shepherd's hut.

One of the instructors was by now trying to induce a CS environment by lighting solid aspirin-like tablets, which once alight quickly produced CS. He was having a problem keeping the tablets alight due to the strong moorland winds. The rest of us were trying to regulate our breathing and ensure we had a tight seal while fitting our respirators. The next thing I heard was:

'Grenade!'

Either Roger or Harry had thrown in a CS hand grenade. The lever sprang off and the grenade spewed out CS, which looks like thick, off-white smoke. I could tell that a couple of the lads were getting nervous and displaying the first stages of panic. This is what CS is intended for – it is a panic-inducing agent.

I also knew that the instructors would be assessing our reactions. We could easily fail on this part of the course. My major problem at the time was my ankle, which hurt like hell after all the exercise. It didn't take long before we couldn't see our hands in front of our faces. The hut was completely enveloped in CS. To be quite honest, whoever had thrown the grenade into the hut had used enough CS to disable Diggle village, never mind ten potential firearms officers. The reason we had been made to sweat now became evident, as the CS actually starts to burn wet or damp parts of your body. It gets between your bollocks, under your arms, into your eyes and also affects your respiratory system. The more CS you experience, the more you are able to withstand. The burning of the extremities isn't a major problem but once it's in your eyes and you start to inhale, it becomes like nothing you can describe. You can breathe, but because it is burning the inside of your throat and lungs, your body starts to induce the fight-or-flight syndrome. I have seen officers trying to run through brick walls under the effects of CS.

I heard the instructor say, 'OK, make your way to my voice in single file.'

One by one we made our way to the voice.

'Take off your respirator and tell me your collar number, warrant number and station.'

Once a student took off his respirator, all you heard was a garbled 'fuck' and a hasty retreat from the hut. Outside, other instructors were waiting for us, issuing instructions.

'Face the wind and don't rub your eyes.'

Most of us by now were bent double coughing our arse through our lungs. CS is great for those with nasal problems because snot drips from your nose in large globules. A particularly nasty trick I learnt over the years was to tell people you don't like to go and wash the CS off. Once they place water onto surfaces affected by CS, it recreates the effects already suffered and you get double your money. The only effective cure for CS is fresh air and wind.

Classification day is always a Friday and, depending on the weather, always in the morning. Those who tell you they are not nervous during classification are liars. There is a considerable amount of pressure during the test shoots. A lot is self-induced. I have seen grown men cry when they have been told they have failed. The pressure comes from not wanting to fail and fear of ridicule from the other lads once you return to your unit. For some it's the chance of a new career within the police service and for some it's the chance to pose and show off their self-imposed importance.

The test shoot was a 50-round shoot, testing five separate disciplines with 10 rounds for each. A score of 90 per cent was required on a half-man target. Most forces in those days used a figure 11 target (full man) and required an 80 per cent pass mark. Therefore, you were only allowed to drop five rounds, with a maximum of two rounds on any discipline. So if you scored only seven on one discipline that was instant failure. In those days a student wasn't given a second chance. A fail was a straight fail and you didn't have a course of redress or grievance procedure. An instructor's word was final. Anyone with aspirations to use firearms within their department had to think of another career path. It was a good system. GMP produced officers who were good shots – they were not necessarily the best tacticians, but their AFOs were safe and competent and could actually hit what they were aiming at. I think I missed with two rounds on my classification and had two 'light strikes' (misfires) during my sense-of-direction disciplines.

Taffy Williams, my individual instructor, decided I dealt with the light strikes safely and in the correct manner and accordingly gave me the score. Taffy was the department's dog-handler and had refused to do a national instructors' course. Because a dog-handler who was competent with firearms was required on the unit, he was allowed to remain. Taffy was as hard as nails and typified dog-handlers of the day. He would never let an officer down and would always be in the thick of it, using his dog to best advantage. Taffy had a habit of eating his dog's vitamin biscuits, stating that they were perfectly OK for human consumption; as I say he typified dog-handlers of the day. If he had been an up-his-arse instructor he might have docked the two light strikes due to my trigger control. Fair play to Taffy, maybe he decided I would make a reasonable AFO anyway.

Once we had finished the shoots we were instructed to make our way to the range house. Heads were down for a few of the lads – they knew they had failed. I knew I had passed my shoot but now other considerations would take preference, for example, course averages, attitude, tactical ability. It wasn't a question of passing just the shoot, there were plenty of other subjects you could fail on.

Police officers have a great sense of humour, many would say quite macabre at times. A good place to get a laugh is on a basic firearms course. The instructors always had one or two students down for the following practical joke. Once we had returned to the range house and thoroughly cleaned our weapons, we were called in to the instructors' room one by one, where the good or bad news was delivered. A student would also be debriefed on his performance over the previous two weeks. No holds were barred, and if you were a lazy, idle, whingeing or bullshitting individual then you would be told in no uncertain terms. On the other hand, if you had applied yourself, demonstrated certain abilities and had potential, these facts would be brought to your attention.

I had observed several of the lads go into the instructors' room, and some had come out elated but others surrounded by a cloud of gloom. Once the lads had the good or bad news, they didn't hang about. In good old tradition they were making their way to the bar at Longsight nick. Longsight bar was Home Office-approved, the beer was subsidised and officers at times acted in an outrageous manner (always out of the eye of the public, of course). It was a great place for lads to let off steam and get pissed without having to endure members of the public, or senior officers if they had any sense, which wasn't often the case.

Both Jab and Tony had come out, given me the thumbs up and shouted, 'See you at Longsight.' I would be a liar if I said I wasn't nervous and had butterflies in my stomach. I didn't want to fail this course. If I passed, I would be involved in a difficult and exciting style of policing. I would also be the youngest AFO in GMP, not bad for a force with the strength of 7,000.

The rest of the lads went in and left, leaving me to the last. I was expecting the last lad out to tell me to go in but he said I would have to wait. I sat waiting for my call thinking what had gone wrong. I was hunched over, twiddling my thumbs and staring at the light green wooden door that led into the instructors' room. My stomach was in knots but I was determined to remain calm and cool. Then the thought struck me, maybe I had failed. How would I put up with the piss-taking or watching the keys to the van, while the lads were engaged on house entry or category A operations. I would have to ask for a move from TAG and return to division. But which division? Not the G, they would all know I had failed.

So much for staying cool, I was working myself up in to a right old panic when the door opened and Mike 'Antro' Antrobus said, 'Oh, you still here? You had better come in.' Five of the instructors were sat on a long bench with an equally long table in front of them. In the middle of the table and on the opposite side to the instructors was a strategically placed chair. Antro indicated for me to sit down. I sat facing the five instructors, all with stern expressions.

'How do you think you have done?'

'OK,' I blurted out in a nervous and shaky voice.

'OK? Is that all you have to say after ten days?'

'Well, I think I've done OK.'

'Have you got anything to say except OK?'

'Well I have applied myself and endeavoured to work hard through the course, which by the way was excellent.' A bit of arse-licking might help.

'Do you think you have passed?' asked Roger.

'I hope so.'

'Fucking hope so! Be positive you dithering woman,' snarled Antro. 'Well, you have failed.'

I had never failed anything in my police career and this was the worst possible thing I could have failed. I knew I couldn't have another chance. I felt like shit and my face must have mirrored that feeling.

'Do you know why you have failed?' asked Antro.

'No sarge.'

'You are too young and aggressive.'

What! I was about to protest when I noticed a couple of the instructors looking away and sniggering. But the detective in me hadn't registered what was happening.

'During some of the scenarios, we noticed you display high aggression, and you could possibly shoot an innocent.'

'Never sarge, I promise I'd never do that.'

I was clutching at straws by making promises. By now Antro's eyes had started to bulge and were quite obviously watering, but I was too desperate to notice. 'In fact you were useless,' was his next retort. I must have looked like a constipated donkey because the instructors burst out laughing.

'We're only pissing about,' said Antro. 'You have passed. Well done, fuck off, you owe me a pint.'

From desperation to elation. What a lousy trick to play. I vowed I would never stoop to that level for a laugh (like fuck!).

The piss-up after the course was outrageous. Everyone turned up, even the lads who had failed. Most of the firearms instructors were there and it was the first time I noticed many of them showing a liking, if not a preference, for TAG officers. Over the years this would become clear, because most firearms instructors had a TAG background. The piss-up went on into the early hours and was joined by members of Four Group when they came off duty. As usual, Jabba was in the thick of it, either taking the piss out of some unfortunate or holding court over his sixteenth pint of Greenall's.

I felt great after passing my course and as if I had really achieved something. I had worked hard to pass – it was not a matter of turning up and eventually, after many chances and lowering the scores, being given a pass, which certainly happens today. Eventually the night faded out, the weekend sped past and normal duties commenced. It wasn't long before I would experience my first firearms operation.

CHAPTER EIGHT

Strike! Strike! Strike!

Most authorised firearms officers are slowly introduced into the fold and may undertake guarding jobs or help move category A prisoners (the worst kind), which are less demanding types of operation. This makes sense for a normal officer who has become an AFO. The first time he carries a firearm can be daunting. To be an effective firearms officer, you need to be familiar with the weapon you are carrying and also comfortable in the new and unfamiliar environment. Once you carry a firearm the threat level increases, so a new AFO will be working in an unfamiliar environment. Coupled with this are the extra criteria governing the use of police-issue firearms.

A firearms officer works within the same framework as an unarmed officer, but with added responsibilities. I wasn't going to have the luxury of being integrated slowly into firearms duties. Historically VA3, the force's firearms unit, consisted of eight instructors. Their duties were to instruct officers in the use of police-issue firearms and to regularly update that training. They were also responsible for planning and participating in most firearms operations within the force area. The use of firearms within the criminal fraternity was increasing and so was the demand for arrests. These criminals were too dangerous for unarmed officers and the workload for VA3 was ever-increasing. They needed more men and needed supplementing from the TAG.

I was instructed to parade at Bootle Street Police Station, the

HQ of the VA3 instructors, at 03.00 the following morning. I was to take my Nomex worksuit (fireproof overalls) with me. The rest of my kit would be issued on arrival. I duly arrived and made my way to the armoury. Bootle Street Police Station is on the junction with Southmill Street in Manchester city centre. It is a magnificent listed building, dating from Edwardian times. The basement was the armoury, and to reach it you descended a flight of stairs from the central yard and followed a winding corridor for about 200 feet to a large wooden fire door.

Inside you were met by a counter from which firearms were issued, or you could make your way into the armoury itself. In those days every conceivable weapon was on display, from small Derringers to a Maxim machine gun used in the First World War. Among the array of weapons were small bays where the permanent instructors kept their personal weapons and kit. In the centre of the armoury were several tables with chairs.

I felt apprehensive and out of my depth; this type of policing was new to me. As soon as I entered, one of the instructors issued me with a radio, a rig (holster and belt), a set of body armour and a Smith & Wesson Model 10 revolver with 12 rounds of .38 +P calibre ammunition. I was informed to sit down with the rest of the instructors and other TAG lads from different units. A few of us mumbled greetings but before I could fully relax and ask what was happening, in walked the DCI. 'Morning gents,' was his introduction. I looked around and noticed about 24 officers within the subterranean room.

The DCI was a Geordie. 'OK, I will make this quick,' he said. 'We need to be on plot no later than 04.30.' He went on to explain that an aggravated burglary had occurred in the Cotswolds. The break-in was at a country residence owned by a wealthy, retired couple. The targets, two Irish brothers living in Manchester, had broken into the country property believing that the occupants had a hidden safe with large amounts of cash within. The two targets had disturbed the occupants while committing their crime in the early hours. The two brothers decided to bind the elderly couple to chairs and then torture the location of the safe from them. During the ordeal, the old man died, without revealing the whereabouts of the safe – because there wasn't one; the brothers had been misinformed.

As they couldn't find a safe, they ransacked the house and stole several antique firearms and ammunition. The old man had been an avid collector. The firearms were ladies' handbag pistols, which are small so they could be concealed in handbags and were used for self-protection in the eighteenth century against vagabonds and ruffians. These two brothers were callous; they left the elderly lady tied up with her dead husband next to her. Reliable information had been received that they had returned to Salford and were 'housed' (located) at two separate addresses in the Salford area. Our job was to 'bump' (enter) the addresses and arrest the male occupants.

The DCI split us up into two 12-man teams and told the sergeants to allocate duties. I was deployed to the Bravo team. Our job was to enter a terraced property on Langworthy Road, Salford. The option of arrest was a fast entry. Two officers were instructed to force the door.

Number one into the property was Jimmy, number two was me. We were to go as fast as possible to the master bedroom, where it was believed the main target would be. Three and four would be downstairs, five and six upstairs, seven and eight downstairs, nine and ten black cover (rear of the property). I had now switched on. I was working with Jimmy, a permanent instructor and ex-marine. Jimmy was a gun buff and what he didn't know about firearms wasn't worth mentioning.

I had never trained for a fast entry, and all sorts were going through my mind. When do I load my pistol? Do I leave it in my holster or do I carry it on the actual entry? What if I fuck up, who makes the arrest? My stomach was in knots. I wanted to ask Jim all these questions but my voice would have betrayed my nerves and I didn't want him to think I was as jittery as a cat on my first job.

The operation was to be a coordinated strike, which meant both addresses were to be entered at exactly the same time, thereby preventing one of the brothers tipping off the other. 04.30 was to be the strike time. Between 04.00 and 05.00, for those who have a normal sleep pattern, is the time the body is at its lowest ebb. Effectively, the body has less fight in it. This was the extent of our briefing. We were told to van up and make our way to the rendezvous points designated for both addresses. By now I thought I would play follow my leader; everything Jim would do I would copy.

Jimmy issued himself a shotgun, a shortened 810 Remington Wingmaster with a mounted Maglite and pistol grips. This is an evil-looking weapon and scores high for psychological domination on looks alone. He loaded with a mix of rifle slug and SG.

All police shotguns are 12-gauge and are complemented with 12-bore shotgun ammunition. 12-bore is an actual ounce of lead in any configuration, from a solid projectile to 567 pellets. Rifle slug was developed for the destruction of cattle, bulls in particular. A shotgun has a smooth-bored barrel, unlike other firearms which have twisted ridges which allow for greater accuracy. This is known as rifling and assists greatly in forensic detection. As the name implies, the ounce of lead is rifled to allow for greater accuracy. The kinetic energy of rifle slug when fired from the shotgun barrel, ballistically 180 ft per second, hitting a car travelling at 60 mph head-on, will momentarily stop the vehicle and enter the engine block.

The rifle slug is an awesome and devastating round. Later on in my career I came across criminals who would create this type of ammunition by melting candle wax into conventional skeet ammunition used for clay pigeon shooting. The initials 'SG' indicate small game – this is nine individual balls, another nasty round. Jim carried the shotgun as his primary weapon.

He also had a holstered revolver with six rounds. In those days we didn't have loading bays and therefore pointed the weapon at a safe place and loaded – first dilemma over. Jim tested his radio, so did I – next dilemma sorted.

By 03.50 everyone was ready and we boarded personnel carriers en route to RVs. The RV is a safe place to park and debus officers without alerting the targets. It is also where the host division deploys unarmed officers to create cordons, preventing members of the public from placing themselves in danger. From Bootle Street to Langworthy Road took 15 minutes maximum. The mood from Bravo team in the van was quiet. We weren't a permanent team, but a mixture of TAG and VA3. Everyone was wrapped up in their own thoughts, with an overriding one of don't fuck up.

Jim took time to talk to me. On first impression he can be quite gruff but over the years I got to know him and found him an excellent instructor with some off-the-wall ideas but nonetheless a lad willing to listen to new and experimental tactics. Jim concisely told me to follow his lead. Once the door was forced we would use speed, surprise and controlled aggression to arrest the target. I wasn't to stand too close to him but to split to areas of responsibility up in the room we entered (angles of fire), make sure my weapon was drawn and finger off the trigger unless I intended to use it. To be honest, I hadn't even considered entering the target premises and the possibility of confronting an armed murderer. I was too busy worrying about fucking up and upsetting Jim.

By 04.15 we were parked and stationary at the RV. The OPs (observation posts) from the CID informed us that there had been no change since 22.00 the previous day regarding the TP (target property). At 04.20 we were instructed to leave the van and in single file make our way to the TP. All this seemed a bit hit and miss to me, but never mind, I had other concerns.

At 04.30 on a dark and mild spring morning, I stood on a

terraced street in Salford with ten other armed officers, two covering the rear. I would be the second man in to a two-up-two-down terraced property in the hope of arresting an Irish gypsy believed to be in possession of a small handgun and wanted for a gruesome murder.

I was 23 years of age, my arsehole was tight enough to extract the tops of beer bottles. My stomach was in knots, but I was enjoying myself. Enjoying myself – should I even think that as a professional police officer? Through my earpiece I heard 'Strike! Strike! Strike!' This was the command to physically smash through the front door and for all teams to enter and arrest.

The strike is called three times in case it is missed over the comms network and an officer is unclear when to initiate action. The door of my property took the full force of a 14lb sledge-hammer wielded by Billy 'Brass' Brains from Stretford TAG. Billy made short work of the door, attacking the hinges and locks. His partner was on standby next to him carrying another sledgehammer in case Billy got tired or if it was a reinforced door. To Billy this would have been an insult, and in seconds Jimmy and I had made an entry.

Jimmy located the stairs and sprinted up them two at a time screaming, 'Armed police, armed police!' Adrenalin had kicked in and I was up Jim's backside, moving equally as fast. Jim had increased our field of vision by activating the Maglite mounted on his shotgun. He booted the first bedroom door he came across and immediately entered. I followed, conscious of keeping my distance. I had my pistol in my right hand, supported by my left and in the on-aim position.

Jimmy immediately made his way to a double bed in the middle of the room. I could hear booming around the rest of the property, 'Armed police, armed police!' and the heavy footsteps of officers running as they continued to enter the property.

Jim had located a man trying to hide amongst the mess of a bed I would normally call a duvet. Jim was screaming at him,

'Armed police, show me your hands!' Everything seemed to slow down and my vision appeared to increase and focus as if I was looking through a telescope. If it was possible, the room had gone quiet although I knew Jim was shouting. The occupant of the bed fit the description of the target, but he wasn't showing hands, he was rummaging amongst the shit he slept in.

My mind had decided what he was doing. I had judged him and now I was going to sentence him. I took the first pressure up on the trigger of my revolver and started to initiate a shot. His hands seemed to be moving in the direction of his bollocks and I had decided he was looking for the small firearm hidden down his Y-fronts. I was clinically going to shoot this individual.

I started to increase the pressure on the trigger and acquire a sight picture, when my bubble was burst. Jim pulled away the bedclothes to reveal a naked male who was pissing himself with fright.

'Handcuff him,' shouted Jim.

I immediately grabbed him, turned him on his belly and handcuffed his arms behind him. Jim told me to stay with him while he made a quick but more thorough search. I heard over the radio, 'House clear, send in the CID'. Within minutes two CID officers made their way into the bedroom and cautioned and arrested the man in the bed on suspicion of murder.

We made our way back to Bootle Street and after a less than concise debrief were told to take the rest of the day off. As I handed in my weapon, Jim winked and said, 'You did OK there Andy.' OK? I nearly shot someone. Hadn't Jim noticed? He couldn't have, because he actually thanked me.

Over the next couple of days I started to justify my actions and even made excuses to myself. What was obvious was my lack of experience and training, but I knew that given the chance again I would make more critical and practical assessments. As years passed, this job would have massive implications for my learning curve as well as for the others I would teach. I also understand now that in times of stress and limited experience in conflict situations, my episode wasn't unique. Most people go through similar emotions until experience and skill kick in.

It wasn't long before I had the chance to develop my house-entry skills.

* * *

To enter a house or target property and arrest a suspected armed offender is not simple. To learn effective entry techniques, GMP had retained an old police post near Bury. Tottington was a detached house, constructed for the Lancashire Constabulary and was used as both a residence and a satellite police station by the local bobby. It even had its own cells. After the amalgamation of various regional forces, Tottington was abandoned and fell into disrepair. Some bright firearms instructor noticed this and realised it was ideal for practising house entries.

In the late 70s, a contingent of GMP firearms instructors went to Hereford to learn experimental house-entry techniques from the Special Air Service. Much of their experience had been gained from operations in Northern Ireland. The specialised entry they taught became known as a 'fast entry' (today known as dynamic entry). Over the years this became more specialised and I pride myself on being one of the instructors who developed it into a credible and effective technique. Other forces nicknamed GMP firearms team the 'Manchester Cowboys' due to this aggressive, intimidating tactic. I would attend seminars, visit other forces, receive visits from outside agencies and listen to criticism about the quick entry technique and other GMP tactics. I would also witness how it became the *en vogue* tactic with certain senior officers within our force.

On the other hand I also saw how others would shit themselves over the thought of authorising such a tactic due to the political climate of the day and the chance of affecting their career progress. I listened to the national schools and certain officers of junior rank state the dangers of the quick entry. My response to them is this: if you have trained in the tactic and – more importantly – experienced an actual operational entry, then stand up and offer criticism.

The majority of the national schools, apart from the Metropolitan Police and the old RUC (for whom I have the greatest respect), are run by officers with limited operational experience, due to their geographical position. I have witnessed so-called chief instructors of national schools and their subordinates openly condemn Manchester's quick entry policy. If they studied Manchester crime trends they'd be more sympathetic. Certainly from the mid-80s onwards, certain areas could easily become flashpoints and large-scale disorder could flare up quickly. The quick entry allowed firearms teams to gain entry, effect arrests and leave the area in minimum time.

Yet most national schools endorse containment: surround the target premises, cordon off roads and attempt to talk the offender out. If we had tried that in the early 90s we would have caused major problems within inner-city Manchester, particularly on the Alex Park Estate in Moss Side. In later years, colleagues of mine were ordered to contain and talk out the Pitt brothers, feared members of one of the notorious drug gangs terrorising Moss Side. Once the operation went ahead, the Pitts quite openly took the piss out of the lads, phoning the press and their solicitors, but more importantly disposing of evidence that could have assisted the investigation. I know this still bothers my former colleagues and makes me angry at the whole lack of professionalism.

Good planning, training, surprise, speed and controlled aggression will always win the day. Offensive tactics are my preferred option, but I am flexible and tactically astute enough to realise when defensive tactics should be employed. It concerns me that when shootings are studied within the mainland, the majority appear to be ones of defence, i.e. containment. To date, Manchester police have had two shootings. One was a defensive containment, the other was offensive and prevented an offender escaping from the scene of the crime and seriously harming or killing members of the police and public. The officer who instigated the shooting was highly trained and skilled, with the ability to make the correct tactical decisions, giving due consideration to Section Three of the Criminal Law Act 1967 (self-defence).

Don't get me wrong; within the instructional staff there will be some excellent junior officers and this includes GMP. But most ranking officers have never experienced operational firearms duties, never mind an angry drunk. These officers will formulate policy, give tactical advice and condemn certain tactics as dangerous. As an experienced firearms officer you have a duty to the public, and more importantly to your colleagues, to arrest criminals who use firearms, and any diverse, underhanded, sneaky and unethical tactic should be considered, although of course, we have to work within the guidelines of the law. However, stating that a tactic is dangerous is, to my mind, more for the sake of the officer's career prospects rather than the police or public. To quote 'dangerous' is simple – I suggest you look outside the envelope.

There have been three shootings that went disastrously wrong when a quick entry tactic was deployed – although, I would argue, not the quick entry style that GMP used. Also, a lack of intelligence, experience or training could have been a major contributory factor. Those incidents occurred in London, West Midlands and Sussex. I will not vilify those officers; however, I question the overall system. I will also try to justify GMP's successful use of the tactic. I have often heard the quote 'a firearms officer's job is a dangerous one' and I would argue that it has an element of risk, but that risk is planned for by good intelligence, correct training and the issue of firearms.

A firearms officer knows that he will be dealing with armed criminals and is therefore prepared. On the other hand an unarmed officer, either a uniformed beat patrol, traffic officer, CID officer or mounted officer deals with a diverse and varied amount of incidents throughout a tour of duty. They are not necessarily geared up or prepared to deal with armed criminals and their risk level is a hell of a lot higher than an armed officer's.

The hours I spent at Tottington were invaluable to me as a keen and eager AFO. As I look back I see it had its failings, but these would be corrected slowly and by an increase in armed operations and a new era of tactical firearms officer. At Tottington we were taught the actual dynamics of entering a two-storey property and making the property safe so that the CID could come in. The instructors explained how the objective was to get in fast and arrest the target. The target could be in any of the rooms inside, so two armed officers would be tasked to each room to make an entry and search, and if they found an adult male he would be handcuffed.

An entry team would generally consist of 12 men, depending on the size of the property. In the early days, two officers were tasked to force an entry. They were known as the MOE team (method of entry) and were usually the biggest, strongest and were able to wield a 14lb sledgehammer. They would top and tail the usual POE (point of entry), which is the front door. This method ensures that they check for bolts above and below. They would then check, with a nod from the team leader, the door handle or latch (you would be amazed how many times a door is found unsecured). This is known as the first rule of MOE. On the command 'Strike! Strike! Strike!' they would professionally and without malice, smash fuck out of the front door. The rest of the team would be in single file, hugging the building line ready to enter as soon as the door was no longer an obstruction.

Progressively the method of entry has become more specialised and officers actually train in many varied and effective items of kit and also other places of entry such as windows, patio doors, walls, ceilings and roofs. As gun crime in Manchester escalated, I would come across Judas gates, electrified doors, pit bulls, steel shutters, floors removed, ground sensors, high-intensity lights, CCTV and a variety of weaponry located near the front door.

The entry team are split into pairs. Each pair is numbered one and two, three and four and so on. Number one and two are generally the most experienced because they can come across numerous tactical problems on entry. They need to be able to think fast and make positive evaluations and assessments.

The problem could be a rucked carpet that prevents the door to a room from opening, thus preventing the smooth progress of the rest of the team. It could be actual contact – this can be a member of the family on the toilet or making themselves something to eat for example – or the suspect deciding to take you on (rare but I have experienced it), or women screaming because you have scared them witless.

Number one and two are always given the primary task of locating the target. Most quick entries tend to take place around 04.30 but a quick entry can be successful at other times too. One thing crucial about the quick entry is the element of surprise – the last thing you want is the suspect sat waiting for you. As 04.30 is the usual entry time, one and two make their way to the room in which intelligence states the target will be located (generally the master bedroom). Number one's primary weapon used to be a shotgun, but later it became the Heckler & Koch MP5. To be honest, the only advantage a long firearm has in a property is that it usually has an illumination device giving the user maximum advantage. Light source is one of the best weapons available – particularly with some of the great kit on the market nowadays.

Later on team members would use self-loading pistols (SLPs), some mounted with torches. A pistol is a great weapon for house entry, but we had our trusty revolvers at Tottington, and live rounds were replaced by wax loads, which were quite good for training, but they stung like fuck when you were hit by one, especially if it was cold.

We were taught the importance of the metre rule. When entering a room, number one would step either right or left out of the doorway. The doorway or any POE is known as the fatal tunnel or coffin corridor. Once stood in this area, a person is silhouetted and highlighted, therefore making them a bigger target. So number one would step one metre in and one metre away from the doorway. Number two would go in the opposite direction but apply the metre rule (one step is roughly a metre). The metre rule also allowed for quick extraction if an officer went down, i.e. shot or injured; the backup team didn't have to enter too far into a hostile zone to make a rescue.

This tactic was changed later, and number two really became the thinking member. Number one was allowed to act instinctively when entering a room, still observing the metre rule. Number two would have to do the opposite. If number one had balls, he would step into an unknown area of responsibility and go firm. Number two would step into a known responsibility (an area obviously free of danger). Number one would issue search commands and number two would clear the room or neutralise the target. Each pair would adopt this standard operating procedure.

Once the room was clear, the team leader was informed and the problem of loft or cellar then approached. A cellar was entered like any other room, however it was difficult due to the descent, which exposed the lower torso. When the team leader was satisfied that the property was clear, he would inform the CID who would conduct a more thorough search for weapons.

During our training at Tottington, the instructors would play the part of the criminal, usually shooting us at any given opportunity. John, one of the sergeants on VA3, adopted and refined the scenarios to be works of art that would have made any thespian proud. John would play the role of a mental defective in possession of a shotgun. He would effect a contact on one of our entries and then run us ragged, discharging black powder blanks throughout the house. John was a great shot and when we had him contained in a room he would demonstrate how useless an entry would be, shooting our hands, arses and vulnerable parts much to his merriment. The point was: once the entry has been compromised, resort to other tactics.

John knew he was in for a friendly kicking once we got hold of him, so he would keep up the barrage as long as possible. I later got to serve under John as my sergeant and would hold him in the highest respect. He is a farmer's son and was brought up with firearms. His ability with a shotgun is formidable, his knowledge of firearms legislation is legendary amongst civilian gun clubs, and John was the scourge of some of those nutters. Although John was operational, he also controlled the civilian gun clubs within GMP. He had a great sense of humour. I have seen him don a beret and pair of milk-bottle-bottom glasses, wear a pair of ill-fitting overalls, carry a Lee Enfield .308 rifle and present himself to a senior officers' firearms familiarisation class as 'force sniper reporting for duty, sir!' in the manner of Benny Hill's Fred Scuttle character. I still laugh at this but I never did see many senior officers do the same.

As I have already stated, training is necessary to ensure the confidence of an officer and the success of an operation. However, it's true that there is no substitute for one critical element: experience. I strongly believe that as the years progressed, the experience I gained, at times, was detrimental to my police career. It meant I knew what I was talking about, and my attitude towards incompetence prevented my full development and increased my frustration at buffoons carrying ranks of responsibility.

In the police service, when a constable has served two years as a probationer, he or she is eligible to take the sergeants' examination. If they pass this exam and successfully complete other tasks, then in effect they should be promoted to sergeant. The next rank available is inspector and the same criteria as constable to sergeant apply. All other ranks are achieved by attending courses and facing panels or boards of suitability. Experience, skill and ability have little place in achieving rank. In essence, if you can study and pass exams, then you can be promoted. The only exception to this is an accelerated promotion scheme, usually for graduate entrants.

In my time in the police I came across too many idiots holding the rank of inspector. I prided myself on being a confident, skilled, professional and inventive firearms officer. I gained these skills by learning from experience. Yet these skills were constantly questioned by people who held higher rank. I would come across either sergeants or inspectors who had been promoted from, say, community contact to the TAG or firearms. They would suddenly be an instant expert on that department and its tactics. They would, without consultation, decide on options of arrest that I and other officers realised were nonsense, unachievable or far-fetched. Sometimes they weren't even good enough to be dangerous. Once these incompetents were questioned in open forum they became defensive and at times vindictive.

During my early years within the teams, the crime and drug squads showed reluctance to use the Firearms Department because of its perceived incompetence. This reluctance was eventually broken down by good liaison, trust among various departments and, importantly, results. It was achieved by officers like myself, demonstrating skills of preparation and planning and studying the gangs and gun crimes. During the 1990s Manchester firearms department had never been as busy. The squads started to share information and openly co-operate with the teams.

CHAPTER NINE

A Day on the Moors

In June 1985 I attended Holcombe Moor army camp near Bury for a five-day shotgun course. This was more relaxed than my Model 10 revolver course, but it was still pass or fail and the pass score was 90 per cent. The shotgun I trained on was the Remington Wingmaster 810 five-round pump action. I was introduced to the variety of rounds: skeet, triple A, 00 buck (SG) and rifle slug. All these rounds were developed for the destruction of animals. In 1985 the primary long arm for firearms officers was the shotgun, so we had to be competent with it and the variety of ammunition available. On a live operation the choice of ammo was up to the individual. An officer was issued with ten rounds, five for the weapon and five as reloads if required. I usually took two rifle slug and eight 00 buck. The shotgun was later replaced by the MP5 9mm, a more suitable weapon for the role required. Nowadays the shotgun's primary functions are the destruction of animals, as a method of entry tool or delivering CS in a variety of ways.

Passing a shotgun course increased my utility as a firearms officer and allowed my supervisors to deploy me to other firearms operations when required. I was still only 24 years of age – the youngest AFO in Manchester – but my knowledge and experience were steadily growing.

Being a TAG officer was rewarding. I attended a five-week advanced driving course and greatly increased my driving skills. Advanced driving instructors are a different breed who are not easy to scare, and although I passed my course, I think the instructor was glad to see the back of me, with the accolade that I was the worst driver he ever had to pass.

I moved on to a three-day foot surveillance course run by the Regional Crime Squad. Part of the course entailed a team of three TAG officers following a policewoman around the women's underwear section of the old Lewis's department store in Manchester city centre. Needless to say all three of us were blown, but we still passed the course with room for improvement.

I also spent time with the military, learning how to spot suspect devices such as incendiary bombs and other nasty contraptions devised by an active Irish Republican Army and also the Animal Liberation Front. I enjoyed it all.

* * *

On April 17, 1984, WPC Yvonne Fletcher was tragically murdered while engaged in crowd control duties outside the Libyan Embassy, London. To date the murderer hasn't been arrested but it is believed he was part of the Libyan delegation within the embassy. During this period Libyan nationals were engaged in a campaign of terrorism in the UK and several Libyans with connections to Manchester University were arrested under the Anti-Terrorism Act. A policewoman with whom I had been in the cadets, and who had since left to attend a course at the university, gave evidence against three Libyans, one of whom had been her lover, charged with conspiracy to commit murder. They were believed to be agents of the Libyan regime and were acting on orders to kill Libyans in the UK that were opposed to the rule of Colonel Gaddafi. The three Libyans would have normally been tried at the secure court in London, but some bright spark within the judicial system decided they would be tried at Minshull Street Crown Court, Manchester.

This led to one of the biggest security operations ever seen in the city.

All the TAG AFOs from Longsight would be responsible for the movement of the prisoners from HMP Strangeways to Minshull Street. Once the prisoners were delivered, TAG would also be in charge of the armed security of the court. Prior to the date of hearing, myself and other AFOs attended a briefing at the Special Branch HQ. We were informed that the threat level was extremely high due to one of the Libyans turning Queen's evidence; we nicknamed him Abosos the Fat Grass.

The trial was to last six weeks. My job was escort officer in a six-man armed team. Each day three traffic vehicles driven by officers from TASS, a special unit consisting of advanced drivers trained in defensive and anti-ambush techniques, would pick us up from Longsight. We would be driven to Bootle Street and issued firearms. I would have a primary weapon of a shotgun and a secondary weapon of a Mod 10 or 13 revolver.

At Strangeways we would meet the 'Oyster' vehicle, a white Transit van driven by prison officers. Inside the Oyster vehicle was one of the Libyans. The traffic vehicles would take up a defensive formation around the Transit van, and on the command of the senior AFO, make our way to Minshull Street court. This movement was completed six times a day and always in rush hour. Each journey used a different route known only to the TAG commander in the advance vehicle.

Minshull is approximately three miles from Strangeways and the journey could take from four to eight minutes. Category A prisoner movements in GMP's early days were fast blasts with sirens and blue lights and to be really honest it gave you a great rush. Your senses were alive and the adrenalin flowing, as the greatest time of danger is always egress and access to secure premises.

One particular morning we were moving the Fat Grass and

were halfway through our route when over the radio net came the word 'Abort' from Force HQ. 'Abort' from Force HQ means the venue is compromised, move the prisoner to a holding area and secure the perimeter. Our nearest holding area was Collyhurst Police Station. TASS lads can drive but when we received the 'abort' they must have notched the speed up another 20 mph. We were in the middle of Manchester in rush-hour traffic and my eyes were about; the rest of the team were the same. I had butterflies in my stomach and my mouth was dry. I was happy when the vehicles were moving but when they slowed to negotiate traffic, my door would be open. At times I would even get out of the car with my shotgun cradled, ready to engage a threat.

GMP had a ludicrous policy of keeping weapons hidden from the eyes of the public. Fuck that, we had just received an 'abort' and I wasn't about to die for a policy developed by some shiny-arse admin wank by hiding my gun so as not to offend or scare a member of the public.

We made our way to Collyhurst in record time. The six of us surrounded the prison van, four of us took defensive positions and two grabbed Abosos. Jabba was one of the officers deployed to Abosos. Jabba's role was to grab the prisoner, run with him through the custody suite and deposit him in a cell, while we covered the movement. Jabba weighed up the options and decided the fastest way to move him was to boot him up the arse as hard as possible. Abosos flew into his cell with the six of us howling with nervous laughter.

After a tense hour of waiting we received another message to transport him to Minshull Street. Later that day we found out that the 'abort' had been called due to intelligence that a suspected Libyan assassination team had been detained at Manchester Airport. Good call in my eyes.

The trial proceeded without any hitches and several months later we were to repeat the whole thing when a team of Irish

National Liberation Army terrorists stood trial. This period of Category A movements had again increased my skill level and experience. I would go on to move IRA prisoners to the Isle of Wight, move cash in transit from the Bank of England, look after supergrasses and Libyan families at risk. My operational experience was growing.

* * *

It was a cold winter's afternoon. Longsight Police Station was an old and decrepit building, condemned twice but kept open for financial reasons. The TAG office was on the top floor and the wind was howling outside. Gusts of snow blew past the window. The chill was fighting through the aged cracks within the exterior and the office was getting colder by the hour.

I was with a few of my team, drinking coffee, when one of the lads came in and the draught blew the door shut.

'There's some type of big job going on,' he said.

'What do you mean?'

'There's loads of activity from the firearms lads.'

A few of us left the office and descended four flights of stairs into a yard big enough for at least 100 vehicles. In one corner was the firearms instructors' blue Land Rover and a couple of the instructors, including Martin, a Brummie who used to be on Group Three but had transferred to firearms. Martin was a force sniper, a natural shot. He is a bloke I have always liked even though he does have some strange ideas at times (well, he is a Brummie). I went over to him.

'Hi mate, what's happening?'

'Fuck off, I can't tell you,' was the caustic reply.

'Come on mate, I won't tell anyone else.' (Fingers crossed)

'No chance, fuck off, you'll find out later.'

We watched the instructors unload kit from the Land Rover. Some of it appeared to be foul weather clothing. It was freezing in the yard and time to go off-duty, so we booked off and went home. I thought no more of the day's events.

At 03.00 the phone woke me from a deep and comfortable sleep. I always sleep well when it's freezing outside.

'Hello,' I answered in a dream-like state.

'PC Hailwood?'

'Who wants to know?'

'This is the force control room inspector, turn out to Longsight Police Station immediately.'

'Yes sir.'

As soon as I heard the words 'turn out' I nearly fell over myself to get out of bed. As the years progressed I would learn the art of dressing quickly in the early hours, but then I was still a novice. I was trying to pull on my socks and thread my arms through a T-shirt at the same time. I clumsily sped downstairs into the garage, attempting to get my motorbike kit on. Eventually I set off, wondering what the turn out was, maybe a murder or even rioting somewhere. I had completely forgotten about Martin.

Once at Longsight I made my way to our office and spoke to a few of the other lads who arrived.

'What's going on?'

'Not sure, but we have to go next door for a firearms briefing.'

I de-robed and placed my bike kit in my locker, put on a pair of trainers and went into the bar. The time was 03.45, the weather outside was atrocious, yet the bar was packed with officers from different TAG units and many of the force snipers. At the front of the room, on a raised stage, was Martin with bits of kit scattered about the floor, including what looked like Blackpool Sands windbreaks (gaudy-coloured orange, yellow and blue plastic items used by families for protection from the wind and sand while on the beach).

Martin was surrounded by briefing boards. I looked for a chair but couldn't find one available. The first rule of a TAG officer was make yourself comfortable, because at any time some senior officer may apply the mushroom option: keep you in the dark and feed you shit. I started to worry; I didn't have a seat. The last time I had been on a briefing this scale was for the arrest of associates of Lennie Pilot, one of Manchester's first supergrasses. That briefing had been conducted at Stretford Police Station by officers from the Regional Crime Squad. Firearms had been issued at the briefing and we were told that we were not allowed to leave the room under any circumstances. Being young and naive I thought this strange until one of the older lads told me it was to prevent corrupt officers tipping off the suspects. I didn't know who I was more scared of, some of the officers in the room or the actual suspects.

Unfortunately Manchester had its share of bent coppers. Although I didn't witness any direct corruption, I was certainly suspicious on one or two occasions. Once I had been waiting in the back of an old van for hours on end to ambush an unarmed robbery team at a Bookers Warehouse in Stockport, when the robbery took place at a Bookers in Rochdale. Strange...

Chris, an ex-marine who had recently joined the unit, shouted over, 'Andy, there's room next to me.' Chris was sat on a bench seat and made room.

'Listen in,' shouted Martin. He immediately gained the attention of the 70 officers in the room and silence descended. Martin informed us that Myra Hindley was en route from prison to Saddleworth Moor with an escort of firearms officers. It was believed she was prepared to divulge the whereabouts of the graves of her and Brady's victims. Our role was to create a tight cordon in an area of two square miles. Sniper observation posts would be deployed, grid references to follow. We were to keep Hindley safe and prevent any intrusion from the media. Hindley's threat assessment was high, therefore firearms would be issued. Sniper OPs would be double-manned and other officers would be deployed as protection officers to the subject.

'I know what you all think of Hindley, myself included,' said Martin. 'For those who have contact with her, remain civil at all times. Remember, this is for the families of the victims. In case the press get wind, we will be running decoy teams with policewomen acting as Hindley. This should confuse the issue. Any questions?'

Lads started asking the usual sensible questions with the odd idiot giving his two-penn'orth. Martin quickly dealt with them. All I was thinking was, I hope I get on the protection teams – at least it will be warm in the Land Rovers. I had noticed that the foul weather kit that Martin had offloaded the previous day had been quickly acquired by the lads in the room. I didn't have much in the way of warm kit in my locker and the Saddleworth Moor is no picnic in the middle of winter.

Martin gave out our deployment and duties. I was partnered with Vinny and was on a sniper OP. Martin explained it was the second most exposed post. Jabba and Alf were given the most exposed; thank fuck for small mercies. I was more than happy to be partnered with Vin. He was an ex-TAG lad, now a dog-handler and a sniper, a raw-boned lad with a great nature and a very experienced police officer with a habit of getting himself in the shit. Vinny is one of those rare lads you can count on 100 per cent in any eventuality and a friend. But I was concerned about my personal welfare – how was I going to keep warm?

Martin began issuing bits of kit, which included a Blackpool windbreak and several hot cans and Mars Bars per team. The only bit of clothing I received was a woollen balaclava. Hot cans are cans with food inside, usually curry, beans and sausage or hotpot. The cans had a self-heating system, which was activated by piercing a certain part of the can, creating some type of chemical reaction. The food within heated up, usually to the temperature of Mount Etna. At times they got so hot your plastic spoon would melt once submerged into the contents.

I asked Vinny how he was for clothing. He quite smugly

showed me several items of kit including a waterproof Henri Lloyd quilted jacket and matching trousers and a set of motorcycle gloves. I quickly scuttled off to the TAG office and furiously went through any and all available kit and uniform scattered about the office. Within five minutes I was much happier than before. I had managed to salvage enough kit to survive the cold. I would look more like a *Big Issue* seller than a policeman, but who would care in the middle of Saddleworth Moor?

By 06.30 the majority of AFOs were in vans and en route to Saddleworth Moor. At about 07.30 the snow had started to fall again and it was still dark. On the approach to the rendezvous point on the moor, we were met by the press, stood around a barrier hastily constructed by two uniformed police officers. They immediately began taking photographs of us within the van, some of which would appear in the following day's edition of the *Sun* newspaper. So much for secrecy, some bent bastard had informed the press.

The vans continued ascending the now-treacherous roads, stopping at times to allow different OP teams to deploy on to the moors. Eventually myself, Vinny, Jabba and Alf were left in our van. Alf was an ex-TAG lad and Jabba knew him quite well. They were chatting away catching up on old times. The van slowed to a halt and Vinny and I deployed. We both made test calls on our radios. The snow had started to fall thickly and the cold hit me instantly. Every bit of kit I had, I immediately donned.

I had been issued with a Mod 10 revolver, which was beneath at least three layers of clothing. Vinny had his personal issue sniper's rifle and old Lee Enfield .308 bolt action weapon. This was in a cover, slung over his shoulder. Vin quickly took a compass bearing and pointed through the gloom to a rock escarpment approximately three-quarters of a mile away. He informed me that this was the site for our OP.

With the Blackpool windbreak tucked under my arm and the hot cans safely ensconced in Vinny's rucksack we set off. The snow had been falling on and off through the night and had drifted, making the going extremely difficult at times. The sun was trying to appear but it created just a gloomy haze due to the thick snow clouds. It took us about 30 minutes to cover the distance and arrive at the site which would be our observation post for the next nine hours.

The rock escarpment was elevated from the normal contour of the land, so once we stood upon it, we were exposed to the wind. The wind was blowing across the valley in about 30 miles an hour gusts and it reduced the temperature to a windchill of possibly minus 17. To avoid windchill we had to drop below the escarpment, but this prevented us from watching our area of responsibility, which was a stretch of miles along the valley floor and sides. We tried all sorts of positions to create maximum shelter and give ourselves all-round obs, but nothing proved suitable. I suggested we use the windbreak and Vinny looked at me as if I was daft. I set about trying to assemble it in the high winds, and Vinny soon joined in.

It was useless. We couldn't force the wooden stakes into the frozen ground and once we had it part-way assembled, it bellowed like a parachute. The only thing it was good for was standing on to create a slight insulation barrier from the frozen earth.

Although we were freezing, both Vinny and myself didn't whinge, we just got on with the job. The majority of the time we would stand on the rocks, viewing the valley below, chatting and telling each other war stories. Toward late morning the snow stopped falling and the sun started to shine through. It is amazing what a lift this gives you. It also increased our field of view. We could see Jabba and Alf's OP and soon raised them on the radio. Vinny took out his rifle and placed it on its bipod. We could now use its telescopic sights to further increase our new field of view.

Both me, Vinny, Jabba and Alf received a radio transmission from Martin. He increased our state of readiness to Condition

Amber. This meant to expect activity in areas of responsibility. Within 20 minutes a Range Rover drove into the valley. It pulled up and out stepped a team of at least ten, including a female. Vinny immediately put the scope on them and stated that the female was indeed Hindley. I took over from Vinny and clearly rested the cross-hairs of the scope on the forehead of Hindley. She was at least half a mile from our OP. I scoped the rest of the party, recognising the AFOs and Peter Topping, the CID officer in charge of the case with several of his investigation team.

They stayed for about 20 minutes and moved off. I never did find out if that area was important to the investigation. I really think Hindley was taking the piss. It is obvious to most that she and Brady didn't bury the victims in arctic conditions and also the look of the terrain really changes when it snows. Even Ray Mears would be hard pushed to find his way about.

I was contemplating whether to have a hot can when Vinny announced we had visitors. Vinny's eagle eyes had spotted three figures way in the distance, making their way along the valley floor towards our location. They were at least a mile away. We placed the scope on them and could clearly make out three adult males dressed in warm weather gear, heading our way.

I raised Martin on the air and informed him of the situation, enquiring if there were hikers or wardens on the moor. He informed me no-one should be there, all entry points had been sealed with uniform personnel. If they continued to our position, we were to arrest them. Marvellous, I thought, what for? There isn't an actual power of arrest for wandering on the moors.

I contacted Jab and informed him of the situation. Jab informed me he had 'eyeball' and it looked like they were going to walk between our two OPs. Martin radioed back stating he would send a mobile backup as soon as possible. It was clear that the three trespassers were making for a point between our OPs and they hadn't seen us. Jabba and I dropped into cover and made our way to a suitable point to enable us to remain covert. Alf and Vinny covered the progress of the trespassers.

Because of the way the land lies on the moors you can quite easily lose visual on someone. This happened to both Jab and me but Vinny still had them covered from his vantage point so he was able to talk us on to the target. The three trespassers were getting nearer to our ambush point. I managed to extract my Model 10 revolver and reluctantly take off my glove, but only from my right hand. The revolver was freezing and so was my hand.

Then I saw the intrepid three. I ran towards them, screaming, 'Armed police, stand still!' They had eyes the size of bulldogs' bollocks as I appeared from nowhere, dressed as a *Big Issue* seller armed with a handgun. I doubt they could hear my shouted warning because of the wind. Then 18 stone of Jabba appeared, in similar garb, pointing a firearm at them, closely followed by Alf in full camouflage kit carrying his rifle. As if they had been struck by lightning, all three hit the deck and curled up in tight defensive balls. This instantly made me laugh and I could see it had done the same to Jab. However, these three could be dangerous so we had to treat them as such.

Vinny soon joined us and he and Alf covered Jab and me as we quickly searched them for weapons. Once we were satisfied they were safe, we stood them up and walked them towards the mobile unit. One of the three identified himself as Steve Panter, a reporter for the *Manchester Evening News*. They were quickly handed over and we returned to cover our posts. This incident helped us pass a good hour and for a while forget about the cold.

Eventually the weather started to deteriorate and it appeared to become colder. We attempted to heat our hot cans, which we believed to be failsafe. However they didn't even get lukewarm and I for one didn't fancy cold vegetable curry. We did get another clear spell for about an hour and a press helicopter buzzed over our positions for ten minutes, which again passed the time.

At about 15.30 the light started to fade, and at 16.30 Jab, Alf, Vinny and me were the last teams to be extracted from the moors. The vans took us back to Longsight with the heaters on full blast. By the time we got back I could hardly keep my eyes open. Usually after a firearms operation, a debrief follows immediately. Martin made the decision to debrief in the bar at Longsight over a few pints. We were all up for that, but after one or two pints, the majority of us couldn't keep our eyes open – the weather had taken its toll.

* * *

My time in TAG was perhaps the best of my police service. I experienced so much. For example, in the mid-80s football hooliganism had reached new heights. TAG were policing virtually every football match in the force area: Manchester City, Manchester United, Oldham, Bury, Wigan, Bolton, Stockport. We would pick up the visiting supporters when they arrived at the various transport stations, round them up like cattle and herd them to the various stadiums. Many a time pitched battles would occur when rival supporters ambushed each other. Some of the violence was terrible. The fans didn't care who got in their way when wreaking havoc and destruction. I saw elderly people battered to the floor, parents assaulted while protecting their children and isolated police officers given horrendous beatings. I was lucky to be working in a tight-knit team who looked after each other, and more importantly were able, at times, to arrest these offenders.

I was working a United game outside White City, Old Trafford. The match had finished and there were running battles all over the city between United and Arsenal fans. My group was working alongside Stretford lads when one of them had a knife pulled on him. He was arresting an Arsenal fan for public order offences when this bloke pulled out a potato peeler and tried to stab him. Talk about unlucky and stupid. I have never seen a person being 'staffed' that many times. In reality, he had pulled a knife on 20 TAG lads. I hope he learned.

Football crowds are a scary place to be in and again I counted myself lucky to be working with a good ten-man team. Prior to a game, we would receive information on the latest 'crews', be it the ICF (Inter-City Firm) from West Ham, Chelsea's Head-hunters, Leeds United's Service Crew or many others. We knew from colleagues in other forces that GMP's Tactical Aid Group was despised by the wrong element of football fans, and they clearly recognised TAG officers by the 'X' displayed on our epaulettes.

TAG wasn't expected to, and didn't, employ soft tactics. We were expected to resolve conflict early and prided ourselves in that style of policing. I do believe that hitting conflict early and hard prevents problems developing. Others would argue that a firm and visual presence should be enough. In this day and age it is probably one of the only options left to public order units. Once the fighting begins, the cameras are only too eager to see an officer strike some poor unfortunate who just happens to find himself in the middle of a hostile football crowd. The media does little to assist police officers these days and I really do not miss policing large public order events.

One that held the Manchester media attention for months to come was dubbed the 'Battle of Brittan'. On March 1, 1985, the then Home Secretary, Leon Brittan, had been invited to give a seminar at the Students' Union in Oxford Road. Special Branch had received information that Brittan would not be allowed to enter the building – left-wing protesters would oppose his entry.

On this particular day my group had been training in the gym at Longsight and had just played our usual game of skilful five-a-side football. One of the lads from Three Group nipped into the gym and told us to get showered, as we were required at a briefing in our unit as soon as possible. He was immediately grabbed by Jab and Jack. Jack was our new boy, an immense figure of 18 stone and as quick-witted as Jab. The Group Three lad was forced to tell the truth, as he could have been 'nut-megging' us (telling lies for a quick prank at our expense). After a short but fair and reasonable amount of pressure, he screamed, 'No duff, it's the truth!' No duff is sacred and prevents cock-ups, somewhat like the fable of the boy who cried wolf. The Group Three lad scuttled off with no hard feelings; he would have done the same to us, circumstances reversed.

We showered and were in the briefing room within 20 minutes. In there was our inspector, ten lads from Group Three and a detective sergeant from Special Branch. I knew the DS as a rugby mate and he would become my inspector for a time in firearms, a great bloke and now a senior officer within the intelligence circles. I will refer to him as the DS.

The DS informed us of the intelligence and that he was to be Brittan's personal protection officer for the day. It seemed obvious to us that, faced with the inevitable crowd of demon-strators outside the Student Union, we would create some type of distraction and take Brittan through the back or emergency entry point, preventing any fuss.

'Negative,' stated the DS. 'He is the Home Secretary and my orders are to take him through the front door and your job is to get him and me in.'

Fair enough, I thought, and so did the other lads. Twenty TAG lads to get one geriatric Home Secretary through the front, no problems. The DS looked at us and asked the experts in public order situations our proposed tactic. After a bit of consulting in whispered tones and knowing glances, the nation-ally revered tactic known as the 'snooker ball wedge' was named as the option of choice. The DS looked suitably impressed. 'OK lads, I will see you at the venue with Mr Brittan. Once I pull up in my car, surround us and take us safely in. Good luck, see you in a couple of hours.' The DS left the room in what appeared to be a confident and upbeat manner.

As soon as he had gone, the room burst into raptures of laughter. 'Snooker ball wedge! What the fuck is that?' chorused most of us in the room. Little did I know that those words and the whole episode would haunt me most of my career.

'Well you had better sort something out,' snarled our inspector.

Twenty bright minds set about devising the snooker ball wedge. It was decided that Jabba and Jack would be the tip of the wedge, and the rest of us, depending on size and weight, would form the outsides. We would place Brittan and the DS in the centre and move in a protective formation until they were safely ensconced within the student union. Once he had delivered the seminar, we would repeat the procedure to safely extract him to his vehicle. In theory, we would slice through any crowd like a hot knife through butter. To make sure we all understood, the formation was drawn onto a dry-wipe board and officers' initials were placed in deployment positions.

'OK, kit up and van up,' shouted Phil.

'Are we wearing argos helmets and full riot kit?' someone asked.

'No need,' was the reply.

Within half an hour each group was in full uniform, ready and waiting in familiar positions within the van. Oxford Road was only five minutes from Longsight Police Station. Personal radios were turned on and some of the lads tuned in to the local channel. The radio net was a hive of activity. It seemed Operation Response had been activated and all available units were en route. Within minutes we were there. It was obvious that this wasn't an ordinary demonstration. Students had turned out in their hundreds. The present police units were having trouble keeping them off the road and assembling them in a safe holding area.

To gain entrance to two large double doors of the Union, you had to go up a flight of seven stone steps, approximately 10 feet wide. The entrance and the steps were completely blocked by at least 200 protesters. It seemed obvious to us that Brittan wouldn't be going anywhere and the sensible option would be to postpone the seminar. We contemplated what would happen next and watched more students line either side of the road, joined by police support units. The order came over the air for Three and Four Group to clear the steps.

You could see the question in Phil's face – surely some senior officer should ask the protesters to move peacefully? But Phil was a mere sergeant, this was the Home Secretary and an order is an order. Helmets were quickly placed on heads, anoraks fastened, chin stops applied, gloves pulled on. In quick formation, Three and Four groups made their way over to the steps.

As soon as we arrived at the steps, the mood of the crowd changed from hidden animosity to open hostility. In those situations the air becomes electric, the noise increases and so does your heart rate. NVCs (non-verbal communications) change. Officers try to remain calm and display a phlegmatic outward appearance, but it's hard when protesters start to chant and invade your personal space.

Phil attempted to speak to them. He asked them to move but they couldn't hear him even if they had tried. They had worked themselves into a bubble of hate and anger. The pushing and shoving started, people began to throw things from behind the front demonstrators, and others started to spit. The atmosphere became charged and the only way to resolve it was for someone to back down, but that couldn't happen.

The order to clear the steps was given. As a unit we moved among the protesters, trying to force a path to the top and then safely clear the steps top to bottom. This wasn't an easy feat and violence soon erupted. Steve's nose burst as someone punched him straight on the button. Broomer's eardrums were damaged with constant thumping. I was repeatedly kicked in the shins. Officers' helmets were pulled from their heads.

TAG lads have a good fitness level, are trained in public disorder and the majority have a natural level of aggression. Any officer can only take so much and the law of the land, be you civilian or police officer, allows you to defend yourself and that may include a pre-emptive strike.

We were not punchbags and didn't intend to be, so the next level of pressure was applied. Twenty TAG lads can look after themselves and 200 students were no match. They went hurtling down the steps and in 15 minutes order was restored and the steps were cleared. The consequences of these actions would be far-reaching and instigate an internal investigation that took years to conduct. As soon as the steps were cleared, the DS and Brittan arrived and we formed the infamous 'snooker ball wedge' around them. All this must have looked very impressive but also caused another reaction from the crowd, who surged forward en masse.

At this stage, it would be fair to say that the majority of us were wound up and the adrenalin was flowing fiercely. As soon as the DS and Brittan were in the centre of the wedge, we set off at a pace unsuitable for an overweight and unfit Home Secretary, leaving the DS behind, protecting Brittan. Into the crowd we forged, again fighting up the steps.

At a later date I had plenty of opportunity to view the film footage taken by the BBC and also a biased presentation from the *Panorama* programme. In the footage you clearly see the wedge leave Brittan behind and a demonstrator run over and smash him on the head. Eventually the DS and Brittan caught up and an entry was effected but not until someone threw a pot of piss on us from an upstairs window. Reinforcements arrived, 34 arrests were made and the stepped area was made sterile. After 30 minutes, Brittan left the building and returned to his hotel.

Many of the protesters complained about the conduct of

police officers and the level of aggression displayed that day. This, along with the media interest and TV footage, caused a major internal investigation. I was investigated and interviewed on several occasions by two separate police forces, and was exonerated on both occasions.

I believe the public should have the right to complain about police officers but don't throw stones in glass houses.

CHAPTER TEN

Manchester Cowboys

I didn't realise it, but my time on TAG was coming to an end. I had just served a four-month attachment on the public order training wing and successfully completed a national instructors' course. The four months on the public order unit were excellent and I met and trained with some good lads from different forces.

My fitness had increased dramatically. I was fit on TAG but I managed to increase my training regime at Sedgley Park, the unit's place of work. I was regularly attending firearms refresher and classification days and felt a small confidence in my ability. Although I enjoyed my attachment to the public order unit my heart wasn't in it, and I was happy to return to normal TAG duties.

I had become the senior PC on my group. Jabba had gone and was causing mayhem at the airport and Phil was acting up in the rank of inspector, so we had several different acting sergeants. One or two were excellent. They were senior TAG lads from different units going through the motions to obtain a substantial rank and didn't make waves. However, you always came across the exception who had little experience of leading ten officers with strong personalities.

When we didn't have a sergeant, the senior PC was left to run the group – not that I made waves. I was still the youngest among them so I had to find different ways of getting them to listen. Over the previous year I had gained a new partner. A loudmouth from Stockport with an attitude problem was the description given to us before he joined the unit. I can only say that this officer was one of the best I have served with: honest, loyal and a great friend. As the years progressed he would find himself at Bruche as a PTI and then on the Firearms Department. To be honest, Steve still has the gift of voicing his opinion and has got me into the shit more than once but my experiences would be fewer without him.

It was late December 1986 and TAG had been drafted over to Salford to assist in house-to-house enquiries into the murder of an elderly lady. It was late morning and Steve had nipped into the mobile incident room parked near to the Cliff, Manchester United's old training ground. He was submitting our house-to-house enquiry forms. I was having a chat with a couple of Stretford lads trying to blag two coffees. Steve wandered over and said, 'Do you want the good news or the bad news?' He had been speaking to Edgey, our new inspector.

'The good news first,' I said.

'We are working our rest days.' That was always good news – it increased our pay considerably.

'All right, give me the bad news.'

'You are going to VO8 as from Monday.'

VO8 was the new designated prefix for the Firearms Department. I smiled at him and told him to stop pulling my wire.

'No duff,' replied Steve, 'Edgey has just told me – go and ask him yourself.' Steve had used no duff, so it was true.

I had secretly harboured a chance to apply for firearms, but I thought I was too young and had a couple more years of development. I hadn't even applied for a transfer and had listened to a couple of other lads who clearly stated they were the next in line to be aides on the department.

In those days VO8 consisted of ten full-time instructors supplemented by two aides, one from divisional duties, the other from TAG. A divisional aide served six months on the department and a TAG aide four months. The idea of the aide system was to screen potential candidates for a full-time post once one became available. An aide would do the same duties as an instructor but would be under scrutiny at all times.

Over the years I had seen TAG lads return to their units dejected after being told that they were unsuitable. Many had pinned their hopes on becoming an instructor and being involved in some of GMP's top jobs. For the record, the term 'aide' became obsolete and was replaced by trainee following the increased awareness of HIV/Aids!

As I walked towards the mobile unit I contemplated how I felt. I was happy, but was I ready? I had recently knocked back an opportunity to transfer to the Dedicated Surveillance Unit, a new and secret unit. Did I want to leave TAG when I was really enjoying my service with the unit? More importantly, was I ready to prove myself in a four-month period?

I bumped into Edgey on his way out. 'Heard the news?' he said with his usual grin.

'I have sir, why didn't you tell me first?'

He shrugged his shoulders. 'You transfer next Monday. Good luck.'

'Who recommended me sir?'

'I don't know – must have been firearms.'

None the wiser in January 1986, at the age of 26, I transferred to VO8. My place of duty moved to Bootle Street in the city centre. I didn't know it, but this would become my main place of work for the next nine years – my time on TAG had finished and I wouldn't return.

* * *

In 1986, firearms was part of the V department. This meant it was a CID department and not, as one would possibly think, uniform operations. Therefore, even though I couldn't detect my way out of a paper bag, I became a detective constable rather than a police constable. For the reader's benefit, to become a detective does not denote a promotion, as certain TV programmes depict, but a change in your duties.

In the 1980s and early 1990s, GMP's CID department was politically very powerful within the force. Most of its senior officers were old-school detectives who believed in simply arresting criminals. They had risen through the ranks during the 50s, 60s, 70s and 80s and they knew a harder style of policing without the restraints of contemporary policing. I have been informed the majority were Masons and I'm not naive enough to deny that some obviously were. I am not a Mason, however Masons are not mass-murderers and as long as the job is done, who cares? I have heard officers claim that they were skipped over for promotion because of Masonic influence. Let me tell you this – they don't have to be Masons to mess up your career!

VO8 consisted of a detective superintendent, detective chief inspector, detective inspector, detective sergeant and detective constable. They were based on the eighth floor of Chester House along with the firearms admin of four civilians. The admin was the place where all records, licences and relevant material for gun owners, gun clubs and registered dealers were collated and kept up to date. The operational side of VO8 was based at Bootle Street and consisted of two detective sergeants, six detective constables, two aides/trainees and a civilian armourer. The subterranean armoury would be the place where I would store my kit, receive my weekly duties and upkeep my personal admin.

On arrival at Bootle Street, I was welcomed by Julian. He had served on VO8 for many years and had taught me to shoot as a cadet. He was now a sergeant. During the majority of my service he would be my supervisor in one guise or another. Julian was black and white, he never had any grey areas, but he had the ability to sit back and watch options develop. He was extremely competent regarding firearms duties and an expert shot. He believed shooting was all about confidence, and that there wasn't a great need to train all the time. I would disagree: he was a natural shot, I wasn't and I had to work hard at it. The more rounds I fired the better I got. I suffered Julian's wrath more than once and probably deserved it. He didn't hold grudges and in those days he used to punish me by threatening not to allow me to play rugby for the force. To be fair he never carried out his threat and I have to say I respected and liked the fella.

I couldn't say the same for a couple of the other instructors, who had high opinions of themselves. I was later to find these opinions unjustified and I would go head-to-head with them over certain new and radical tactics. But for now I would have to keep my mouth shut and try to get along.

I was issued with my kit and my personal weapons. My kit consisted of a Bristol Armour ballistic helmet with visor, a set of blue overalls, a set of heavyweight armour shield body armour and ballistic nylon plates, a leather rig (gun belt, holster and magazine pouches), a Henri Lloyd waterproof over-jacket, a large holdall, a personal radio, binoculars and a three-cell Maglite torch. My personal weapons were a Mod 13 Smith & Wesson revolver, Mod 586 Smith & Wesson revolver, a two-inch Smith & Wesson revolver, a 9mm Hi-Power Browning SLP and an 810 Remington Wingmaster shotgun.

I felt very important having all this kit but I would come to realise I couldn't possibly use it all, particularly the weapons. I was also issued a pager, and instructed to inform a supervisory officer if I was going out of the force area while off-duty. I was now operational and waiting for my first job. It didn't take long before I had my first turnout.

It was 17.00 and I was over at Longsight nick in the gym, training with a few of my TAG mates, when the pager activated with the number of the force control room. I was told to return to Bootle Street immediately. When I got there the lads were already in full kit. I was told to kit up and arm myself with a Mod 13 and shotgun.

Once dressed, I noticed that two of the team, Jim and Keith, had already left. Julian informed me they were en route to Longsight (where I had just come from – what a surprise), as were the DCI and the DI. I was told to grab two more Mod 13s and ammo for the bosses. I made my way to the enclosed yard, jumped in the back of a personnel carrier and waited for us to screech out of the yard, when one of the lads asked me what I was doing.

I looked at him blankly, and in an excited voice stated the obvious: 'Sitting here.'

Julian leaned over from the front passenger seat and said, 'You drive, Andy.'

No problem. I jumped over into the driver's seat. I was used to driving three-litre Transit vans on emergency calls, so a two-litre personnel carrier was no problem. I activated the sirens and lights and sped out of the yard. Longsight is approximately 12 minutes from Bootle Street. We made it in six. I noticed there wasn't much conversation in the van; a few of the instructors didn't like speed or more likely my driving. We made our way to the CID office on the fourth floor at Longsight nick. The office is a large unit, approximately half the size of a football pitch.

The place was packed with CID officers, several TAG lads, a couple of dog-handlers and our two bosses. We made our way over to the bosses. The DCI was a Geordie called Malc, and the DI was known as Cowboy. I wondered why but I kept my thoughts to myself. Malc briefed us on what was happening. We had a hostage situation, a male suspect was holding a female against her will in a vehicle, he had a handgun pressed to her head and had soaked both of them in petrol.

The vehicle was parked on waste ground on the Anson estate in Longsight. The Anson is a rough, rundown council estate of drab 1960s architecture. Uniform patrols had the couple under observations and were attempting to enter into dialogue. Jim and Keith were en route to assess the situation.

Julian took charge. 'Right, get into the van, let's get down there and give Keith and Jim a hand.' Julian looked at the bosses and confirmed we had authority to issue. Malc nodded and mentioned some ACC's name.

Once at the scene Jimmy explained it was a domestic dispute gone wrong. The pair had been an item but had broken up. As usual the bloke couldn't accept this and after a row had taken her hostage, threatening to kill both of them. Jimmy thought he was armed with a flintlock pistol, possibly a replica or a souvenir from Spain; Jim had noticed the hammer was pulled back. This was good obs from Jim; the hammer was the piece that struck the pan, which ignited the ball once the trigger was pulled. A genuine flintlock had to be cocked to enable it to work. We had no choice but to continue on the same risk assessment.

By now the light had dropped and it was starting to get cold. The target vehicle was a light blue four-door Ford Escort. The man was sat in the driver's seat with his left arm around the woman and what appeared to be a handgun in his right hand, pressed against the woman's temple. The woman was sat in the passenger seat with her window half open. The petrol flap of the vehicle was open with the cap missing, replaced by an old rag. The vehicle was parked at the bottom of the street in the middle of a concrete base surrounded by the graffiti-covered garages of the residents.

Jimmy had issued himself with a mini-Ruger carbine and moved to a position to create what's called 'sniper lock' – in effect he had the target in his sights. The rest of us deployed on either side of the vehicle but out of sight. We were using a brick wall for cover. I heard through my earpiece that a negotiator was en route and we were not to take action unless necessary. I was next to Malc who was stamping his feet, shivering and shaking like a jelly.

My colleagues Rod (left) and Foz training in Manchester. Both are wearing goggles for eye protection and carrying Heckler & Koch MP5s, our standard issue firearms.

The author aged 17 (in quilted waistcoat, holding sign) as a Greater Manchester Police cadet, on an Outward Bound course at Ullswater in the Lake District.

My tormentor Jabba (far left) and colleagues in the Tactical Aid Group, having just completed the famous Three Peaks walk in Yorkshire. You had to be fit to cut the mustard on TAG. I'm kneeling on the right, as far from Jab as possible.

A full TAG team up on the M62 near Saddleworth Moor. Snow blocked the motorway and we had to rescue stranded lorry drivers.

A firearms team training for room clearance in low light. The adrenalin surge when you enter a hostile target premises is incredible.

Right-wing fanatic and cop killer Anthony Hughes, who gunned down Inspector Ray Codling (inset) on a service station on the M62 motorway before blowing his own brains out.
© *Manchester Evening News*

Delroy Brown, leader of Moss Side's murderous Doddington Gang, who were infiltrated by a tenacious police officer codenamed Delta.

Parvo Corkovic, the prolific Salford armed robber I chased on foot. I don't make a habit of praising villains but Corky certainly had balls.

A nasty-looking 762 Ruger sniper rifle, part of the Firearms Department kit. We had some interesting weaponry.

Practising hostage rescue: (above) abseiling down the side of a building in Manchester city centre, and (below) storming a train at a military installation in the West Midlands. The train windows are smashed in with a pick, then in you go.

I try to work out how to break into a Nat West bank in Salford after sensors inside had alerted us that members of a robbery gang were inside.

On the roof of the bank, looking for an entry point. Once inside, I fell through a ceiling, damaging my back and legs – injuries that ultimately led to my leaving the force.

Storming a building in a built-up area. This is the sort of operation the Special Forces are renowned for, but police forces around the country are much more likely to need these skills on a day-to-day basis.

A GMP firearms team seeking to arrest a gang on a shooting spree in the Bolton, Bury and Rochdale areas. The gang gunned down five innocent bystanders in an attempt to slow down their police pursuers before they were caught.
© Chris Mangall

'Fucking great,' he muttered.

The streets around the vehicle had been cordoned off and residents were sent home. It was now dark but street lamps and police blue flashing lights illuminated the area. I could see the boss was getting impatient, and he called Julian over.

'Lets rush them,' he whispered in his Geordie accent.

Julian advised against it, relaying the contents of the last radio message.

'It's fucking freezing,' complained Malc.

'We just have to contain and wait,' said Julian.

This was the obvious safe option – unless the suspect created problems. The suspect had stopped talking to uniform officers and sat completely still. We were approximately 50 feet from the vehicle, but couldn't really get a good visual.

Over the radio came Jim's voice. 'I think he has fallen asleep.'

This was the excuse Malc needed. 'Right, we are going in,' he stated. Without any further planning, he broke cover, shouting, 'Strike! Strike! Strike!' and led the charge. The rest of us followed. Malc was on the driver's side and yanked the door open. Out tumbled the suspect. He was quickly grabbed and handcuffed. His weapon lay where he fell, a wooden-gripped flintlock pistol. We later found out it was a toy. One of the lads reached through the driver's side to unlock the passenger door and release the terrified woman. The suspect was handed over to CID officers. This was normal protocol; once an arrest had been made VO8 generally took no further part in proceedings and returned to unit if safe to do so.

In my eyes, everything had happened too quickly, with no planning. What if the driver's door had been locked like the passenger's? None of us had designated positions; we almost fell over each other. What if there had been a shooting on either side? What medical facilities did we have? The whole operation was like the Keystone Cops.

But one thing I had noticed was that I functioned. I thought clearly and had the ability to debrief the incident to myself. During all my times on firearms, I knew I could make clinical decisions. I was at my best when the operation was at its highest level. I could out-plan and offer more tactical options during an emergency or deliberate plan than most people. This may sound conceited but I was confident in my abilities. I believe that I started to gain these skills after my first house entry, when I almost shot the suspect.

I kept these thoughts to myself, but as with all my other firearms operations I filed them away. I would rely on these experiences in later years.

Julian asked the boss if he was coming back to Bootle Street for the debrief.

'No chance, I will just get last orders if I'm quick,' was the reply.

We returned to Bootle Street, de-kitted and sat round the tables in the centre of the armoury. Julian opened the debrief, and not much of the incident was mentioned. The lads acted as if this was the norm for the DCI. I kept my mouth shut and listened. It had been a busy couple of days. One thing was clear: I loved every minute of it. Maybe I enjoyed the adrenalin rush as well.

* * *

The weeks progressed quickly in VO8. A normal day's duty would be 08.00 parade at Bootle Street and grab a quick cup of tea. We would prepare the kit needed to take to one of the training venues. Weapons, ammunition and targets were loaded into the van. By 09.30 we'd be at one of the training venues used by GMP, usually Diggle. We also used an indoor range at Salford Police Station (later condemned) or another at Rochdale. At times throughout the year we also had access to Swynnerton Army Camp in Staffordshire, which housed a close-quarters battle range, or Holcombe army camp. The students would already be waiting for us and by 10.00 we would be on range instructing the force's AFOs. Depending on the type of course, basic, refresher or classification we would usually be back at Bootle Street and off-duty by 16.00.

In theory that was how the day ran, but more often than not a pager would activate and we would be required to attend a firearms incident somewhere within the force area. These events had an impact on the students' training and development and early on in my VO8 service I was hearing rumours of an increase in staff.

VO8, or the firearms unit of today, do not generate work, apart from the ARVs (armed response vehicles). The unit is reliant on the various squads or divisions within the force area to determine how busy they get. The squads investigate criminal activity and from intelligence (either technical or human) and evidence decide when to arrest suspects. Divisions are generally more reactive; for example, a uniform patrol may disturb an armed robbery in progress or a shooting and require armed assistance. Although each division has its own CID, they have similar resources and requirements as the squads.

VO8 was also required to assist at Manchester Airport due to the terrorist problems in the Middle East. The Israeli El-Al flight was inbound and outbound every Monday and Thursday and the threat assessment was at its highest level. In January 1986, VO8 was stretched to its limit. I would say on average I was on an actual armed operation at least twice a week.

I believe the reason we were so busy was the increase in armed crime. Manchester – and at times other regions' criminals – were using easily available firearms in committing crime. In the mid-80s a definite crime trend towards armed robberies had been identified. Cash in transit or banks and building societies were the flavour of the day and the sawn-off shotgun was the weapon of preference.

During the rest of my career I would come across a full range of weaponry, from handguns, shotguns, grenades to sub-machine guns and assault rifles. All weapons frighten me but the one I detest is the shotgun. The usual belief is that a shotgun barrel is shortened to enable a wider shot pattern. This is not true; it actually tightens the shot pattern. A shotgun used by criminals is shortened for one reason only – concealment. It is a simple weapon to shoot – point and pull the trigger – and depending on the ammunition used, is reasonably accurate.

The other weapons I have mentioned are much harder to master and are difficult unless in skilled hands. Shotguns were easy to obtain. One source was burglaries from rural properties. Many farmers have one shotgun on ticket (registered) and several off the ticket. Therefore when a burglary is reported they would usually only mention the one weapon stolen. To be fair though, there are other sources available to the criminal community.

I was learning to teach the arts of shooting stance, grip, trigger control, sight picture and so on. I was also learning how to put together an actual shooting discipline and then deliver it to the students. On every armed operation an AFO wears body armour so I started to introduce shoots with students wearing body armour. This caused a great deal of hostility towards me, and also between heads of departments.

In those days the force had an assortment of AFOs. Virtually every department had AFOs, including the Regional and Serious Crime Squads, the airport, the TAG, Special Branch and normal uniform patrol officers. Some of those officers volunteered to become AFOs because they knew once they were involved in a protracted firearms incident the chances of overtime greatly increased. It also allowed them to have the pick of the jobs assigned to their particular department's speciality, at times allowing for 'cushy numbers'. This wasn't the case for all AFOs, many being professional and dedicated, but more than a small minority benefited from this system. Once shooting disciplines become harder, for instance wearing body armour, the small minority started to make waves, whingeing to their supervisory officers and also other firearms instructors.

My firm belief is that you train for reality and once the basics of aimed shooting are mastered, then it should be the norm to re-class, refresh and practise in the equipment you would wear on a live job. The practice of wearing body armour would become the norm while participating in any type of shoot.

Back in the days when I was a cadet at Diggle, employed as the monkey pulling the wire, I had been threatened on two occasions, both times by CID officers. At first I thought they were joking, but I soon realised they weren't. The threat was in relation to the timed exposure I had given; they suggested I was economical with my exposure times and it would be prudent to leave the targets exposed a little longer. As a cadet this bothered me and although I didn't back down I certainly stayed out of their way. I actually saw one of those officers break down in tears when he was told he had failed his classification and was NFT (non-further training).

Several years on, those type of officers still existed and would be openly hostile towards me and on later occasions try to 'mix me a bottle'. I can honestly say these wankers never bothered me. Maybe it was the arrogance of youth, the confidence in my own abilities or surviving for four years on the TAG.

I had been on VO8 for only two months and the department had increased its strength by a further four officers. Two were TAG lads who had aided prior to me, Bob and Pete, Leaky was another ex-TAG, and traffic lad Stuart had come from the airport. Bob and Pete were sound, Pete a practical joker and Bob a big, hard, no-nonsense lad. Leaky, 'the little shit', was unassuming, not the biggest in stature but an ultimate professional with a snappy personality and the ability to sleep anywhere. Stuart was the complete opposite to these lads – a quiet person without an ounce of aggression.

It was the middle of the week and we were going to Diggle when the pagers activated. A quick call to the force control room and we turned around, the blue lights and sirens activated and we speedily returned to Bootle Street. There Keith, one of the sergeants and old hands, quickly briefed us. We were to get into civvies and kit up. Instead of heavyweight body armour we would don covert armour. Rigs were replaced by pancake holsters and radios hidden as best as possible. The majority of us kept a baggy civvy coat to cover our bulky kit. Shotguns were usually kept in Adidas training bags or even black bin liners.

Keith told us that members of the Dedicated Surveillance Unit (DSU) were following a team of four Manchester criminals who were driving a Volvo Estate. The team had been under surveillance since yesterday and the vehicle had been followed from Manchester to the East End of London. The four suspects were believed to be armed and had engaged in a big drug deal with criminal members of the Turkish community. They had bought a large quantity of amphetamines. The consignment was on board the Volvo, which was returning to Manchester. Three vehicles from the DSU were making their way to Bootle Street to pick up nine VO8 staff (three per vehicle). We were to drive to Burtonwood service station on the M62, tag onto the end of the surveillance and, when safe to do so, effect a stop and armed arrest of the suspects.

It wasn't long before the DSU drivers arrived and we were speeding out of the city towards the M62. The DSU are purely a surveillance unit and its officers are always unarmed. You might question the wisdom of having unarmed drivers in an armed operation, but GMP has always had a policy that doesn't allow drivers who are involved in fast, progressive and offensive driving to be armed. The reason they give is that the driver is under a lot of stress and could act adversely once involved in an armed deployment. I believe this to be an antiquated and short-sighted policy. It has at times been a rod for their own back and they have had to relax the rules for the armed response patrols.

An officer with the correct training and right attitude has no problems switching from one role to another. This has been proved many times. I have lost count of the times myself or my colleagues have raced from one side of Manchester to another and then been involved in the arrest of armed criminals. If that isn't good evidence, I don't know what is. Another argument I have heard is that an armed officer cannot adopt the role of a surveillance officer. Again, this is rubbish. I think without too much research you would find that the military and overseas police forces would count this as normal practice. But for some reason in GMP there is massive reluctance to multi-skill a firearms officer. Again this is possibly due to the incompetents sat in their ivory towers.

In 20 minutes we were at Burtonwood, where a small contingent of CID officers and the senior command were in the car park. Keith and Harry made their way over and were updated on the state of the surveillance. The target vehicle was on the M62, approximately half an hour from Burtonwood and travelling towards Manchester. Keith wanted ideas for a plan and a couple of senior instructors voiced their opinions. I knew my place and this was all new to me, so I would keep my mouth shut unless asked for my opinion and wait for my deployment duties. After a short period it was decided that a liveried motorway patrol vehicle would be used.

The motorway patrol, in company with Harry, would move through the surveillance with the three DSU vehicles behind the patrol but not too conspicuously. When Harry believed it was safe, the motorway patrol would signal the Volvo to pull over onto the hard shoulder. The motorway patrol would position itself in front of the Volvo, quickly followed by the three DSU vehicles taking rear and side positions, effectively boxing in the Volvo. Members of our team would then approach the vehicle and arrest the occupants. The plan was quickly agreed on and deployment duties were given. I was in the second DSU vehicle, which would take a side position. Our role would be to cover the rest of the team who would approach and arrest.

One of the DSU officers had been listening to the radio and shouted that the convoy had passed Burtonwood, average speed 80mph, heading in the direction Salford and the M602. We immediately jumped into the vehicles and established comms. Harry was the passenger in a motorway Range Rover, which quickly took the lead. We accelerated off the slip road, our speed quickly reaching 100mph. The rear end of the surveillance had to work to catch up.

Not much was said in our vehicle; I was listening for an update from the DSU driver who had switched his comms to his earpiece. I could start to feel the adrenalin flow as the speed of the vehicle and the operation started to effect chemical changes in my body. As long as I didn't let it take over this was a good thing – it would allow me to operate on a better plane.

The driver started relaying, 'Target vehicle in sight'. Then our radios came alive. Harry was on the net. 'Pull back, pull back,' was the command. We reduced our speed a little; Harry was looking for a safe spot to stop. I took my Mod 13 from its holster and placed it on my lap. I wanted every advantage once we pulled the target vehicle over. I didn't want to be struggling with my holster. The net came alive again. 'Standby, standby.' Harry had found a safe spot for the arrest, but we were still travelling at over 70mph.

Harry's vehicle had activated its blue lights and was indicating to the Volvo to pull over. The Volvo pulled over onto the hard shoulder and the occupants were clearly looking at the traffic car, and hadn't a clue about us. 'Strike! Strike! Strike!'

We moved to the Volvo's off-side, the other DSU vehicles were at the rear, and the motorway patrol was in front. The Volvo was boxed in. I jumped out of the rear off-side of my vehicle and immediately started to cover the occupants of the vehicle. My colleagues were doing the same and everyone was shouting.

'Armed police, armed police, get your hands up.'

I started to worry: my back was exposed to the motorway traffic. Six VO8 ran towards the Volvo, Harry included; they were crossing our line of fire. They then attacked the Volvo's doors, which were fortunately open and in minutes three of the occupants were belly-down and handcuffed on the tarmac. Harry and another instructor, Parker, a really annoying and pedantic bloke, were struggling with the passenger, trying to drag him from the vehicle, but he wasn't moving. The pair of them were going red in the face but couldn't budge him. Leaky leant into the Volvo from the driver's seat and released the seat belt – out popped the passenger, dropping on top of Parker and Harry. He was quickly cuffed.

The occupants had a look of surprise and then fear. There was no doubt that they hadn't spotted any police activity. We were to later find out that the suspects were from Salford and the front passenger was related to the McPhees, a notorious criminal family.

The motorway section had responded quickly to the incident and our stretch of the highway had been closed off. The occupants and the car were searched and two handguns and a large quantity of amphetamines were recovered. Within minutes the prisoners were handed over to the CID and we were heading to Bootle Street.

'Five minutes, debrief in the armoury,' shouted Keith.

A brew was made and we took our positions round the tables. It was decided that our response had been good, the new DSU were good to work with, and Parker and Harry laughed over their incident with the seat belt. All in all a good job, time to clean up and get home.

This time I wasn't left with my own thoughts: Leaky and Bob clearly had issues, and we made our way to the canteen so we wouldn't be overheard. We evaluated the action. Arcs of fire had been crossed – what would have happened if the arrest team had a compromise? Would the cover team have been able to deal with it? The surveillance was moving faster than anticipated and we were almost off the motorway – only just on the M602 – when the strike was called. Did we have an option for arrest in the city? What if the doors had been locked? How could we have gained access to the vehicle? The senior instructors seemed to have fucked up with the front passenger and seat belt.

We agreed that although the result was great, the execution of the plan was inadequate. Although we were new, we could see failings. If these weren't corrected, someone was bound to get hurt. We also agreed it wasn't the right time to speak out. Maybe it was a one-off, although I doubted it. Some weeks later I spoke to a couple of DSU lads I knew, and they too voiced concerns about the arrests.

CHAPTER ELEVEN

Robbers and Terrorists

Three months had passed and I couldn't believe how busy the department was. If I wasn't engaged instructing I would be employed on an operation somewhere.

I received some disturbing news – my position on TAG had been filled. Edgey had recruited an officer from the D Division and had effectively replaced me. This bothered me, as I had only one month left in my position as an aide. If I failed to make the grade, or upset one or two of the small-minded instructors, I would be out on my rear without a place of duty. All that would be left was a return to division. I didn't fancy that – life was much more exciting where I was. I intended to get stuck in, learn as much as possible and try not to upset the few back-stabbing instructors.

More importantly, I had to disassociate myself from Ian. He was one of the new breed of officer required for the Firearms Department. He was ex-TAG and had been a permanent instructor for two years. He was motivated, fit and highly skilled. He had the ability to switch to a different mode of operating, which I admired; he could demonstrate a high control of aggression when required. This certainly frightened, and assisted in the capitulation of, armed suspects, but it also scared one or two instructors shitless. I had played rugby with Ian since I was 18 so we have been close friends for many years, but in those early days of firearms I had to keep my respect for him in check in case this adversely affected my chances on the department.

Ironically it was Ian who told me I had a permanent place on the department. He had been over at Chester House and the superintendent, who incidentally later become the commander of the CID, had asked how I was fitting in. Ian quickly told him I would be suitable for a permanent place if one came available. 'As it happens we are increasing by a further two constables,' he told Ian. 'Tell Hailwood he's got a place.' And so, in April 1986 I transferred permanently to VO8.

Within days of my transfer, myself and the rest of the team were over at Longsight. It was 07.00 on a sunny and comfortably warm morning. Twelve VO8 staff had been told to parade at the Regional Crime Squad office. We were to be kitted for a covert operation (civilian clothes), and would be working in company with officers from the RCS.

We made our way to the Regional's office and found ourselves seats. The office was packed with RCS officers and a few suits who I didn't recognise, but when they spoke, a couple had southern accents. One of the DIs from the Regional walked to the front of the room, accompanied by another bloke who was well groomed and dressed in what appeared to be a very expensive grey suit.

'Morning, gents. I'm DCI Oliver from the Met's Flying Squad.' This certainly got our attention. My favourite TV cop was and still is DI Regan in *The Sweeney*. The DCI went on to give one of the best and most thorough briefings I had ever received. A team of four of London's most wanted criminals were in Manchester planning an armed robbery for later that morning. The men had been under surveillance since the previous day; in fact the Met's fixed-wing aircraft had followed them to Manchester.

The MO of this team was to steal a high-powered motorbike, which two of them would use as a 'third eye' to watch for any sign of interference from the police or the public. The other two would be responsible for attacking a delivery of cash in transit.

Once a 'tin can' (security van) stopped outside a bank or building society and the guard started to deliver or collect cash, the gang would attack the lone guard, quickly soaking him in petrol and holding a naked flame near him. The intention was to make the driver of the tin can hand over all the cash collected to prevent his colleague being badly burned.

DCI Oliver said that this MO had been successful on several occasions. The last time it had been used a member of the public had been shot by the team on the motorbike. The latest update on the gang was that they had stolen a lime-green Kawasaki high-performance motorcycle in the early hours. They possessed shotguns and revolvers. It was believed that a known Manchester criminal had 'sold' this job to the London gang. It was not unusual for criminals to research and plan robberies and then sell them on. He went on to inform us that intelligence suggested that the robbery would occur in Rusholme, south of the city centre.

The 12 of us were deployed to four RCS vehicles. As usual the drivers would be from the squads and unarmed. There would also be a command vehicle with senior detectives on board. The DI from the RCS was one of those sad eccentrics who turned out on a job wearing a Shemagh (Arab-style) headdress. I didn't know what the Flying Squad thought of him, but he certainly embarrassed us and his lads.

It wasn't long before we deployed and split into two separate convoys. It was hard to understand what was actually occurring on the ground. The mobile surveillance was busy following the suspects, but all the radio transmissions were being relayed to the driver, who had a different comms system to ours. It was ludicrous. We had to build a mental picture of what was happening on the ground from what the driver told us. At times this picture could be disastrously wrong. Surveillance drivers, particularly those transporting a firearms team, have to work hard. They have to keep up with the surveillance, which severely tests their driving skills. They have to listen to the surveillance commentary and respond accordingly. They have to keep the firearms convoy together and update the firearms officers within the vehicle on what is occurring. Surveillance changes second by second and a relay of radio transmissions can already be history once it's been received. If a surveillance driver has a firearms officer like me in the vehicle, he will face a constant barrage of questions. I will be relentless in gathering as much information as I can, sometimes to the annoyance of the driver.

It would obviously make sense to train firearms officers in the basics of mobile surveillance and ensure the radio systems were compatible. This is too easy a solution and for many years there was reluctance to multi-skill. We therefore had to adapt and work within difficult and stupid boundaries. At least this allowed me to experience problems from an early stage and learn how to conquer them. Therefore, as the years progressed and other so-called experts questioned or rubbished a tactic, I could explain why and how we had arrived at that decision. To be honest I got sick and tired of explaining to some of these gutless know-alls, and upset them to my own cost.

From an update from our driver I realised our two-car firearms convoy had tagged onto the arse-end of the surveillance on the motorcycle. In my vehicle, Harry was in the front passenger seat, John in the rear near-side and I was in the rear off-side. We were the lead vehicle, with another firearms vehicle behind us. Each vehicle had the usual weapons: each officer had a revolver and extra ammo plus in my vehicle I was armed with a shotgun.

In another vehicle, Smiggs, a cool, laid-back ex-TAG lad, was, unusually, armed with a Heckler & Koch MP5 9mm carbine. We had only taken delivery of a consignment of these weapons a few weeks earlier and were still evaluating their suitability. They would later become the primary weapon for most police forces around the country.

Our convoy was now in Owens Park/Fallowfield, an area with a high student population. An update from our driver informed us that the robbery gang had been following a Securicor van along Wilmslow Road. The other two members were in a stolen, high-performance Fiat saloon. They had split up but were still in the area. It appeared that the tin can was collecting cash and the gang were waiting for the most financially opportune moment to commit the robbery.

The driver in the other vehicle nodded his head and acknowledged a radio transmission received through his earpiece. He turned towards us. 'We've got Condition Red from the command vehicle,' he said. This meant authority had been given to arrest the gang. It was now up to us.

John made sure Smiggs had received the OK. Everything seemed to notch up a gear. I don't think any of us were quite clear on exactly where the two on the Kawasaki were, but our driver dropped a gear and we found ourselves hurtling through the streets of Fallowfield. Driving at these speeds quickly disorientates you, and John and I were flung about the vehicle. Above the noise of the engine, John tried to calm the driver and find out what the gang was doing. The driver had let the adrenalin get the better of him and was tear-arsing through the streets. All we could do was hold on. Through the rear windscreen I could see the other vehicle stuck to us like glue. The RCS driver appeared to have grown horns and was hunched over the wheel of his vehicle, looking like Lucifer himself. Smiggs, usually calm and cool, was ashen and his eyes were the size of golf balls.

Because of the excitement of the chase, I couldn't help but laugh. John looked at me as if I was daft, but soon went back to our predicament as we rocketed around a bend. The driver dropped another gear, accelerated and took off down a narrow alleyway. Because of the created illusion we appeared to be travelling at Mach 1, with the walls and entry gates flying past us.

The driver shouted, 'There they are!' and into view came a lime-green Kawasaki with two riders on board. The pillion passenger was looking behind, and around his chest he was carrying a khaki satchel. The motorcycle tried to accelerate away, and normally he would have succeeded, but some quick-thinking RCS driver had got his vehicle in front of them, creating a barrier. The motorcycle rider was furiously trying to find a route round the RCS vehicle, and we were gaining on them. Disaster almost struck as we hit the alleyway wall on the off-side and my window popped, showering us with glass, and sparks flew as we careered down the alleyway. The driver stamped on his brakes and we fishtailed down the alley, myself and John stretching our arms in front of us to avoid smashing into the front seats. I had to do this with one arm while I held onto my shotgun.

The motorcycle rider had crashed the bike and he and his passenger were sliding along the alleyway on their sides. The bike hit a wall and as with all lucky criminals the rider picked himself up and started to limp away. The pillion passenger was more dazed and was on his knees. Our vehicle came to a halt and Harry was out and running towards the pillion passenger. I couldn't get out of my side of the car, as the vehicle was boxed in by the wall, and John was struggling to open his door, which had jammed. I started to climb over the front seat. Smiggs went hurtling past me screaming 'Armed police stand still!' I was after the driver.

Harry was by now struggling with the pillion passenger. The passenger was at least 6ft 4ins and solid. He appeared young beneath his helmet and was getting the better of Harry. I took in the scene and was horrified to see a revolver on the roof of the RCS vehicle. As I ran towards the struggling pair I could see the pillion passenger glance at the revolver and start to make his way towards it with Harry hanging all over him. I had no option but to smash the barrel of my shotgun into the visored area of his helmet. He fell back, hurt and visibly shaken. I screamed at him, 'Armed police, armed police.' As if a light had been turned on, he seemed to comprehend, and was quickly handcuffed. I noticed Harry get up and place the revolver from the roof of the vehicle into his empty holster.

The pillion passenger's satchel was searched and a loaded .357 Magnum revolver with six rounds of hollow point ammo was found, along with a Zippo lighter and a small container of petrol. Smiggs was walking back with his prisoner, who was securely handcuffed. Smiggs had also recovered a firearm. The prisoners were made to lie on the floor at the scene. This wait lasted at least 30 minutes, which is unusual for GMP, but the Flying Squad insisted that scenes of crime officers attended and all evidence was photographed in situ. During this wait I saw Harry walk over to our DI. He seemed to be looking at me and remonstrating. Smiggs joined in the discussion and Harry walked off. I later found out that Harry had complained about my use of the shotgun on the suspect and said that I was dangerous. He omitted to tell the DI about the revolver on the roof of the vehicle. Fortunately for me, Smiggs had seen what had happened and defended my actions, leaving Harry fuming.

This was part of a great learning curve for me. I realised that at times it's not just the criminals you're working against but your colleagues as well.

The other team had an equally good result. They had arrested the two suspects in the Fiat and recovered two shotguns. Eventually we returned to Longsight, where the Flying Squad DCI thanked us and asked for statements of evidence. In the weeks that followed we would be requested to give evidence at the Old Bailey in London. It had been an ambition of mine to give evidence in one of the oldest and most historic courts in England. However, the team we arrested pleaded guilty while the other team pleaded not guilty, so I never achieved it.

Once back at Bootle Street we quickly dekitted and held a team debrief. Smiggs was impressed with the MP5, notably its psychological impact. While being chased, his prisoner had looked back and seen Smiggs with the MP5. He stopped dead in his tracks. Smiggs said that he was mumbling something about a machine gun. To be fair, Smiggs would always undersell himself. What became clear on the debrief was the massive confusion that had arisen once the authority for the arrest had been given. We needed a better tactic and option.

* * *

It wasn't long before Bob and I found ourselves on a six-week national firearms instructors course at Bishop's Garth, West Yorkshire. We were there to learn teaching techniques and different styles of instructing. We would have to demonstrate that we understood what we had been taught by delivering lessons to our class of 12 other students from forces throughout the country. We would have to prove that we were competent enough to teach the skills of shooting with the four separate police issue weapons. We would also have to pass an instructors' classification shoot on all four weapons. The pass mark for the instructors' classification was 90 per cent.

The West Yorkshire force was known for its prowess in shooting. Several of their instructors were in the England police pistol team, and they rightly prided themselves in teaching the disciplines of shooting. I learned a great deal from their instructors in the use of handguns. The handguns to be used on the course were a Smith & Wesson 2-inch revolver, Smith & Wesson 4-inch revolver and a 9mm C/Z SLP. The other weapon to classify on was the 810 Remington Wingmaster shotgun.

The classification shoots don't take place until the sixth week and a fair amount of pressure builds prior to them. In those days there was no second chance: a fail was a fail. In GMP, if an officer failed an instructor's classification then he was transferred out of the department – usually back to uniform duties. Bob and I passed the shoots with a fair amount of relief.

The instructors' course wasn't just about shooting, it also covered the use of police tactics in firearms situations. This is where my interest lies. I don't get pissed up on shooting – in fact it bores me. I know I must be skilled with my firearms, but I also believe that the best tactical option puts you in a better position to take the shot. The better the tactical decision, the easier the shot, so to speak.

It became clear from early on that the West Yorkshire instructors lacked operational tactical experience. They were excellent at quoting the 'Blue Book' (Home Office guidelines for the use of firearms) but they didn't realise that the Blue Book was inadequate when it came to live operations. I got sick of them quoting the so-called golden rule: never approach the known location of an armed suspect. How can you possibly arrest someone if you don't approach their location?

Remember your priorities: the public, the police, the suspect. How could I forget that I had become a police officer to serve and protect the public? My loyalties would always be to my colleagues. A non-politically correct and honest answer towards giving the offender any consideration was, 'I couldn't give a flying fuck!' If a criminal decides to arm himself in the pursuit of crime, don't expect me or any of my colleagues to consider his value. Having spoken to criminals who have used firearms, the majority understand the risks and don't expect any quarter from the police. I'm not suggesting we execute them – far from it – but many good officers have lost their lives to criminals using weapons. I didn't intend to be another one of them.

The Yorkshire instructors kept on relating one actual operation they had experienced, which was the pursuit of an armed offender in a vehicle. Bob and I found that although we respected their obvious teaching skills, they were weak when it came to teaching tactics. During my career I attended many police firearms schools of training and only a small minority had the credentials to teach tactics. The reason they could was because their force was busy gaining invaluable experience by arresting armed criminals. Examples are the Met and Northern Ireland. My last experience of a national school was a few years ago at West Mercia. The facilities were fantastic and the instructors nice enough lads, but their experience was limited in operational firearms policing.

Both Bob and I weren't about to rock the boat, and kept our mouths tightly shut. All we needed was the instructors' qualification, which would allow us to return to the force and continue with VO8. So we returned to the force as qualified instructors. This allowed us to give tactical advice to senior officers, something that would become more important as armed crime increased. It also allowed us to carry our Browning Hi-Power SLPs on anti-terrorist duties.

It may sound stupid to the reader, but in my early days as an instructor, someone in their ivory tower insisted that only qualified instructors could carry SLPs and they could only be used for anti-terrorist operations. VO8 had the role of policing the Israeli El-Al flights, and for the next five years, until Manchester Airport increased its AFOs, VO8 would deploy eight officers armed with SLPs and either the H&K MP5 carbine or the H&K 33 assault weapon, a medium range weapon with a .223 carbine round.

I often questioned why an officer not qualified as an instructor couldn't carry an SLP. As long as he had qualified and proved he was competent with the weapon, what was the problem?

The reason semi-automatic weapons were carried at the airport was because of terrorist incidents at Rome and Vienna airports. Terrorists had attacked the El-Al passengers, killing and wounding many. Months later we were able to read the officers' response reports from those incidents. What was noticeable was that officers had quickly run out of ammunition while engaged in a firefight with the terrorists. A recommendation was that officers should carry SLPs while engaged in anti-terrorist duties.

SLPs came in hundreds of varieties and calibres, but the 9mm round was favoured by both the military and police. Most SLPs have a magazine capacity of seven to 15 rounds with an extra magazine; this considerably increased an officer's capability. Over the years VO8's SLP was the Browning Hi-Power. Mine was so old it had an emblem of a Nazi eagle stamped on it. Smiggs called it a butcher's gun, which in essence was true. It wasn't the most accurate of weapons, but it increased firepower close up. The Browning was eventually replaced by a weapon called the AT84.

GMP, in its wisdom, decided to purchase an Eastern Bloc weapon that no-one had heard of. It was inexpensive and that certainly played a part in the decision. There was a delay of nine months before it was delivered. The suppliers suggested that one consignment had been on board a ship that had sunk during rough weather. Eventually another consignment turned up (possibly from the seabed). When we shot the guns, either the magazine fell out or the foresight dropped off. These were replaced by the Beretta 92F, but this was phased out and replaced by the Glock 17. The Glock 17 has become the primary weapon for all AFOs in Manchester and the revolver has slipped away into history.

About this time the department size increased again to two teams of two sergeants and eight constables each. Our duties were split; we had a week of instructing and a week on duty. This meant one team would be in charge of instructing the AFOs throughout the force at various venues, and the other team would be operational – on 24-hour standby (eight on duty) and responsible for any firearms operation within the force. This week also included team training – something that was badly lacking and would help the development of VO8 considerably. After every week we rotated duties.

During this period, several of the operational team were called over to the Special Branch office at Chester House. My team was on training duties. Some operational instructors had disappeared – no-one had seen them for several days, and they weren't responding to pagers. One by one the operational team were disappearing and the training team was having to replace them on ops. Then training was cancelled and the department was put on standby.

Only the bosses knew what had happened to our missing colleagues, and we were still diminishing in numbers. An instructor would be told to grab his operational kit and parade at Chester House and that's the last we saw of them. By now we were down to a team of eight and relying on TAG to assist us. We also started to hear the rumours that GMP's Special Branch was working alongside the Secret Intelligence Service in a joint operation to arrest an active IRA service unit which had infiltrated the Manchester area and was believed to be trying to plant explosives. Once the rumours started to circulate, those of us remaining were trying our hardest to get on the job.

Eventually my turn came. I was called to parade at the SB office with a covert option. That evening I reported for duty and made my way there. After identifying myself, I was allowed in. The SB office takes up virtually half a floor at Chester House and is divided into sub-sections or desks: one for dealing with Irish matters, the other for the Middle East and another for Eastern Bloc.

On this particular evening the office was crammed with members of the Special Branch, SIS and my missing colleagues. I immediately saw Laimond and Smiggs. Laimond was an ex-Para and had been with the department for many years. He was another Brummie and had the caustic wit of the West Midlands. I liked and respected him. He wasn't one to go behind your back: if he had a problem it was face to face. Not that I ever had a problem with him. Laimond and Smiggs looked knackered and as I walked over they both smiled. I knew they had something to tell me. The three of us made a conspiratorial huddle as I asked what was going on. They briefly updated me. The officers in the room were the full technical and surveillance team for an Irish active service unit operating in the northwest. The ASU was in possession of explosives and firearms, some of which had been buried in a cache in Macclesfield forest. Over the last week Smiggs and Laimond had been responsible for the protection of the surveillance teams. They had been operating with limited sleep and were absolutely knackered.

As I looked about the room I recognised a few faces from the SB but the majority were unfamiliar. What was of interest was the arsenal of weaponry on display, from stainless steel revolvers to the MP5 Kurtz, a more concealable version of the MP5. I turned back to Laimond and Smiggs, who were still grinning.

'So tell me what's happened.'

They looked around to ensure no-one was listening and in whispers informed me that they had been stuck in the back of an old Ford Escort while their driver tried to keep up with a progressive surveillance. It appeared to be going on for hours as the team followed the suspects around the northwest. As the surveillance progressed, the hours ticked away. By now Smiggs and Laimond were totally disorientated but they noticed their driver was driving erratically and both of them were increasingly concerned for their safety. The final straw came when he started to nod off at the wheel and Smiggs had to regain control. The driver announced he was too tired to carry on; he climbed into the rear and fell immediately into a deep sleep. They tried to wake him but he was completely out of it. They knew they had a responsibility for the safety of the surveillance team, but they didn't have a clue where they were. It was the early hours of the morning and the weather was atrocious. A heavy mist had settled, so visibility was limited. The van they were in belonged to the SIS and they didn't have a clue how to work the comms. Smiggs jumped behind the wheel and set off looking for the nearest landmark when their predicament took an even worse turn. The petrol gauge indicated empty.

Now it's not in either of those two's nature to blow out a fellow officer. The sensible course of action would have been to find a telephone kiosk and ring headquarters. However, this would drop the fast-asleep SIS officer in the shit with his senior officers. As they pondered their predicament they noticed that they were driving over a bridge. Laimond, being a keen caravan-touring anorak, recognised that they were on the Menai Bridge to Anglesey, Wales. He also knew of the location of a garage. Within minutes they had pulled onto a petrol forecourt and proceeded to fuel up the van. At this precise moment another vehicle pulled up and out stepped the suspects. Laimond and Smiggs were now in the middle of one of the country's most important anti-terrorist operations.

Smiggs giggled as he described their next tactically orien-tated surveillance move: Laimond jumped back into the front passenger seat and lit his pipe. That took care of his predica-ment. Smiggs dropped his head and eyes, made his way to the cashier and paid for his petrol, acting as though he was the only person on the forecourt. He said his heart was in his mouth and the blood pumping around his ears; he felt as though he was treading water as he walked back to the van. He was also thinking how he was going to explain to senior members of MI6 how they had come face to face with the UK's most wanted terrorists. The two of them decided retreat was the best course of action and made their way back to Chester House. On the way back the driver woke up, asking for an update. This time he received the full wrath of Laimond's caustic vocabulary. It later transpired that the suspects had been lost by the full surveillance and that Smiggs and Laimond's incident allowed the intelligence cell to track their lost movements: my colleagues had actually saved the day.

A technical team had been practising on a Ford Capri, an exact copy of the vehicle used by the ASU. Within minutes they could enter it and plant covert listening devices. That night an operation had been planned to plant covert kit into the suspects' Capri. It is often said that the IRA are extremely competent while planning atrocities. This team we were following were no exception. They would always complete anti-surveillance drills while on the move.

Their MO for the end of the day would be to park up the Capri near St Mary's Hospital in Manchester. They would open the hatch of the Capri, reverse it slowly into bushes in the car park and then close the hatch. It would be quite easy to spot any interference with the vehicle by the broken foliage. The two suspects would split up and take different routes to a small bedsit in Didsbury. Prior to leaving the flat they would varnish the lino floor in the interior entrance of the flat. The varnish would remain tacky and reveal tell-tale footprints of unwanted visitors.

I was to be part of a firearms team that would create a perimeter protection on the SIS technical team, while they planted listening devices in the Capri. The suspects had been surveilled to the flat at Didsbury and appeared to be settled for the night. The surveillance would remain on the flat, while the technical team got to work. However confident the senior command were regarding the suspects' location, they had the foresight to plan ahead, and in case the technical team were compromised, a firearms team would be 'on plot' to provide protection.

I remained at Chester House chatting with Laimond and Smiggs and a few of the other lads involved. As usual with our downtime, we would tell war stories, catch up on sleep or our competitive nature would take over. For hours on end we would play the alphabet game. You choose a subject such as cars, countries or sports people and go through the alphabet naming either one, two or three, depending on the number of players in the game. We set a time limit and when you lost three lives you were out. Cheating was expected, as was collaboration with other players. The arguing involved generally took longer than the game, but it passed the hours.

It was about 03.00 when a member of the Special Branch approached our table of arguing and contesting players. He asked who was Andy and I identified myself. He told me I would be responsible for protecting the technical team, who were making the final preparations and were in the downstairs car park. I grabbed my kit, including an MP5, and joined them. Little conversation took place between us, in fact the majority of the time they ignored me as if I was a necessary hindrance.

The team drove out to St Mary's and on arrival immediately deployed to the Capri, which was reversed into bushes in the side car park. I wasn't given any instructions at all. I knew I had to look after the team so I deployed to Hathersage Road and kept a careful watch. It was now approximately 03.30 and I stuck out like a sore thumb, walking along Hathersage Road. To make matters worse I didn't have a case for the weapon, which I had beneath my coat. I also didn't have a comms link with control – I was effectively working cold. I made my way back to the technical team, who had by now extracted the vehicle from the bushes. One officer was furiously sketching the place of every leaf and twig.

It felt like 30 minutes but it was more like 10, before the team had successfully placed covert devices and returned the vehicle to its correct position. We quickly returned to our transport and made for Chester House. The whole operation took less than an hour from start to finish. When I think about it, I realise I wasn't scared or nervous, which I would have expected, but more puzzled and confused. I hadn't been briefed properly, I didn't have a comms link and the technical team didn't utter a word to me. They do call them the Secret Service though, and true to their name they were pretty secret with me.

I booked off-duty in the early hours, and for the next three to four days resumed normal duties. A small amount of training had resumed, but the majority of VO8 were still involved in the anti-terrorist operation.

About eight of the remaining team were en route to Diggle when our pagers activated. After a quick radio transmission we were informed to make our way to Chester House, and the Special Branch office immediately. Blue lights and sirens were activated and Jim took us for a 15-minute terror ride through the streets of Manchester until we arrived. After Jim's white-knuckle drive, we shakily carried all our operational kit to the lifts and ascended to the ninth floor. As we entered the SB offices we were faced by a barrage of activity and a feelgood atmosphere of success. Radios were blaring and orders were being issued.

As soon as we walked in, Malc, our DCI, grabbed Julian and pointed to an area of glass partitioning which appeared to be sterile of any activity. He firmly told us to go into the area and kit up as he dragged Julian away. Within five minutes Julian returned and while putting on his kit, told us what had happened.

At 10.00 that day two members of the ASU, codenamed Echo and Foxtrot, had been arrested by our VO8 colleagues on Trafford Wharf. We had been brought over to conduct a house entry at the bedsit flat in Didsbury. Julian went on to explain that the SIS suspected another member of the ASU might be present at the flat and that a covert OP was monitoring the area. However, due to the location of the bedsit – inside a building containing 14 flats – the OP was having difficulty confirming occupation. We were not allowed any association with officers of the operational team due to cross-contamination of evidence.

Julian decided we would contain the premises and call out the occupants. We all agreed with this option, as the element of surprise had been lost because two suspects had already been arrested. We also didn't fully trust our command structure. Although the press wasn't aware of the arrest, it wouldn't be unusual for a leak to occur and the *Manchester Evening News* to sensationally publish 'IRA Suspects Arrested In Manchester' in the afternoon edition. Our safety could have been seriously compromised while attempting to arrest a third suspect who had been alerted.

Julian was busy giving deployment duties when Malc stuck his head round the door.

'Look lively, lads, the Chief Constable is on his way to congratulate you.'

Sir James Anderton, GMP's controversial head, wanted to speak to us. We looked around and started laughing.

'Did you say congratulate us, boss?'

'Yes, he thinks you're the team who arrested Echo and Foxtrot.'

'Well tell him we're not,' said Julian.

'Fuck that, he wants someone to thank and that's you lot,' snarled our DCI.

I for one respected our Chief Constable. Perhaps not all his comments, but he was a man I admired and was proud to have served under.

Malc dodged out of the way and GMP's senior command structure walked into the room. Mr Anderton, who was dressed in full uniform and displaying a full beard, had a commanding presence. I can't say the same for some of his staff officers. We stood respectfully to attention while Mr Anderton shook our hands one by one and thanked us for our brave contribution toward the anti-terrorist operation. I had a half-grin on my face but soon lost it when I received a withering look from my superintendent. As soon as he had left, we were back to business and within minutes were en route for Didsbury.

This is the time you start to think, we are going up against one of the world's most proficient terrorist organisations. If the suspect is alerted, will he surrender or decide to fight it out? Could we successfully arrest him, would we safely gain entry into the flat, taking into account the explosives the cell had access to? As these thoughts swirled through my mind, my earpiece started to pick up transmissions.

'Smiggs to Julian. Smiggs to Julian.'

'Go ahead Smiggs.'

'Make your way to an RV on Barlow Moor Road.'

We all thought Smiggs was on the other armed team. As we arrived at the RV it became clear that Smiggs and Laimond were part of the OP team at the target premises. Smiggs quickly updated us. The IRA use scanners and also the chances of IEDs (improvised explosive devices) were high so radio transmissions were to be kept to a minimum. The bedsit was difficult to access, and Smiggs had reccied a direct route, but he still couldn't confirm whether the flat was occupied.

As we made further kit preparation, two of the team had been tasked with MOE duties. A radio message came through from command; on no account were we to attempt entry. Intelligence suggested the property would be booby trapped. We were to contain and await the bomb disposal team from London. I had to laugh, the two lads who were tasked with the entry looked as though they had been kicked in the bollocks.

We made our way to the target premises (TP) with Smiggs leading the way. The TP was on the second floor of Edwardian maisonettes, which had been converted into bedsits. It was like a rabbit warren, with corridors running all through the property. I'm sure nowadays a fire safety officer would condemn the place. We entered the building, made our way to the TP and quickly began to evacuate the other residents. Most responded quickly once they took in our dress and weapons.

The TP was effectively 'locked down'. All we had to do was

literally sit and wait for the Explosive Ordnance Department (EOD) team to arrive.

The hours passed without any movement from the TP. Julian received a radio instruction to go outside, as the bomb disposal team had arrived. He returned with a member of the EOD. They went to the front door, which was fitted with a Yale lock. The EOD officer had a good look at it as Julian covered him with his revolver in the on-aim position. He stealthily retreated and he and Julian went back outside. I was thinking that within minutes we would hear the whirl and hum of a caterpillar-tracked remote control vehicle fitted with a water-fired disruption system. I had a vision of the vehicle being guided to the POE and then two loud explosions as the door was quickly and efficiently removed.

By now we were pretty certain that the flat was unoccupied. Although we hadn't advertised our presence it wouldn't take a genius to realise that something was going on outside. We still couldn't take the risk – a suspect could be in the premises and we had little choice but to wait and see what developed.

Julian returned to our position and gathered us around him. 'Right this is what is going to happen.' We looked at him in expectation, pretty certain the EOD would have some nasty trick up their sleeves. 'We are sending for the key of the flat for the prisoners' property, then I need a volunteer to open the door.' He looked at us as if we would be clambering over each other to volunteer. I think I fell over Smiggs, who had fallen over Jim to get out of Julian's gaze.

'Is that the fuckin plan?' gasped Laimond, echoing all our thoughts.

'Well yes – the EOD say they have nothing to force the door,' said Julian. We were all backing away from him as if he had the plague.

Apart from my TAG training I had little experience with explosives, and what I had usually ended up with the military blowing us up in what they called a 'bit of fun'. None of us was keen to open the door and effect an entry – surely that was what the bomb disposal team was for? Julian explained that the bomb disposal team dealt with unexploded bombs and that they were not really equipped for booby traps, but once the door was unsecured they had a bit of kit to help us.

It quickly dawned on Julian that he wasn't going to get a volunteer and moodily he stated he would do it. Another half hour passed and eventually a member of the SB arrived with a key. Julian, with definite reluctance in his step, made his way to the door.

From a safe distance the rest of us bravely covered him. He inserted the key, and with eyes the size of milk bottle bottoms, slowly released the catch, and we slowly released our breaths. Julian produced the 'special kit' from his pocket – a fishing rod and hook. Not any fishing line, however, but one with the breaking strain to capture a baby whale.

What the bomb disposal expert had ascertained on his recce was that the target door opened outwards. Julian attached the hook to part of the door and started to walk backwards while he unravelled the line. Julian reached my position. I was horrified, as it was obvious what he intended to do. I looked at him with pleading eyes to 'fuck off'. He smiled and yanked the line. My only bit of cover was a flight of five stairs and the two of us fought for a position of protection.

Incredibly we didn't hear a loud explosive bang.

The door of the TP was wide open and we could see into the bedsit. The bomb disposal team was called up, and after tentatively peering into the flat from a secure distance declared it safe. All that remained for us to do was search and clear the flat. After a great deal of shouting and announcing our presence, we effected an entry.

The flat was quickly cleared and I don't think there was one of us who wasn't relieved to depart the scene. In subsequent months all the GMP officers involved in the operation were awarded chief constable commendations. When I received mine it was addressed to 'Clive Halewood'. No-one had heard of him, and I suppose there was a subliminal message regarding the whole operation.

CHAPTER TWELVE

Laugh At Death

We had many unanswered questions about our tactics. The quick entry was tried and tested, but wasn't the finished article. The option of overt and covert ambush needed more planning and good intelligence, while vehicle strikes were on a virtual wing and prayer. Our approaches from the RV to the target premises were ad hoc.

Due to the new team structure, which had again been increased with two new sergeants and two constables joining us, we could now start to train ourselves. We had to consider entry by stealth. Manchester didn't then have a hostage-rescue capability, but the SAS rescue at the Iranian embassy had highlighted the benefits of having one. We were also at times entering properties and searching with the aid of ballistic shields. The shields varied in size, and the largest and most used was approximately 7ft by 2ft 6ins and constructed of Kevlar with a bulletproof glass aperture. The tactics involved needed research and at times visits to other forces. Officers needed to practise and be confident in their use.

If our week's duty was operations, then the day would consist of physical training for one to two hours. After a quick shower the team would make their way to a disused building such as a hospital, old farmhouse or old police station, and there we would rehearse and practise our tactical options. Incredibly, this system met a lot of resistance and at times caused splits and friction among our unit. The older instructors, including the sergeants, showed massive reluctance to do physical training and practise tactics. Some of them simply hated physical training and didn't see a need for it. Others didn't have the ability to look ahead and see what was occurring in the criminal fraternity – especially the widespread increase of drugs and guns.

Some of the older instructors believed that the training and instructing of the force's AFOs was more important than our own improvement and increased potential. For me the essence of being a credible and competent firearms officer is an extremely high standard of physical fitness. Failure to have this decreased your operational ability.

A proficient firearms officer, able to function when called upon to arrest gunmen, requires every advantage. His shooting skills should be of a high standard and his tactical awareness should be second to none. That officer will be required to carry heavy loads such as ballistic shields, door-opening equipment and double-span ladders, sometimes for long periods depending on his final assault position (point of entry or arrest) – even over walls, hedges, gates, through awkward and narrow spaces, or up 21 flights of stairs if he's heading for the top flat in a multi-occupancy high-rise building.

Once the officer arrives he has to use the kit, maybe to gain entry. Once inside he must work quickly, coolly, and aggressively towards the arrest of a suspect. Not all suspects roll over and give up once challenged; some will fight or try to run. An officer may achieve all this and still have to fire his weapon. He would be absolutely useless if he was a fat pool of lard lying on the floor unable to complete his tasks.

I, therefore, fiercely argue my case: a fully trained firearms officer must be fit and conversant with the required skills. This has and always would be my ethos. Boxers have a good motto: train hard, fight easy. I believe this wholeheartedly. Police officers by nature can be lazy but a good firearms officer has to have a high degree of motivation. At times this gets mistaken for arrogance, as it sometimes does in professional sportsmen. This can cause friction amongst the departments. I know I was guilty of arrogance at times – but I had a massive belief in my ability as a tactical firearms officer. This was earned through hours and days of extremely hard physical and tactical training. I also researched my enemy (the armed criminal) and new tactics any outside agency could show me. One of the most important advantages I had was my experience. This couldn't be replaced, and every new experience was filed away mentally; one day I might need it.

A major problem my colleagues and I faced was the enemy within. I have mentioned that police officers can be lazy; they can also be jealous and destructive. I would come across this time and time again. It's the nature of some people to like to see others fail. I saw this amongst our own unit and in some prima donnas in other units. Some officers were not prepared to integrate their skills and had the misconception that firearms officers are numbskulls recruited from the TAG. Put a door in front of a tactical firearms officer and he will smash it down no problem, but don't ask him to think about using a key – that would be too difficult. This was the common misconception. Many of the prima donnas, including certain senior officers, didn't like the way they were spoken to either.

Firearms incidents develop quickly and are unpredictable. The early stages can be crucial if they are to lead to a quick and effective conclusion. If I was called upon to give advice, I might have had to drive many miles at speed, or even fly in the force helicopter, to present myself to the commander of the incident. Experience would be screaming at me to deploy a recce team immediately, as it takes time. I might need certain facts, such as offenders, offences, weapons and authorisation. I could save a commander hours if he listened to my abrupt tone. I don't have time for the formality of respecting the rank.

Many commanders and firearms inspectors are bags of wind

and nerves and this shows by their dithering and lack of decision-making. I didn't have time to consider their lack of bottle: carry the rank, carry the consequences. I was sharp, decisive, considerate and confident and if they listened they could only benefit. Many commanders recognised this in me and let me operate. Others hated me and would be destructive in hidden and, I suppose, subtle ways. I make no apologies: I believed I was acting in the best interest of my colleagues and members of the public.

I was also aware of certain officers claiming credit for my operational plans, to better their positions. Antro, who would later become my DCI, once said of me that I got the job done but at times needed a restraining lead. My answer to Antro, who I like and respect, is 'bollocks'. You wouldn't believe how many times the lead was off and what we did to get the job done.

* * *

We had finished training and showered. We had outgrown the armoury and been given a room above it on the ground floor. This was known as the crew room and was used for downtime and briefings. As usual, our competitive nature was in full flow and we were arguing about who should make a brew. We had decided to toss a coin and were playing last-man-standing-makes-the-brew when the phone rang.

Jim answered it and after a few questions and nods he replaced the receiver. 'There's been a shooting in Rochdale. Two women down and a suspect housed,' he said in his usual clipped vocabulary. 'Housed' meant a suspect was in situ at a premises.

We grabbed our kit and weapons, jumped into the personnel carrier and Land Rover, and sped out of the city towards Rochdale Police Station. It takes about 30 minutes to reach from Bootle Street and the drivers had the accelerators floored and sirens and lights on all the way. A 'blue run' like this is always exhilarating and at times frightening, depending on who is driving. Traffic parted for us as we flew along.

John and Graham were already there when we arrived. John had been promoted and was now the sergeant in charge of admin and enquiries at Chester House. Graham was one of the older instructors who had recently moved from Bootle Street to assist John and Harry. Graham is a great character and easygoing (for someone from Bolton). I thought him a badly underestimated instructor because of his easy nature. I had learned a lot from him and valued his presence.

John hadn't been idle since his arrival at Rochdale and had up-to-date intelligence. An elderly male who lived in a semi-detached house on a local council estate had shot two women, one of them in the back while she was hanging out washing. It was the result of an ongoing domestic dispute between the man and two women who were his neighbours; he believed they were slowly trying to poison his beloved Alsatian dog. Both women had been taken to hospital; one died on arrival.

John had done some digging and ascertained that the man was a registered firearms certificate holder. He possessed several handguns, including a .44 Magnum revolver. He was also an ex-soldier, having served many years in the military. John believed the woman died from gunshots from a .44 calibre wadcutter round – a flat-faced bullet used by target shooters that leaves a clear, crisp hole in a paper target. A horrendous missile, it would create massive trauma on impact. The man was last seen in his property shouting at neighbours that he would 'send them all to hell'.

The P Division (Rochdale) had put plainclothes observations on his property and had heard further gunshots but had not seen the occupant or the dog. John had quickly replaced the observers with armed officers from the TAG. The target premises was a council property with two rooms downstairs and two rooms and a bathroom upstairs. It was positioned off-centre in a row of 30 properties in a cul-de-sac.

TAG officers took up positions of cover on what we called the white and black aspects of the property (front and back respectively). Once they were in position they confirmed over the radio. The division had already contained the area and all roads leading towards the house had been cordoned off. Our approach would be from the red aspect (right as you're looking at the front) and the black. The approach from the white was too exposed. John told us to kit-up and move to the designated rendezvous.

Once there, we deployed and started to prep the ballistic shields. I had a Remington Wingmaster shotgun as my primary weapon. Bob had grabbed a shield and Martin a 14lb sledgehammer. Graham was equipped with another shield. The rest of the team made sure all their kit was fastened down. I looked around and noticed the usual activity: marked police vehicles and senior officers giving instructions. Unusually, an assistant chief constable had turned out wearing the latest police fashion – a fluorescent yellow jacket. At one stage I saw him wander down the road towards the target premises. He must have had a death wish, dressed in that jacket. As long as he stayed away from us, I wasn't bothered.

Our approach would be through the gardens and over the hedges of the next-door properties. I immediately struck out, putting cover on the team, climbing over the hedges and gates. Bob and Martin were not far behind but a few of the other instructors were lagging back; carrying the kit was taking its toll. Eventually we made it to the house. We decided to gain a foothold by forcing an entry. We would hold there and try to establish comms. We'd go in through the back door, which didn't appear too solid. We positioned ourselves along the building line of the property and Graham and I covered Martin, who lifted his sledgehammer. We keenly listened for any movement before Martin started to sledge the door.

By now the adrenalin had kicked in and I felt I was operating on a different level. I felt calm but with senses totally tuned into the environment. I was conscious that the suspect had already shot and killed someone; he would be pretty desperate. Believe me, that concentrates your mind.

Blam!

Martin whacked the door.

Blam! Blam!

The sledge was bouncing off, causing little damage. Every now and then you get a bastard of a door and this proved to be one. Martin was no wimp but he was tiring and when a door doesn't start to go in immediately you worry. I moved in and nudged him with my foot. Martin took hold of the shotgun and I grabbed the sledgehammer. I was thinking, Oh fuck, what if he decides to shoot through the door? These fears go through your mind, but you still stand there determined to put the door in. I gave it my best but also tired quickly and felt a nudge in my calf. Martin, now rested, replaced me and I took back the shotgun.

Smash!

The door virtually swung off its hinges; Martin had done it. Bob placed the shield in the doorway. He and I had been developing tactics on the large shields and worked as a pair. Number one carried and moved the shield and dictated how the search progressed and what the next move would be. He also shouted challenges; in essence he was the eyes and ears and mouth of the team.

'We are armed police officers!' screamed Bob. 'Show yourself!'

It was important that the team then fell as quiet as possible, as the challenge may instigate movement and determine presence. But all I could hear was the drone of either a TV or a radio.

Bob relayed what he could see. 'Kitchen directly in front, approximately eight foot by six foot, no suspect. Table and chairs, doorway, open to our right.'

The team now had a clear search objective. We would clear

the kitchen and hold on the first doorway. The rule of thumb on a slow shield search is the fewer numbers the better: clear an objective and ferry the team through into a safe area. Bob and I cleared the kitchen, moving as stealthily as possible. Our intention if compromised was to go to a firm position and deal with the threat. Being on the other side of a shield search can be daunting, as the shields progressively close you down in an intimidating manner.

With the kitchen cleared, Bob again threw out a challenge: 'Armed police, show yourself.'

No response. From the doorway Bob looked through the glass aperture in the shield.

'Stairway to our left, living room directly ahead. Graham, take your shield and clear the living room. We will hold on the stairs.'

Graham acknowledged this and had started to move with Jim as his partner when the earpieces came alive with a radio transmission.

'John to the team. I have received info that the suspect is in possession of grenades.'

Graham backtracked to the kitchen – quickly. Fuck, we were in a predicament. What do we do? This was the unspoken question on all our faces.

I for one didn't fancy stepping out of the property and getting a grenade dropped on my swede. I shrugged and said, 'Let's carry on.' We looked at each other and silently nodded.

'Keep going.'

The ante was upped with every step and every move we made would be critical; there was no room for error. My senses were almost screaming to lock on to a noise or movement. I covered my arcs of fire – both eyes wide open – with the shotgun mounted in my shoulder. My finger was always on the safety button; within half a second I could depress the safety, move my forefinger to the trigger and fire. We turned off our radios; we didn't need the interference of a squelch or unwanted transmission. Our ears ranged like radar, trying to locate any noise or movement.

Graham and Jim moved into the living room and with great purpose and skill cleared the room and gave the universal 'OK' hand signal (forefinger and thumb in a circle). Bob and I held the stairs. We had a flight of 13 steps to clear, with a bathroom ahead and two bedrooms adjoining on a landing looking over the stairs. This wasn't a pleasant place to be. If he had a grenade, all he had to do was lob it over and we were fucked. My instincts screamed at me to run up the stairs and clear the rooms quickly. I knew Bob would be thinking the same. It took all our discipline to continue with the slow search.

I felt a nudge in my back and Graham whispered in my ear, 'I don't know where the fuck he has come from but we have a divisional dog-handler with us.' Somehow he had decided to join us. This was typical of dog-handlers; they are an unusual breed, never afraid and always eager to help. I also realised what Graham was thinking, and whispered to Bob, 'We have dog man, let's send his dog up.' Bob agreed and the dog man was brought forward.

My experience using dogs in firearms situations has never been good. I know other forces use them with success, but every time we used one it bit one of the team or, on one memorable occasion, got stuck in a loft – the handler took over an hour to get it down. But this time none of us had a problem sending a dog upstairs. The handler was told to stay behind the shield and let Rover go. The dog set off upstairs and disappeared along the landing.

After a few minutes it reappeared and the dog-handler set it off again. Within seconds it shot down the stairs, almost knocking Bob and his shield over, and fled out of the back door with the handler on its heels.

In other circumstances it would have been funny, but we were both wondering why it had happened. We could now smell a foul stench from upstairs that started to make us gag. Bob decided to move up the stairs. Clearing stairs slowly is hard and generally requires another officer. Jim joined us as we progressed, Bob with the shield, me covering ahead and Jim acting as a contortionist covering the unseen area of the landing behind the balcony.

Graham, some ten feet behind, brought his shield up. I could visually clear the bathroom. We moved onto the landing where the smell was horrendous. In a quick co-ordinated movement the two shield men placed their shields in the doorways of the bedrooms, and Jim and I took up positions behind them.

We would clear one room at a time. If both rooms are searched at the same time and a shooting occurs there is a possibility that stray rounds may go through walls – particularly plasterboard – and injure occupants on the other side. Bob was the search co-ordinator and decided we would search first.

'Wall ahead – no visual – room opens up to the left.'

Bob moved into the room. 'Contact – don't move. Armed police!'

Bob had seen the occupant and I tried to get a visual on him. At times on a shield you have to be brutal, so I rammed Bob over to his right and got the offender in my sights.

'Relax Andy, he's dead,' said Bob quietly. 'And so is his dog.'

We moved into the room. On the bed was a sad sight: an elderly man was cuddled up to an Alsatian dog. The man was obviously dead; half his head was missing from a clear gunshot wound and he had a stainless steel revolver in his hand. The dog had also been shot in the head. The bed was a bloody mess, with brains and gore dripping on the floor. We finished our search and informed Jim and Graham to continue with theirs. At no stage would we relax until we were certain the house was safe. Intelligence is not always correct and other factors may have crept into the equation. The only time you are safe is when the premises has been completely and thoroughly searched.

Jim gave the all-clear. Radios were switched back on and division informed. The sight we had seen was sad, but we wouldn't be dwelling on it. This may sound callous, but many years ago an old bobby told me, 'Son, laugh at death. If you don't it will drive you daft.' What he meant is that death is obviously serious, but in the police you will constantly come across it and if you let it affect you, you will dwell on it and eventually those thoughts will catch you up.

The smell was still bothering us and I thought it was from the corpses. Then Assistant Chief Constable Phillips entered the property in his bright yellow jacket. He walked upstairs giving us the obligatory 'well done,' and went into the bedroom.

Bob had discovered the source of the smell and was trying to scrape dogshit off his boots. The police dog must have come across the scene and literally shit itself with fright and then fucked off. While searching, Bob had stood in the dog crap and spread it all over the landing.

We looked at each other and smiled. I suppose we should have warned the ACC but it appealed to our small-minded sense of humour not to. He quickly made his way out with a pristine white handkerchief pressed to his mouth and nose and we watched him through the bedroom window, scraping his brightly polished shoes along the grass verges as he returned to the rendezvous point.

CHAPTER THIRTEEN

Procedures and Operations

A couple of colleagues and I still had concerns about our tactical capability. The option of entering target properties using either slow or quick entry was coming together and we felt confident in them. I spent some time perfecting my recce techniques and was using that in the planning of operations. Briefings were becoming crucial – the days of quickly relating the brief facts of an incident and then attempting to arrest were a thing of the past.

Experience dictated our briefing skills and we identified the need for two types of plan: an immediate action plan and a deliberate action plan. The immediate (IA) would be later renamed emergency action plan. Let me explain how this system works. An IA is a response to a spontaneous operation. For example, a shooting occurs and uniformed officers contain the offender in a property. A response from the teams, depending upon the location of the shooting, usually took between 30 and 60 minutes.

The first pair of firearms officers at the scene would be expected to throw together an IA. This had to include a recce of the property and area. A recce is most important because it is the first time a member of our team gets real, up-to-date information. Our terminology was changing and abbreviations were used to assist in brevity while planning.

The recce team would be expected to plan timings. It was important to know how long it would take a team to position itself on the primary POE (point of entry). At the holding area, which in most cases would be police stations, the recce team would quickly acquire a room and start to prepare a briefing. Using dry-wipe boards or flip charts they would put down the team's deployment and their duties expected. This would be in clear and concise writing for all to see and would be deliberately left on display. The reason this was done was so an officer could quickly see what was expected of him while the rest of the plan was revealed. He could check who was working with him, what kit was required, where he would be positioned in a vehicle. This is done almost subtly and with a psychological purpose. The team member wouldn't be thinking what his role was while the plan was outlined, missing vital intelligence.

On arrival the team would quickly make themselves available for any job. The planning team might require the assembly of door-opening kit, preparation of ladders or preparation of special munitions. There is no place for idleness; if you haven't got a job you ask for one and if you are not given one you make sure you are available for one at a second's notice.

The planning team may even set the room out in such a way that the seating may emulate the team positioning while engaged on the operation. Once the preparation is completed, the team gets ready for the actual briefing. Information is related first, and this must include as much relevant intelligence as possible. Offenders, descriptions, weapons, offences, MOs of offenders, vehicles, powers of arrest, associates such as family – the list must be concise and relevant.

Intention is the next phase of the briefing. This will be the tactic used to effect the arrest of the offender(s). It will also include the department we would be acting on behalf of. Intention may break the tactical options into phases in case one fails, then we will move to another option, and so on.

Method comes next, and this includes how we will get to the arrest zone and order of march: the phases of the operation and each member's duties. The method is the crucial part of the plan. If the method is wrong, the plan will fail.

Admin follows method, and this includes powers of entry, warrants, acts and sections we would operate under, also details of the nearest hospital. It also includes the senior officer authorising the operation.

Finally, communications: which radio channel we would operate on, channels for the division we were working on and also the department we were representing. Mobile phone numbers would be included.

After the briefing, the briefing officer would ask, 'Any questions?' If he had briefed well then there would be limited questions. If it was a bad briefing then he could be expected to be ripped apart and his plan changed until it was safe and workable. I pride myself on my briefing skills and have taught many officers the benefits of being able to brief. If you can brief then it proves you have a greater understanding of how a plan works.

After questions, a comms check takes place, and every officer ensures his radio works. From the holding area a team will embus vehicles in a logical order, first out last in. From the holding area we would move to the rendezvous point (RVP). The RVP is a safe area near to the target premises but not near enough to compromise the operation. Superstore car parks such as B&Q or Tesco are good RVPs. This is where the senior commander, TAG adviser and the logistical side of the operation wait.

From the RVP the team will have streamlined and would be only in the necessary transport required to take them to the FUP (form-up point). At the FUP the team becomes tactical. Every officer takes care to avoid unnecessary noise. The lead scout, usually one of the planning team, moves from the vehicles and takes up a kneeling position and shoulder-mounts his MP5 in the direction the team is heading.

Once the team have quietly alighted from the vehicles they

will take up the correct order of march behind the scout. Once they are satisfied that they are ready, e.g. kit such as ladders or shields prepped, they will kneel down. This indicates readiness for the next phase of the plan. Any officer remaining standing indicates he has a problem.

Once all the team are kneeling, the back-up man (rear man) presses his radio's 'send' button three times in quick succession. This is the signal for the scout to lead on. At times a team can be over 20 strong, lined up along an inner city street. It could be in the early hours of the morning or in rush hour but the SOP remains the same. In my years of operations I have seen postmen walk past, milkmen drive past, the paper boy or girl cycle past and not give us a moment's notice.

From the FUP we could move to a JOP (jump-off point). Part of the team may split to cover front, rear or side aspects. The rest of the team would move on to their respective FAPs (final assault positions). The FAP is usually as far as a team can go without compromising the operation. It may be a garden gate, a rear yard gate, a front door, level one or two windows. More often than not the FAP is a point of entry. Once each FAP is reached, a radio transmission is sent to indicate that the team is ready. A team leader or assault co-ordinator acknowledges this and 'Strike! Strike! Strike!' is called.

Once the stronghold (area where the offender is suspected to be) is breached and secured, the team will wait for the arrival of divisional vans to transport prisoners, search teams and sometimes senior officers who have been waiting at the RVP. I insisted, on my operations, that a team left as it arrived, in the same order of march, covering the same areas of fire as before. For example, at the height of the gang wars in Moss Side, we had received good intelligence to suggest that the gangs wanted to kill a member of the Tactical Firearms Unit. I wouldn't allow us to relax until we left the area.

An immediate action plan has to encompass all these

operational phases to make it successful. Therefore the briefing officers/planning team have to be skilled and experienced. The briefing described above, which is known as the IIMAC system, should take 15 minutes maximum.

A deliberate action plan (DA) can take days and can be changed and refined up to the day of the operation. A feature of a DA is rehearsal time. This allows officers to rehearse their duties, which may be effecting entry through a patio window, placing ladders at a POE with four officers climbing through it or a room search. This allows officers to implant 'muscle memory', a good advantage while engaged on an operation. I felt that our house entry techniques were good but still had room for improvement. The greatest concern was our lack of a structured vehicle arrest drill.

As I have already mentioned, GMP had formed a Dedicated Surveillance Unit. These officers were highly skilled in mobile and foot surveillance. They were starting to get results and their workload was increasing. Because of their success, department commanders were using them on Manchester's armed criminals. By conventional surveillance methods, the DSU were at the same time collating and gathering enough evidence to arrest these suspects. At times they would witness them commit crimes using firearms.

The role of a surveillance officer is not to break cover unless circumstances dictate – to prevent loss of life or to prevent serious injury for example. On two occasions that I know of, surveillance officers had no option but to take action while watching an armed suspect. On each occasion, the officer had firearms pointed at them, a frightening experience. The DSU were screaming out for a safer option.

We were also concerned about our lack of hostage rescue capability. Every now and then an armed suspect would barricade himself in a property, take pot shots at members of the public and cause a general nuisance. The only option was to contain the premises from a safe distance, ensure the public were safe and, as long as he was alone, sit and wait it out. The offender usually gave himself up after the usual threats and demands.

We were concerned, because it wouldn't be long before Manchester experienced its first hostage-taking incident. Hostage-taking isn't unusual. Many forces had experiences of hostage-taking, for example the Balcombe Siege and the Northolt Siege in London. The Balcombe Siege occurred when a dis-covered IRA cell took two elderly occupants of a flat hostage after a botched police operation. The Northolt Siege saw an intervention by the Metropolitan Police's SO19 to prevent the loss of life of a young girl after her mother had been stabbed to death by her common law husband.

With limited knowledge we were practising intervention techniques into old properties, trying to learn hostage rescue. We knew the theory, but practical application was proving difficult. We had started to ask other forces how they developed hostage rescue. The majority had been to Hereford and had some input from the Special Air Service. We made requests to attend Hereford. The requests were refused by management, for the reason that we had a Labour-controlled police authority, which would object! None of us thought to question that excuse. As I think back now, it was again small-minded people who wouldn't allow us to progress. At times it was such hard work with some of our sergeants and inspectors. A good example of this small mindedness comes to mind.

We were suffering minor problems while forcing entry on wooden and PVC doors. If the MOE man hit the wooden architrave surrounding the door or the door itself, they could badly splinter. At times you would get dust and debris in your eyes. This could limit your operational ability – blinking bits of crap out of your eyes while arresting an armed suspect. Also the offenders we were arresting were not always in the best of health, many suffering from the HIV virus, full-blown AIDS or hepatitis B. These people, contrary to popular belief, can be sly when being arrested and will attempt to spit at you or cause bleeding by biting and scratching. They are often also in possession of drug paraphernalia such as needles.

I made a request for eye protection: Bollé goggles and gloves. We needed something that was not too cumbersome and would not mist up. The gloves had to be tight-fitting, and made of hard-wearing material but flexible enough to shoot with. This request was considered a joke by some of my supervisors. The terms 'robocop', 'gunfighter' and other phrases were offered. It took another 18 months before they were issued – and that was due to the Health and Safety at Work Act.

The West Midlands Firearms Department offered themselves as the experts on hostage rescue training and became known as '24 SAS Regiment'. Ian and Pete eventually got to go on one of their courses and managed to bring some good ideas back. I later attended a national hostage rescue abseil course in the West Midlands and found some of their instructors to be excellent. I met a few of their operational officers and, as with all firearms teams, experienced the usual wankers, more than I would like to see on a close team.

It wasn't long before an answer to our problems came. Leaky and Vinny had been researching body armour and brought a rep over from Armourshield, a Manchester-based company. While chatting with the rep, a bloke called Mel Parry, it became clear that he was extremely knowledgeable. In fact he was a retired soldier, formerly of the SAS. Over a coffee, Leaky and Vinny opened up regarding our tactical limitations. Mel offered a solution in the form of Peter Moore, an ex-special forces soldier who was serving on the Surrey firearms team. Mel went on to say that Pete was involved in some interesting projects regarding tactics and suggested a phone call to him to arrange a visit.

After the usual reports and questions and answers, our

management decided to allow four of us to visit Surrey. They probably thought, what could a small force like Surrey teach GMP, and to be honest I think all four of us believed the same. However, it was a chance to travel south and look at another force without the interference of the national schools.

The four were myself, Leaky, Dino and Rod. Dino was a sergeant on the unit who believed in progressing tactics and didn't care who he upset. He was later promoted to inspector within the department and became more of a political animal. Rod had come from my old TAG group, a real laid-back character, which would deceive some people. He is always cool under pressure and able to make the correct tactical decisions. Rod would spend many years on the department. Before joining, we had been great friends and to this day remain extremely close.

On a bright and very early June morning, the four of us met at Openshaw complex, collected a pool vehicle and drove 200-odd miles to Mount Brown, the police headquarters of Surrey Constabulary. To the four of us from Manchester, it was like being on holiday. Mount Brown is a lovely complex just outside Guildford, set in a rural location.

As soon as we arrived and checked in at reception, we were treated with a respect and friendliness unusual for police forces – they are normally suspicious and uncommunicative. Pete was summoned and quickly introduced himself. He is in his mid-40s, very slim and wiry, almost bald and with a mischievous grin. He has an aura of confidence and endless motivation and enthusiasm.

Pete introduced us to a couple of his colleagues and took us to the canteen for lunch. He took us to a table and sat down with an officer of assistant chief constable rank, introduced us and started chatting to the ACC as if they were mates. This stunned us, as in GMP you very rarely saw an ACC, never mind sat with them and discussed the weather over lunch. The ACC was an amiable bloke, but the four of us answered any questions tendered in a limited 'yes sir, no sir' vocabulary. We only relaxed when he left the table. What we did find out was that Pete was a sergeant on his team. This would not be unusual but for the fact that Pete had been promoted by his chief constable, in a rare and largely unheard of way. According to police regulations, a chief constable has the privilege, if he so deems, to promote a maximum of six constables to sergeant in any 12-month period. The circumstances have to be exceptional such as bravery or outstanding duties. Peter had been promoted in this way.

During lunch the four of us had been planning the rest of the day. We thought Pete might show us around the range for half an hour. After that we would unload our kit in our rooms, get a kip, do a bit of training and, as in keeping with police tradition, familiarise ourselves with the local towns or city (in case we got lost) by going on the piss.

I mentioned that Pete is self-motivated and has endless amounts of enthusiasm. We were to feel the full force of his energetic presence. He worked us to 22.00 without a break. If we weren't shooting on his range we would be discussing tactics. If Pete had an idea, we would be rehearsing and practising it. He ran us round his range area and if we weren't running, we would be crawling as we practised movement by stealth. If he heard you, a bucket of water was waiting to be thrown on you.

Pete has a huge collection of video footage of firearms incidents and operations throughout the world, some of it classified. If he was stuck for an answer, he would consult his library and play a video. He was a mine of knowledge and we were milking him for anything and everything. From special munitions to co-ordinated sniper shoots, Pete had an answer. The first eight hours flew by and each one of us was impressed.

I know Pete was also impressed with our commitment, and he had purposely made the day hard to see what we were made of. We hadn't moaned or whinged, we had soaked it up. Eventually he called a halt, saying he had a home to go to and he would see us in the canteen at 08.00 for breakfast and expect another full day. We didn't get to see the nightlife but had a leisurely pint in the bar on site and were in bed for midnight, knackered.

The following day Pete collected us from the canteen and took us to a disused hospital, where he led us through hostage rescue drills and introduced us to munitions such as the stun grenade, Hatton rounds and RIP rounds. The stun grenade, or flash bang, was developed by the SAS as a distraction device, either a single bang or a multi bang grenade of 180 decibels. It is used to disable people by noise and light alone. Pete discussed its use, its advantages and disadvantages. He then made us experience them by walking among them going off as he threw them into rooms we were entering.

Hatton rounds are 12-bore, graphite-loaded shotgun cartridges, and are an effective entry tool when used on door hinges and locks. Once the shotgun is fired the Hatton round dumps all its energy into a lock or hinge, blowing the item off the door but not into the room, therefore minimising the threat to innocents held hostage. The RIP round, long and short range, is again a 12-bore shotgun cartridge filled with CS, designed to be fired into rooms through doors or into vehicles. The CS is in a highly concentrated form and an extremely effective incapacitator.

Pete worked us through the day, climbing through windows, crawling through tunnels, entering doorways and demonstrating the drills. He was always constructive, patient and amusing with his assessment of us. It was dark by the time we left the hospital. Pete explained he wouldn't be with us in the morning due to a job that had come in but we could make use of his library until he joined us.

The following morning the four of us blearily made our way to the range and Pete's library: we had eventually sampled the delights of Surrey's hostelries. We started to search through and view his videos. Leaky had become interested with a bit of kit that Pete had shown us known as an 'aim point'. This is a sighting system mounted on top of a weapon such as a mini-Ruger carbine. Once the system is properly adjusted and aligned, the shooter keeps both eyes open and looks through its optical lens. The lens superimposes a red dot on the target, and unlike a laser the recipient can't see the dot. The aim point system is accurate up to 150 feet and greatly assists accurate shooting. After years of painstaking arguments and trials, Leaky would get this system adopted throughout GMP.

All tactical carbines and some shotguns are mounted with aim points thanks to Leaky's determination. While Leaky was discussing the aim point with a couple of Surrey firearms officers, I had spotted a tape entitled 'Vehicle Drills'. After watching it, I knew I had the answer to the DSU's problems. I ran off a copy because I needed to painstakingly study the drills and see how to adapt them for GMP.

During the short period we had with Pete, we had learned and gained answers to many of our worrying tactical problems. Pete eventually arrived back at the range – we had been holding on to thank him for all his efforts. We were due back at GMP that evening. We thanked Pete and Surrey for their valuable assistance and time. We had learned some invaluable lessons, many of which would be passed on to GMP – but not without problems and obstructive personnel.

We knew we would be questioned on our return about what we had learned. I was certainly prepared for this and viewed the tape of Surrey's vehicle drills each evening at home. Surrey used two firearm vehicles with four armed officers on board each. The vehicles were part of the surveillance, and once the decision to arrest was made, they would move through the convoy and, when appropriate, using surprise as a key element, arrest the occupants of the target vehicle. The drill could also be used on more than one target vehicle.

I knew I was hindered by GMP's policy of using unarmed

drivers, so I would have to bastardise Surrey's drills. During the nights I would play and stop the video, making sketches and notes. I needed to keep the drills simple but I also had to know every element of the tactic. I believed this would be the answer to our problems while involved in operational surveillances.

It wasn't long before Keith asked me to present to the department what we had learnt at Surrey. I don't know why he asked me. My suspicious side thinks perhaps he wanted me to stand in front of 20 of my colleagues and look like a jerk with ill-prepared information. The reasonable side tells me he was giving me and the department a chance to progress.

On the day of the presentation, all of the department was gathered, including the inspectors and staff from Chester House. Approximately 25 crammed into the crew room. I can't make a speech at a wedding without making a hash of it but when it comes to briefing or presenting tactics in front of a group, be it ten or a hundred, I don't have a problem. For me the key to confidence is to know your subject. I was fully prepared and knew I had support from many of my colleagues; however there were enough in the room who I knew were completely obstructive to changes.

I presented our findings in a logical order regarding the new munitions, the hostage rescue drills and the aim point system. Apart from the hostage rescue drills, there was a murmur of approval regarding the munitions and aim point systems. I kept the vehicle drills to the last. By way of introducing them I had already sketched out diagrams and tactical positioning on the briefing boards in the crew room. I revealed the diagrams and proceeded to explain the tactic and how the lead vehicle, when called to do so by the surveillance team leader, would move to the off-side of the target vehicle; the next vehicle would position itself at the rear. An armed officer carrying a mini-Ruger .223 carbine would get out of the lead vehicle and shout a challenge at the target vehicle. This would create a distraction while four

AFOs would assault the target vehicle; three from the back-up vehicle and one from the lead vehicle. They would quickly, firmly and aggressively disable the occupants of the vehicle by laying them on the floor.

During my presentation I noticed the usual contingent grumbling and pointing. I asked for questions. Harry and Parker got up, making a noise to attract the rest of the unit's attention, and said, 'Fuckin' nonsense, it's dangerous, fancy attacking a target's vehicle.' I was ready for this and asked Harry what he had done on the M602 when arresting one of the McPhees – hadn't he and Parker run over to a target's vehicle? He didn't have an answer and both of them stormed out of the room saying, 'It's dangerous, you won't catch us being involved.'

Harry and Parker were older instructors and certainly Harry held a lot of influence over many of the other instructors. I could see some worried faces and the questions and comments came thick and fast.

'It won't work.'

'Why don't we use shields?'

'It's too complicated.'

Eventually I answered their concerns and told them it was in its infancy and I needed the surveillance unit's thoughts on it.

Many of the lads including Ian, Jim and Smiggs were for it but believed it needed a lot more work. I wasn't naive enough to believe it didn't and the next day I arranged to meet some of the DSU. I was to present the drills to Dave Fiddler, a detective sergeant and a serious surveillance operator with years of experience, and his oppo, Ian Wolstenholme, another extremely skilled surveillance man. Both had years of experience but were progressive, enthusiastic and fair-minded. I had worked with them and knew they liked my attitude towards arresting armed criminals. Both were the lynchpins of the DSU and certainly Dave was a gifted and skilled taskmaster who worked his team hard but fair. He didn't suffer fools, and I had seen him bollock individual team members, including even sergeants if they messed up – he was a respecter of skill rather than rank.

Dave and Ian couldn't have been more respectful toward the tactic and immediately rubber-stamped it. All we needed to do now was to teach it by rehearsing, practising and drilling. Dave got the authority from his bosses to put resources, depending upon operational commitments, into it; his bosses in turn influenced the firearms command, who endorsed further training.

For the next several weeks the two departments regularly held training sessions. The surveillance officers watched 'dry drills' as the firearms team, instructed by me, assaulted the target vehicle. We would then jump into vehicles and with myself and Dave as the 'hare' (target vehicle), drive around Manchester practising the surveillance side of the tactic, moving the strike team up through the convoy. At the end of the sessions, we would pull over and debrief what had gone right or wrong.

The DSU used numbered communications over the radio net. At times they even spoke to each other in numbers over a pint. It was a brilliant system and Dave ensured all his operatives spoke a second language of numbers. Everything from pedestrian male or female to a piece of street furniture was identified by a number. This enabled the surveillance commentary to be fast, concise, accurate and up to date. A mobile surveillance changes second by second and is only effective if a picture is built by radio transmissions.

The number system also allowed a secure net – anyone scanning police transmissions would know there was a surveillance nearby but not necessarily what was being said. I always found the majority of the DSU to be excellent operators, motivated and intelligent. It was generally the sergeants who were tossers. As the tactic started to evolve, we would run in three firearms vehicles, Alpha, Bravo, Charlie – each driven by a surveillance operative.

Each vehicle's duties and equipment were exactly the same, as this allowed the driver to be flexible. Each firearms officer knew what his responsibility was, whether he became Alpha, Bravo or Charlie vehicle. Once a decision by command to arrest was given, then the eyeball of the surveillance would be looking for a suitable position to initiate the strike. This was done by colour-coding the team's alertness.

Condition Green is a limited condition of alertness, basically the command for strike is not imminent. Condition Amber is a heightened level of alertness, weapons are prepped, the target has now put itself in the 'loop'. Officers start to mentally rehearse their drills and positions of responsibility. The drivers start to make steady progress towards the target.

Condition Red, the arrest is imminent. The eyeball has identified a suitable spot for the arrest, such as a traffic queue, traffic lights or an engineered stop. The drivers are aggressively making progress to place the Alpha, Bravo, Charlie vehicles in the correct tactical position. 'Strike! Strike! Strike!' is called and the distraction and assault takes place.

Dave and I had replicated the place of the target on many occasions and were confident we were progressing. It was decided that senior officers from firearms and the DSU would become the target, to observe for themselves the workings of the tactic. We had reservations about the involvement of senior officers, but it worked out for the best, and after a short surveillance and an arrest, their feedback was nothing but positive and we were given the green light to go live.

It had taken weeks of hard work but with the help and support of Dave, Ian and several of my firearms colleagues, the tactic had been officially sanctioned by GMP's command. It is a good feeling to know that this tactic is still being used and has progressed in GMP and also that other forces have adopted it.

Some years later, one of my colleagues attended the National Firearms Instructors Conference, an annual event. He informed me that a sergeant from Merseyside had presented this tactic to the audience, claiming ownership. He was also offering the services of Merseyside to instruct in its use. When I heard this I was blazing and phoned Pete in Surrey straight away. Pete calmed me down and said, 'Does it matter who owns or claims it, as long as it's being used – and by the sounds of it, with a degree of success. Let him have the credit.' Of course, Peter was right.

I have also sat in a classroom while instructors from West Mercia have decried its use – what the fuck would they know amongst the cider plantations of mid-England? However, there is an old saying, 'the proof is in the pudding' and although the tactic had been sanctioned, we hadn't actually gone live with it.

* * *

It wasn't long before I received a call to attend the Serious Crime Squad's office at Longsight. Their primary function was the collation of evidence for the arrest of suspects responsible for armed robberies. I was to make my presence known to DCI Glenn (not his real name), the officer in charge of the SCS. I quickly found him and introduced myself. Glenn's 'handle' (name for brevity on the radio) was Digger. He was appropriately named, as once he got information on a suspect regarding serious offences, he would use all lawful means to arrest him, digging up as much info as possible. During the ensuing years, he would recognise my qualities and I was privileged to plan many of his armed operations.

DCI Glenn informed me that the SCS, in company with the DSU, had over a period of several months been working on a team of armed robbers: Peter John Hamlett, Craig Bulger and Anthony Ryan. Hamlett was the brains behind the team, a career criminal with a streak of guile. Some years ago he managed to access Longsight Police Station and leave behind his calling card, a packet of five Hamlet cigars. For many years he was the

Regional Crime Squad's most wanted criminal. It always appeared to me that when the RCS were unproductive, Hamlett would resurface as their number one suspect. I was never impressed with the RCS; most of the time they were a bunch of bunglers, plucking Hamlett out of the drawer when times were hard. I've lost track of the times I have been part of an RCS operation to arrest Hamlett, without a positive result.

Craig Bulger had allegedly progressed from a catalogue of minor offences to a career as an armed robber. Anthony Ryan was the muscle of the team and, to be fair, a real hard case. All three were East Manchester located and were actively looking at post offices and cash in transit deliveries in the same area. It was believed they were about to commit an armed robbery. Mr Glenn wanted options from me. I said that because the information was imprecise – we didn't have a specific post office or cash delivery location – an ambush would be difficult. Because the DSU had been working on the team, I suggested a vehicle drill option. After explaining the new tactic to him, he agreed. He would seek approval from his senior command. I was to get on planning for the following day.

I drove over to the DSU office and sought out Dave Fiddler. Dave knew about the job and was only too eager to assist. He would have three surveillance vehicles and drivers at Bootle Street for 06.30 the following day. I returned to Bootle Street and put together my operational order.

At 05.30, eight members of the VO8 operational team and one inspector sat in front of me. I had set the room out as if the chairs simulated the interior of a vehicle. Three chairs were positioned as the front near-side passenger and the rear near-side and off-side passengers. The trio of chairs were designated Alpha, Bravo and Charlie vehicles.

Each officer noted the deployment board and sat in his designated position. I had given myself the Alpha two position (rear off-side) with Dino as Alpha one (front near-side). I then opened the briefing with the information, intention, method, admin and communications. I stressed the importance of getting the tactic right and how much hinged on its success. Fortunately the majority of the team were supportive. I had planned a rehearsal phase at Openshaw Complex once we had been collected by the DSU drivers.

The lads were busy with final kit checks. Comms was checked between us. The majority of us were doing our best to hide our bulky kit. We were wearing covert body armour/pancake holsters, side arms and radio systems. Door-opening kit and shields were prepped in case we had to enter premises. Some poor fucker was given the first aid kit. I insisted that everyone carried a first field dressing and a gorgle airway but he needed more kit in case one of us or a suspect was shot. It's a necessary item but can be quite bulky.

At 06.30 three DSU officers turned up. I briefed them and designated their vehicles, Alpha, Bravo and Charlie, then we made our way to Openshaw. For the next 40 minutes we ran through our deployment drills, making sure we were crystal clear on our duties. The Alpha vehicle and the Alpha one (Dino) would be in charge of the team and would be monitoring the radio. Our inspector had disappeared to the control room, along with Mr Glenn and members of the DSU.

The control room was a radio room in the DSU's office. Mr Glenn would monitor the conventional surveillance on the three targets and once he decided that there was enough evidence he would give the order to arrest. We could also hear the conventional surveillance on the targets.

Most of the DSU were reporting in with locations of laying-up points near to the targets' addresses. Hamlett and team had stolen a couple of Renault 5 GTSs and hidden them. It was believed these vehicles would be their transport for the robbery. A usual MO for armed robbers, once they have committed a robbery, is to speed away from the crime to the location of another stolen vehicle, usually on the other side of a river or motorway, where access can only be gained by foot along a bridge or narrow alleyway. If the police are chasing, they abandon the first vehicle, run across the bridge and into the other vehicle, preventing the police from continuing the pursuit in vehicles.

The radio soon became busy with reports of movement at all addresses. The DSU drivers constantly translated the numbered lingo for us. Over the years I became reasonably familiar with the numbers and could slowly work out what was happening. The three targets had met up and were making their way to garages suspected of housing the stolen Renaults. A confirmation came through that the gang had split into two, one lot in one Renault and one lot in the other. This is the time when the adrenalin kicks in and the positive excitement of realising that the job could be on.

Firearms teams stand down more times than expected, for all sorts of reasons. A robbery team may only be rehearsing. They may be psyching themselves up to do the job and something will spook them – something as simple as a badly parked van. A member of the team can be sick or even have overslept. I have known them to get lost en route to a robbery. It is still important to collate as much damning evidence as possible. At times the senior CID officer has to consider whether he has enough evidence to fit the crime – has the gang done enough to get 20 years in prison? Will the evidence stand up in a court of law once a smart-arsed defence barrister starts to unravel it?

But this was looking good; the gang were making their way to a post office which the surveillance had seen them recce a few times. Our driver informed us that Mr Glenn was trying to ascertain whether a 'happy bag' had been spotted. A happy bag is something their team keeps its robbery kit – guns, masks, tape – in. A call sign confirmed a sighting of a happy bag in Hamlett's vehicle.

The gang parked one of the Renaults a mile from a post office in Blackley and all three of them (ridiculously) crammed into a Renault 5 and continued towards the post office. The surveillance commentary increased in content and our three vehicles were on the road speeding towards the surveillance. Dino put the team onto Condition Amber. We were busy in the vehicles, mentally preparing ourselves.

The DSU drivers aggressively drove through the morning rush-hour traffic. The driver was shouting the status of the gang over the noise of the engine.

'OK, we're on the arse end of surveillance – now!'

I looked behind me and shouted to Dino, 'Bravo and Charlie with us.'

All of a sudden, the surveillance driver slowed down.

'The Renault has stopped and all three targets are on foot, they have separated and are walking in the opposite direction of the post office,' he said.

'Have they got the happy bags?' I asked.

'Stand by.' He radioed my request through. Then, 'Negative.'

The surveillance team leader split his resources, deploying teams to each target. Another message came through: Bulger had flagged a taxi and was en route towards Clayton in the rear off-side position. It appeared the gang was not about to commit the robbery – and then we received the command to arrest Bulger. We accelerated towards the limited surveillance on Bulger. Hamlett had jumped on a bus bound for the city centre and Ryan was still on foot.

Bravo and Charlie vehicles were directly behind us. 'OK, we're back with the surveillance,' shouted our driver. Dino calmly transmitted Condition Red to the rest of our team. We could clearly see the brown Vauxhall Cavalier taxi in front of us. Bulger was in the rear off-side and the vehicle was being driven by an elderly male. He was an unknown quantity but he would be treated as hostile until handcuffed.

The conventional surveillance was pulling away, allowing our three-vehicle convoy a clear route and then – for no explicable reason – our driver turned left into a one-way street.

Dino was screaming at him: 'What the fuck are you playing at?' He just looked at Dino with a confused expression. Fortunately the tactic allows for such contingencies: Bravo became Alpha and Charlie became Bravo.

Rod, as Bravo one, took over the comms as our driver reversed out.

'Standby, standby,' could clearly be heard over our radio net as Rod's team approached the taxi. I was screaming inside about the cock-up and felt like punching the DSU driver, but losing my temper wouldn't help.

'Strike! Strike! Strike!'

The taxi was forced to a halt and the Bravo Two officer was pointing a mini-Ruger at the taxi, screaming, 'Armed police!' Both occupants were looking shocked and bewildered at the vehicle on their off-side with someone shouting at them. Then the taxi's two front doors were ripped open and the driver was covered by one of our team pointing a sidearm, clearly stating, 'Look at me, look at me, do not move.'

'Locked doors' had been screamed and Rod was busy smashing the rear off-side and near-side windows so the covering officers could access the car. Within seconds, the taxi had been assaulted and disabled, all doors were open and the two occupants were covered by armed officers. Both the taxi driver and Bulger looked totally confused and were made to lie on the floor and were handcuffed. By now we had joined the operation and the lads were smiling at me. They knew how much this operation meant to me but somehow the surveillance driver had made the wrong turn.

Bulger was searched and a six-inch knife was found in his waistband. A divisional van was summoned and he was taken to Collyhurst Police Station. After some questioning, the taxi driver was dusted down and released.

We returned to Bootle Street with orders to standby for further instructions. We started to debrief the operation and the use of the tactic. A debrief is important to any operation but it is for everyone to be honest. It's not about how well you did and a nice pat on the back. It's about how to further and better a tactic, how to learn from it, and being honest about your mistakes (if you have made any) so everyone can benefit from it. We were happy that the tactic was a success, but why had our driver turned left at a crucial moment and also, what had happened to Hamlett and Ryan?

I later found out that our driver had previously been threatened by a target with a handgun. While on a surveillance, a target had discovered his presence and had pointed a weapon at him until he could escape. This obviously had an impact on our driver, who needless to say wasn't used in that role again.

For reasons never discovered, the gang had become spooked in the process of planning their crime and had decided to abort the robbery. Still, Mr Glenn was confident that he had enough evidence to arrest and convict the team and had given the order to arrest.

Hamlett and Ryan had been followed to their home addresses and it had been decided to arrest them in the early hours. Both addresses were subject to a quick entry at 04.30 the following day. Hamlett was arrested without any fuss.

Ryan was confronted on the landing of his terraced house. He was completely naked but, true to his status as a hard man, he stood in front of Jim and Pete without any sign of fear, which is very rare in such circumstances. He decided he wanted to fight, which probably wasn't the best decision he ever made. Needless to say he was arrested with a bit of fuss.

The importance of this whole episode led to the development of Manchester's vehicle drills, later designated a MASTS (Mobile Armed Support To Surveillance).

CHAPTER FOURTEEN

The Strangeways Riot

I had been expecting my pager to activate all day. When it finally did, I was in such a hurry that I was stopped for speeding by the local police. After a quick explanation, I was allowed on my way to Bootle Street, where I quickly kitted out with the rest of my team and headed to one of our vehicles.

It was April 1990 and the media was in a frenzy over the day's events. HMP Strangeways had been the scene of fierce and serious disorder. Prisoners had taken control of most of the jail and had already caused thousands of pounds of damage. Several were making rooftop protests and the local and national TV were broadcasting regular updates.

The yard at Bootle Street, five minutes' drive from the prison, was a hive of activity: personnel vans were picking up support units, TAG officers were kitting up in full riot complement, vans containing public order shields were leaving for Strangeways. I started chatting with a couple of TAG lads who I knew well and received the usual police rumours.

'You won't believe it Andy, the nonces have been attacked, some are hanging from the landings with syringes sticking from their necks. They reckon, at least twenty are dead.'

It's hard not to get wrapped up in this type of atmosphere, particularly when we heard stories of prison officers being held hostage by some of the more desperate inmates. I for one was not bothered about any executed nonces (paedophiles) but the prison officer rumours concerned me.

We jumped into the vans and sped out of the yard towards Collyhurst, the headquarters for the B Division, where Strangeways is located and where the commander had the responsibility of policing the prison. As we made our way we discussed why the Firearms Department had been turned out. It seemed obvious to us that the rumours of hostages must be true, others why would we have been activated?

On our arrival we were sent to the canteen, where our bosses were waiting. We jumped into the lifts and at the last possible moment pushed out the person nearest to the door so he would have to walk the five floors to the canteen carrying all his kit. This childish prank always amused us and as soon as we got into a lift we were always vying for the best position.

We were soon seated and listening to our detective inspector explain that he was unclear about the current situation but there was a possibility of hostages. He had been summoned to the scene and we were to consider Collyhurst as our holding area until he had further intelligence.

I knew the DI well; he had been Leon Brittan's protection officer. 'Andy, you will come with me?' he said, more as an instruction than a question. I grabbed the Range Rover keys off one of the lads and within minutes we were at Sherborne Street, virtually outside of the prison. The DI made his way to a gaggle of senior officers and was soon in deep and animated discussion. I had no inclination to join them but instead took in the scene. By now the chaos and confusion of the early stages of a large-scale incident had been replaced by cordons and gatherings of support units from virtually every division, plus members of the Tactical Aid Group. The perimeter of the prison was surrounded by uniformed officers. Junctions were blocked and traffic had been re-routed.

I took the time to wander about and take in what had happened. I had been inside Strangeways many times, usually transporting prisoners. I had also been on a familiarization of the prison in the event of an incident of this nature. I had been given guided tours of the interior, its construction and the labyrinth of Victorian sewers. I was also familiar with many of the cell doors and how to make an effective entry. I hated the place; it was depressing and forbidding, exactly how a prison should be. It had been constructed in Victorian times and was straight out of a Dickens novel. I found the whole place frightening.

As I returned to the DI, he grabbed me and said, 'Are you armed?'

'Yes.'

'Well lock it away in the Range Rover. The bosses are not sure if we have a hostage situation, but you are to recce the prison and try to establish a route in.'

I looked at him bewildered. 'What, on my own?' My arse had already started twitching.

'Yes, we haven't got time to get anyone else down here.'

'I'll need a guide,' I nervously stammered.

'Find one. I have got to speak to the ACC. I will see you here in an hour.' He promptly fucked off.

I did as I was instructed and locked my SLP in the gun safe in the Range Rover, then went to a side gate on Sherborne Street and told the prison officer there of my intentions. He looked at me as if I was daft but let me inside. Once inside the perimeter walls, I could see the extent of the damage. Walls were fire blackened, glazed windows were smashed and piles of rubble littered the area.

Strangeways is a massive complex and I had entered from the east wing. The interior was manned by prison officers from their C and R (control and restraint) teams. These are usually big, no-nonsense lads – I had played enough rugby against them to know. I headed over to a team and explained my dilemma. They were quite unfazed and amusedly pointed me in the direction where the main activity had occurred.

As I made my way to the first building block, someone shouted, 'Don't get caught, you will not sit down for weeks.' It was bad enough being in the prison but the thought of getting caught filled me with dread. I good-naturedly acknowledged their comment as I hastily retreated towards the gate I'd come in at, noting their amused faces.

I went to the Range Rover, unlocked it and holstered my Beretta, along with another thirty rounds of ammo. Although it was against regulations, there was no way I was getting caught. Then I walked past the C and R team who had just watched my hasty departure, and entered a long, single-storey, pre-fabricated building with rooms on either side of a central corridor. It had been devastated: water pipes had been ripped from walls, pools of water were everywhere, furniture was trashed, paint had been splattered on the walls.

As I went further into the building, the light diminished. The building appeared to go on for another 150 metres, with rooms either side. My imagination began to work overtime in the gloom. I started to think about the bodies hanging from the landings.

I had been walking along the corridor as if I was on a Sunday outing. If I was going to establish a route in, I decided I had better wise up. I took my Beretta from its holster, switched on a mini Maglite, and started to tactically clear the building, searching and moving. For the next thirty minutes I cleared room after room. Each had been trashed and ruined. I eventually came to a secure door at the end of the corridor. This was a reinforced prison door with the appropriate locks. Through the glass aperture I could see into a small part of the main prison area. I could actually see part of the landings, surprisingly enough without bodies hanging from them.

This door was firmly locked and had a semblance of a barricade behind it. The part of the prison I could see was minus any prisoners but again showed evidence of the riot. I hastily returned and breathed a deep sigh of relief when I stepped outside. I had been crapping myself all the way through that search.

I spent some time with the control and restraint teams, who were genuinely disgruntled with the way the riot had been handled. To a man they said that had they been utilized early and been allowed to do what they are trained to do, they believed the problem would have been dealt with without escalation. They believed the politics of the era prevented an early resolution. As I left the C and R lads, I couldn't help but reflect that it wasn't only the police service that was led by donkeys.

I met the DI back at the Range Rover and briefed him. He also appeared pissed off with the commanders. He told me that all prison officers had been accounted for and that the Firearms Department was to remain on standby. Orders from above stated firmly that we were not to become involved in anything within the prison but leave it to the negotiators. I tried to explain the need for rehearsals and tactical drills in case we were requested but again he stated firmly that we were to leave it to the negotiators.

All I could do was inwardly smile to myself and think back to an incident in Stockport, which a negotiator resolved.

* * *

It started at the Pennine Shooting Club in Stockport. A fellow called Peter Crack had been diagnosed with terminal cancer, and before he died he decided he would seek revenge on a few characters that had done him harm. He would shoot those he had a grievance with, and to do this he would steal a gun. He enrolled at the Pennine Club, and whilst in possession of a .22 revolver, tried to leave the club. A firefight followed between him and gun club members, without anyone being hurt. Crack escaped and subsequently shot dead two people he believed had done him harm.

Somehow Crack ended up in a Stockport suburb in an unoccupied property. The police had been called to the reports of someone breaking in. A uniformed officer attended and was threatened at gunpoint. We were contacted and, on a night when the heavens let loose, my team and I had surrounded the property. Dino, my team sergeant, started negotiating with Crack, trying to persuade him to peacefully surrender.

Crack pointed the weapon at us a couple of times and we ducked behind ballistic shields. We were not taking any chances; he had already killed two people. There is a syndrome known as 'suicide by cop' and we wondered whether this was what Crack intended. Suicide by cop is where someone wants to die but instead of taking their own life, they place the police in a position where they have to shoot.

I had Crack in my sights twice from a position in the back of the garden and actually started to take up pressure on the trigger of the MP5 but fortunately hadn't been quick enough to take a shot. I was also in a dilemma because of the weapon I had – I needed ammunition capable of covering 100 metres, drilling patio windows and then the suspect himself, and the MP5 was not the best option.

For the next eight hours it bucketed down as Dino used all his communication skills to entice Crack to surrender. In the early hours of the morning, the command decided to turn out a nationally trained negotiator of chief superintendent rank. This man was highly trained in techniques developed by the FBI to deal with desperate offenders. Dino had done an excellent job over the last eight hours but it was time to hand over to the expert.

We heard over the radio net that the negotiator had been brought to the scene and at any minute he was about to enter into important and protracted negotiations. I then heard a further comms message confirming negotiations had commenced.

Within minutes I heard a muffled crack, an obvious gunshot that made me duck instinctively. The radio net came alive with confirmation of a gunshot. It appeared our suspect had shot himself. A search team was sent into the property and confirmed it.

I'm not decrying the use of negotiators but Dino had kept Crack alive for at least eight hours by using his skills as a police officer. A highly trained negotiator arrived at the scene and within minutes of establishing dialogue, the suspect killed himself. It makes you think, doesn't it?

* * *

The DI asked what I was thinking as I got into the Range Rover.

'Remember Stockport?' I said.

He shrugged his shoulders and smiled back.

Throughout my service, I came across many negotiators. Some were excellent, others incompetent. The trouble is that they are usually of senior officer rank and therefore want to know the ins and outs of a duck's arse. That would be generally okay for an incident that doesn't require an intervention. However, if an intervention may be a tactical consideration, then the less the negotiator knows, the better. By simply knowing, they may give away a vital part of a plan.

Some years later I was involved in a siege over the Christmas period in the Lancashire town of Wigan. The festivities had become too much for one individual, who had recently split up from his girlfriend. The heartbreak of the bust-up caused him to hold his ex-girlfriend at gunpoint. He then barricaded himself in a small terraced house, threatening to kill himself and his girlfriend.

The department was turned out and it soon became a major

incident, with all the force's resources deployed to Wigan. By now we had a reasonable hostage rescue capability and at once containment and negotiations commenced. Rehearsals and drills started in preparation for an assault and breach of the house.

During this phase I was tasked with a close target reconnaissance (CTR). The Technical Support Unit had full camera coverage of all aspects of the property and these were being relayed to the command and negotiators' cell. From this camera coverage we could see that the front door was partially open and from negotiators' intelligence we believed the hostage and hostage taker (dubbed X-ray) were barricaded into the front upstairs bedroom.

I was tasked to make a covert entry and establish a safe route in for the hostage rescue team, if possible up to the bedroom door. I made my way to the front door with Foz. I was aware that X-ray was distracted by intense negotiation between him and the specialist negotiation team.

Foz and I crept into the property and commenced our reconnaissance. We quickly confirmed X-ray's stronghold as the upstairs bedroom and identified a poor attempt of a barricade at the foot of the stairs. Neither of us are the stealthiest of blokes but we managed to exit without alerting the X-ray.

However, as we were leaving, one of the negotiators happened to glance at a monitor that was linked to the camera covering the front door. According to Joe, the negotiator cell's firearms liaison, the negotiator almost had kittens, stammering and blustering and threatening to sack the idiots that had entered the property without his consent. He was obviously unaware of our orders to conduct a CTR and had missed the entry phase but clocked our extraction phase on the monitor. Fortunately there was a more experienced negotiator who calmed the situation down and informed him to wind his neck back in.

We eventually assaulted the property in the early hours whilst X-ray had left the barricaded bedroom to help himself to a sandwich in the downstairs kitchen. His girlfriend was rescued and appeared nonplussed by the whole affair. I suppose that says a lot for the resilience of Wiganers and also the advantages and disadvantages of negotiators.

CHAPTER FIFTEEN

Crossing the Line

Armed robbers had hit a warehouse near the Quays in Salford. Three masked men burst in brandishing sawn-off shotguns, terrorised staff and stole an articulated lorry containing branded footwear. The consignment was worth a small fortune.

An informant tipped off the Salford CID office that the footwear had been driven to a large holding area in Salford, where it was transferred to another wagon. A surveillance team had been tasked with finding the stolen lorry and the holding area. Within hours, they had not only found the spot but were tailing a large wagon believed to contain the shoes. Because the offenders were believed to be armed, the CID and the DSU requested armed back-up.

My team were at Diggle, running through shooting disciplines, when our pagers started to bleep. One of the lads made his way to the range house and, after a quick phone call, ran back panting to tell us we were needed at Salford Police HQ at The Crescent. Pete and I sprinted ahead to get the two sets of vehicles keys first – we'd both been scared to death when Jimmy was behind the wheel on a blue run and no way were we letting him drive.

We loaded up the vans and sped down the narrow country lanes of Diggle, then stuck on the sirens and lights. Pete and I were both advanced drivers and shot through the busier towns of Ashton-under-Lyne and Openshaw in a protected formation, covering each other as we negotiated junctions and crossroads. It took us 35 minutes to reach The Crescent.

A few of the surveillance team were in the car park. Me, Rod and Pete walked over to them and were brought up to speed on the events. Meanwhile Jim and Parker went to the CID office and were told authority had been granted for a vehicle strike on the wagon. As they returned, I noticed another vehicle pulling into the yard. It was driven by the sergeant in charge of the DSU. His handle was Disco and I knew him to be conceited and prone to sulking if he didn't get his own way. As I was contemplating this complication, Pete came up with a valid point.

'We've rehearsed and gone live on normal cars. We haven't thought about assaulting a lorry.'

He was right. The height of some articulated vehicles would certainly give the occupants an advantage. I asked Jim if we had any info on the suspects. He informed me that they were two 'no marks', possibly associated with the McDonalds, an active robbery team from Salford with a reputation for violence. The informant had confirmed that the robbers in the wagon were armed. Because vehicle drills were my baby, it fell on me to produce an immediate action plan.

I went over to Disco, who already had a face like a slapped arse, and asked him to assign three DSU operatives to us. He uninterestedly pointed to a couple of his team, both in small hatchback vehicles.

'Are you fucking joking?' I snapped. 'You know we need bigger vehicles.'

This was typical of him: some days he could be really co-operative and others a mard-arse. Today he was a mard-arse. I was thinking I wouldn't have this problem with Dave when Ian drove into the yard. He quickly realised what was happening and with a mischievous wink radioed for three suitable vehicles with trained drivers.

As we waited, I quickly briefed and deployed our team into Alpha, Bravo and Charlie call signs. Ian brought me up to date on the robbers. They were parked in Trafford Park outside a mobile canteen having a brew and a sandwich. This would have been an ideal time to arrest them but we were still waiting for our drivers. I gathered our team together and held a Chinese parliament, inviting ideas and options. It became obvious that we would have to be flexible and change the plan from a vehicle drill to maybe a foot strike or ambush. Disco's face was a picture when he heard the two other options.

'That's not our role,' he objected. In a sense he was right, but we needed transport and his team supplied it. My best course of action was to ignore him.

The vehicles screamed into the yard, all driven by good operators. I quickly briefed them and we set off to Trafford Park. The DSU radio net was alive with numbered transmission. It was obvious the wagon was mobile again, with a conventional surveillance in tow.

I started to badger my driver for up-to-date descriptions of the suspects and the wagon they were in. He radioed my request to the 'eyeball', and within seconds I knew that the suspects were both male, white and 30 to 35 years old. One was about 5ft 10ins, fat with a shaven head. The other was slightly slimmer with a mop of black curly hair.

The vehicle was a box wagon, approximately 18 feet long with a separate cab which was elevated and reached by built-in steps. Curly was driving the wagon, which was heading north towards the M61 motorway.

This could cause us a problem. If the wagon left the force area, our firearms authority was useless. Authority is usually granted for the force it is issued in, and an assistant chief constable would have to consult with his opposite number in the affected force to allow a cross-border authority. More often than not, such authority is refused unless life is in danger. If we crossed into Lancashire, I wasn't going to hold my breath.

Our driver said the wagon was heading towards Chorley. It was now in Lancashire and we didn't have a firearms authority.

The offenders could still be arrested but without firearms unless certain circumstances prevailed. The next update said the wagon had come off at Junction 8 and was westbound towards the M6. All we could do was hang back and wait and see where they led us.

'M6 southbound,' our driver informed us.

For the next hour we stuck on the end of the surveillance, trying to make sense of the wagon's movements. It can be hard to guess what a criminal is planning. I have been on many surveillances and the suspects have displayed the most extra-ordinary movement patterns. Maybe they suspect a police presence and it's their attempt at anti-surveillance procedures, perhaps they have time to kill, or sometimes they are not the sharpest tools in the box and end up getting lost.

We were now heading south towards Cheshire and again our authority would be useless. Maybe the wagon would return to Manchester and we could start planning the strike. The conven-tional surveillance team were not having a hard time following the wagon and my team were pretty relaxed. This happens on operations – you can get a sudden surge of activity with everyone rushing around with orders and radio transmission cluttering the airwaves, vehicles driving off at speed towards the offenders, officers running towards vehicles and grabbing kit, team mem-bers being thrown about as the vehicle rockets away while you are trying to arrange or prep kit in the back. Then a lull occurs: the offenders become inactive and you just have to sit and wait it out. This is known as Condition Green. Many of my colleagues will take this opportunity to sleep, others will read or chat and some will get up to mischief.

On one surveillance, Rod and Foz were the number two and three of a vehicle strike team. They were sat on the back of a surveillance vehicle chatting away. Foz had recently joined VO8 from Heywood TAG. He is one of the most easygoing characters I've had the privilege to call a friend. Foz only has one speed –

his speed. Nothing is done hastily, everything is calculated and planned. He would become an extremely competent and skilled operative and one of the most loyal individuals I have ever known.

Unknown to Rod and Foz, their vehicle had a faulty radio, known as a 'carrier'. This means the press-to-talk button has become stuck in the activation mode and anything they say will be transmitted. Foz's voice came on to the net, chuckling.

'That Antro is a crucifier of fashion.'

Rod started laughing. 'Yeah, have you seen the penny round collared T-shirt he's got on?'

Foz giggled. 'He looks like a reject from the *Randall and Hopkirk* series.'

I was in a surveillance vehicle with my team when we heard this transmission. They were referring to our chief inspector, who was part of the operation and had attended the morning's briefing wearing a ridiculous T-shirt. We started laughing, clearly recognising Foz and Rod's voice.

I quickly made a mobile phone call to Rod and informed him they had a carrier. 'Oh fuck,' we heard over the net, then white noise. The lads in our vehicle were splitting their sides and wondering if Antro had heard it, when the squelch of the radio came alive.

'Mister Antro is a great boss,' said Foz.

'One of the best,' said Rod.

Then they unanimously agreed, 'We couldn't work for a better bloke,' and the transmissions ceased. We were pissing ourselves with laughter, wondering what the outcome would be. Fair dos to Antro, he never mentioned it, not that he wasn't without a sense of humour.

★ ★ ★

Over the years I would work closely with Foz and he would give me some great laughs. In the early 1990s my team was sent to

Lancashire to help protect the Conservative Party's annual conference at the Winter Gardens in Blackpool. At this stage, GMP had replaced the Model 10 Smith & Wesson revolver with the 9mm 92F Beretta self-loading pistol. An officer now had a weapon that carried 15 rounds rather than six and could carry a spare magazine with another 15 rounds – a decent amount of ammunition if he was to be in a firefight.

Lancashire Police, however, insisted that my team were to carry revolvers instead of SLPs while on duty in the Winter Gardens. We questioned this decision but were told that Lancashire, being a national firearms training school, didn't see the need for SLPs. So, prior to our secondment, we had to reclassify the antiquated revolver. It was ludicrous.

All governments have a high risk assessment and the Tory government of the day was no exception. The IRA was still active, although its weapon of choice was generally explosives. If it had realised how poorly armed the protection officers were, a determined assault with fully automatic weapons would have had a reasonable chance of success. Each one of us was shocked by Lancashire's decision. We were even more shocked by their tactical planning. When we arrived at Hutton, Lancashire's training HQ near Preston, a chief inspector from their firearms school briefed us on our duties. Each morning we would be expected to travel from Hutton to Blackpool, a 30-minute journey, in a coach supplied by a local transport company. We asked where the bus was kept and if it would be searched each day.

'That is totally unnecessary,' stated the chief inspector.

Lancashire expected us to treat the week's operation seriously, but couldn't even bother to have secure transport for its protection officers. It doesn't need me to state the obvious. The IRA wouldn't have had to try hard to blow the bus – and us – apart. I was disgusted and switched off for the rest of his briefing. As soon as it was over, Mick, our sergeant, and myself as the senior AFO, briefed our lads. In the event of an attack, our main objective would be our own protection. We would rendezvous by Blackpool Tower and if one of the team was missing we would return for him as a unit.

We had limited firepower and idiots for tactical advisers. I had full confidence in my team's abilities; each one of them had a fair amount of bottle and would never let each other or members of the public down. But the planning of the conference came under that old saying, lions led by donkeys.

As the week progressed, the logistics turned into a shambles. Half of the team were issued revolvers without ammunition, the other half had ammunition without revolvers. It was a case of swapping bits of kit with the officers we relieved, who were from Staffordshire and seemed as pissed off as us.

At some stage during the operation, Foz wandered over to the Golden Mile and bought a pair of joke milk-bottle-bottom glasses that gave him the appearance of Cosmo Smallpiece, the leering Les Dawson character. At any opportunity, Foz would put on these glasses and mimic Cosmo. This would have us in hysterics, particularly when he did it in the presence of Tory MPs. You could see them looking at him in a quizzical manner, wondering if this bodyguard was all there.

Foz decided he would get a laugh when handing in his weapon. At the end of a tour of duty we would return to Hutton and hand over our weapons to the instructors at the Lancs firearms school. They took this job extremely seriously and had you queuing like kids in a dinner line. The majority of them were jobsworths who spent an eternity checking your revolver before booking it in. Foz put on his glasses, shouted 'Where's the front of the queue?' and put his arms out in front of him and started shuffling. The lads in the queue looked up and started smiling.

Foz then asked, 'Can someone show me where to hand this in?' and patted his revolver in his holster.

One of the lads quickly cottoned on to the prank and shouted,

'Here mate, let me help you,' and grabbed his arm and led him to the instructor's desk at the front of the queue. Two of the instructors looked up and saw this blind buffoon in front of them.

Foz shouted, 'Andy, is this thing safe?' and again patted his holstered weapon.

The Lancashire instructors looked at him in utter amazement which quickly turned to disdain. We were by now howling with laughter; this prank had appealed to our childish humour. However the Lancashire instructors were obviously upset with his show of so-called unprofessionalism and completely ignored Foz. This didn't deter Foz and his impersonation of Cosmo was getting better.

Some weeks later back in force, Foz and I were summoned to Rochdale HQ. Two lads from the Serious Crime Squad had arrested someone who had a handgun. We had been asked to check it out and ensure it was safe. We arrived and the two SCS lads greeted me excitedly, quite rightly happy about the recovery of a gun. Neither of them knew Foz, who I introduced as a firearms expert. The lads were suitably impressed when I told them he was the 'dog's bollocks' and if he couldn't identify the weapon, no-one could.

Lying on a nearby table was a Second World War, 9mm parabellum German Luger. Foz had mentally identified it and stated, 'Right, stand back,' and indicated to the detectives to move away, with great sweeping movements. They looked at each other and hesitantly stepped back. Foz theatrically pulled out a pair of rubber gloves and leisurely placed them on. He then arranged a notebook and pen, and with a deliberate and slow movement removed his glasses from his breast pocket. He made a great show of cleaning the lenses as the two detective constables looked on. Foz put the glasses on.

Instantly he said, 'Fuck, it's gone dark, grab my arm Andy.'

The two DCs looked half amused and half confused.

'Lead me to the gun,' Foz announced. I took him over to the Luger. Foz started slapping the table deliberately near the firearm.

'Where the fuck is it?' he demanded. The two DCs had backed off towards the wall with incredulous looks. My stomach was in knots trying to hold back the laughter and my eyes were smarting with mirth.

'Is it safe?' asked Foz.

'Hold on,' I said.

The two DCs had now retreated so their backs were against the office walls and they couldn't go any further.

'Is the safety on?' Foz enquired.

'Fucking Jesus,' one of the detectives blurted out. This was too much and all four of us fell about howling with laughter. The two DCs had quickly appreciated the prank and were roaring with laughter. A slightly different result to the Lancashire instructors.

* * *

'They are exiting the motorway and heading for Crewe town centre,' shouted our driver. Then a surprising radio message came over from command and control in Manchester: 'Authority has been granted for the use of firearms in Cheshire.' This was unusual, but we could start planning for a strike.

The wagon was heading along the A roads towards the town centre when it took a turn towards Crewe speedway track. Within minutes we were in an area of allotments serviced by narrow, black cinder tracks. The nearby buildings were wooden shacks, used to store garden produce and equipment.

Most of the surveillance had to pull off due to the restrictive area the wagon was negotiating. Several times the wagon stopped at gates obstructing the roadways. Fatty would have to get out and open and close the gate and it meant the wagon was becoming harder to follow. A tractor would get a lot of looking at in an area like this, never mind a family saloon.

Fortunately the wagon pulled up outside a shack that wouldn't have been out of place in the Florida Everglades. Fatty and Curly immediately started to unload, humping parcels and boxes into the shack. We had two options: arrest them at the shack or take them in the wagon if they decided to leave in it. An arrest at the shack would be difficult due to the large expanse of open ground around it. At the white aspect was a small hillock and then 500 feet of ploughed field. At the black aspect was at least three-quarters of a mile of ploughed field towards the speedway track. Red and green aspects were unapproachable. Our decision was made for us.

The suspects unloaded their consignment and manoeuvred the vehicle towards the route out. On the way in we had driven through at least three gates. The middle gate was ideal for an ambush, flanked on two aspects by derelict shacks. This would be our FAP. We hastily retreated; we didn't have much time and rehearsals were out of the question.

The surveillance drivers deposited six of us at the FAP. I had decided that three of our team would remain with the surveillance at the lay-up point further up the track in case our ambush failed. The six of us hastily planned our actions. We would split into two teams of three, our areas of responsibility were the off-side and near-side doors of the wagon. Each team would have a foot on the ground (sniper lock). Another would attack the door and the other standby for MOE and arrest duties.

We split up and took cover in the derelict shacks. We could hear the engine of the wagon rumbling towards us. Rod had jammed the handle of the gate, making it difficult to open. As soon as the wagon stopped at the gate and Fatty got out, I would call the strike.

We had minutes to go and my mind was racing. What if the wagon smashed through the gate? I stood with Rod and Jim, hidden in the shack. Jim would cover mine and Rod's movements as we ran towards a three-ton lorry. The plan didn't sound so great at this stage and the adrenalin was causing my stomach to flip.

I heard the harsh grinding of gears and the unmistakeable sound of air brakes. I risked a quick look; Fatty was out and struggling with the gate.

'Strike! Strike! Strike!' I shouted over the air.

Jim stepped out of cover and aimed his mini-Ruger at the wagon, screaming, 'Armed police!'

I sprinted towards the driver's side. Pete and his team were dealing with Fatty – from the corner of my eye I saw them drop him to the floor. Crunch – I heard the driver trying to put the wagon into gear. Crunch – he was trying to reverse away. My duties were MOE and prisoner handling. I ran towards the wagon and almost left the ground as I smashed a crowbar into the windscreen. I needed to regain our advantage. The driver was thinking and that wasn't good.

Rod was on the door screaming 'Locked doors, locked doors!' I jumped onto the steps and shattered the driver's window. I could see Pete pointing his pistol at the driver from the passenger door.

'Armed police, turn off the engine,' he growled.

The driver looked terrified and quickly complied. I dragged him from the cab and cuffed him. Jim moved into the arrest area and covered the prisoners as Rod and I cleared the rear of the wagon. The back of the wagon was empty. We could now start to come down from our instantaneous adrenalin fix.

I made a radio call to the lay-up point team that we had arrested the suspects and could the DSU radio Cheshire Constabulary and ask for assistance in the way of vans to transport the prisoners. Stuart, who had been part of the LUP team, informed me we had a small problem and he would be with me in seconds. As I looked up I could see Stuart and his team walking towards us, minus the DSU. I walked over to him and asked what had happened. In Stuart's unflappable and polite way, he said Disco had decided to pull off all his team and return to Manchester, stating he wasn't going to be used as VO8's transport. Fucking marvellous. We were stuck in the middle of nowhere in an alien force with two suspects and the location possibly of stolen goods.

Fortunately Ian from the DSU saved the day. Although he had been ordered back to force, he had the foresight to contact the CID at Salford and tell them our predicament. Meanwhile a couple of our team had found a telephone kiosk (these were the days before mobile phones) and informed command of our situation. Eventually officers from Cheshire turned up shortly followed by the Salford CID.

Most of us ended up in the custody suite at Crewe Police Station armed to the teeth, explaining to a geriatric sergeant the circumstances of the arrests. The old sergeant looked totally bewildered and appeared only too happy to see the back of us as the prisoners were taken into custody. We made our way into the canteen and waited for transport back to Manchester.

Eventually we arrived back at Bootle Street and after a constructive debrief we continued sounding off in the Nag's Head. Some time through the night we heard from the Salford CID that the full consignment of footwear had been recovered, along with two shotguns and ammunition, at the shack in Crewe.

* * *

There is always the danger on any armed operation that things can go wrong – fatally wrong. Firearms are lethal weapons. That's why we spend so much time training to get it right.

In the mid-80s the Home Office presented findings on shootings by police officers within the UK. In several incidents, officers had shot and killed or seriously injured innocent people, including a child. After full judicial enquiries, the officers had been exonerated of serious charges such as murder or manslaughter. However, the enquiries revealed a lack of adequate tactical training. The Home Office study also raised concerns regarding the number of AFOs within many of the major police forces.

A recommendation to streamline the system, creating teams and delivering regular training, was part of their diagnosis. To be fair to GMP, they had recognised this fact and had seriously limited the use of AFOs from the crime squads and divisions. However, they were still reliant on AFOs from the Tactical Aid Group.

The command structure decided to hand over some firearms duties to the TAG, such as the movement of category A prisoners – those deemed the worst risk – and armed guard duties. In theory, this would free VO8 to concentrate on team training, AFO instruction and operations. And for a period, this new system appeared to work.

VO8 gained a full strength of 40. We were split into three teams, working a three-week rota. Week one would be instructional duties; for that week your team would be responsible for teaching the AFOs within force, running basic courses, refresher days and so on. On week two, your team would rotate to operational duties and would be responsible for any operations within the force area. The team would be on duty from 08.00– 16.00 at Bootle Street. If the team was not engaged on an operation then it would self-train on tactical options.

During the off-duty period, the team would be placed on standby, with instructions not to leave the force area unless you lived outside it and not to consume alcohol. This allowed GMP a full response of 60 minutes to any incident. Week three would be advice duties. The team was broken down into pairs and given a shift pattern, for example one pair would work 06.00– 14.00, the next pair 14.00–22.00 and the next pair 22.00–

0600; another pair would have been on rest days. The advice team was equipped with a three-litre Range Rover, a box of pistols and shotguns, and ammunition. This allowed GMP an immediate response to any incident. The advice team would be responsible for planning immediate action options and turning out the operational team.

For several years GMP operated this system. I found it one of the best. It allowed a firearms officer to develop his strengths. Some were more inclined towards instructional duties, others operational. It allowed an officer to gain experience, knowledge and understanding of the level of armed crime patterns within the force.

* * *

On the first weekend in September, 1989, I was on operational duties when my pager went at 09.30. I checked the number and contacted the crew room at Bootle Street. The advice team had requested a full turnout to Bootle Street.

Within 40 minutes, I was there with the rest of my team, being briefed. There'd been an armed robbery at a building society on Deansgate, the main city centre thoroughfare. The offender had threatened cashiers with a handgun but they'd refused to hand over any cash. This had deterred the offender and he fled empty-handed. He hailed a double-decker bus, climbed on board, went up the stairs and sat at the back. He was in a panic and possibly not in full possession of his mental faculties. At this stage he fired his gun – two 9mm rounds were recovered from the back seats. Several passengers sitting upstairs fled downstairs. The driver also heard the shots and stopped the bus. He and the passengers then legged it. The offender also left and flagged down a taxi.

The incident was reported within minutes and attending officers quickly contacted the taxi company, who said that the offender had been dropped off at a premises in Wythenshawe, a massive council estate in south Manchester. Further enquiries revealed that the occupant of the address was an Anthony Hughes, recently out of prison. He had been imprisoned for the theft of a 9mm handgun from Diggle Range.

Some of our team heard alarm bells. About 18 months before, Anthony Hughes had attended Diggle as a probationer shooter; before handguns became illegal, Diggle was a civilian pistol-shooting club. The police used it from 08.00–17.00 Monday to Friday and the rest of the time it was used by civilian gun clubs. One of the gun club members had his vehicle broken into and a 9mm Tangfolio self-loading pistol with ammunition was taken. Hughes was suspected.

After enquiries by the CID, the following morning my team made a forced entry into Hughes's property in Wythenshawe. He lived in a typical two-up, two-down council maisonette. We quickly arrested Hughes in his bedroom, which was a shrine to the Third Reich. His bedroom was adorned with pictures of Adolf Hitler and swastika flags. He also had quantities of kill-your-mates weekly magazines such as *Combat & Survival* and *Soldier of Fortune*. Hughes himself was an insipid individual, approximately 5ft 8ins, with lank and greasy hair, a pale complexion and skinny build, and he stank like a polecat. CID searched the premises but failed to recover the handgun. In interview, Hughes denied having it. He was put before a judge, who took a dim view of his denial and delivered a custodial sentence.

Hughes was convicted on the damning evidence of his finger-prints found on the exterior and interior of the boot of the vehicle at Diggle. It didn't take a genius to follow Hughes's next steps. Once he had completed his prison sentence, he had recovered the stolen pistol and decided to commit a robbery.

The advice team had been granted authority for a house entry at Hughes's premises in Wythenshawe. The local CID had managed to get two OPs on the premises and were monitoring the property from a safe distance. The latest intelligence was 'no movement'. This meant there was a lack of sightings and it was unclear whether the property was occupied. The advice team had given us our duties and we started to prep kit with the usual sense of urgency.

At this stage of VO8's history the shotgun had been replaced by the H&K MP5 – an all-round better-suited weapon. The MP5 is a small carbine, with an effective range of 300 feet. It is extremely accurate and easy to shoot, with a double magazine complement. It has the capacity of 30 or 60 rounds depending on the size of the magazine.

The police MP5 is single shot, but reloads after each shot as long as the magazine is loaded and the trigger pulled. The reader may have seen the MP5 used as a machine gun with bursts of rounds being fired. This is generally for the military – burst fire can be inaccurate, however the military require that facility at times. The police have little need for a burst fire system.

MP5 magazines were loaded, shields prepared, door-opening kit checked and radios tested. Within minutes we were aboard our vehicles and hurtling out of the city centre towards Wythenshawe. The advice team had gone ahead and were liaising with senior officers on the division. They were also locating a rendezvous point.

As we sped towards Wythenshawe a message from the advice team came through: 'No RVP available – suggest initiate strike from vehicles.'

This was a good call. Wythenshawe is one of the largest council estates in Europe. I would hate to brand all its occupants with the same label but it does have its fair share of what we termed 'shit' – lowlifes and criminals who delighted in other people's misery and liked nothing better than to hinder the police. Once a police operation was instigated on the estate, the crap came out of the woodwork, intent on giving the police a hard time. The tactic of early resolution was employed on many estates in Manchester. Get in quick and out even quicker. This could prevent long and protracted incidents of containment, closure of roads and evacuation of people.

While the law-abiding would assist, the shit would do everything in their power – even warning the suspects if possible – to hinder an operation. On many occasions I experienced this, a classic case being in the high-rise flats off Victoria Avenue, Blackley, in the north of Manchester. The flats are in clusters of three, and if our team was spotted moving among the floors of the flats then all hell would be let loose, with tenants shouting and banging, warning the occupants of each block that the police were about. This would certainly mess up our plans and we would find ourselves legging up flights of stairs to secure premises. These occurrences actively made us develop a joint covert and overt option for entering flats in multi-occupancy high-rise buildings.

It was noon on a summer Saturday; the estate would be busier than normal. The advice team had suggested we drive straight to the target premises and deploy from our vehicles. Four of the team would immediately 'contain' the property by covering the front and back. Two of the team with a double man 'wham ram' – the latest bit of door-opening technology – would smash down the door. For those of you who have seen the great Kirk Douglas movie *The Vikings*, these were the battering rams they used to assault the castle and this was our latest bit of kit and extremely effective it was too. Two of the team would go upstairs, the next two downstairs, the next two upstairs and the final two (sometimes the MOE team) downstairs. A premises could be contained within a minute using this tactic.

Dino shouted from the front passenger seat to the rest of us in the rear of the van that we would go with the advice team's option. I for one had no problem with this tactic; we had used it successfully on many occasions and practised it regularly. We could adapt it to either a quick entry or a shield entry. Dino suggested we go to a quick entry.

Leaky was driving and knew Wythenshawe well. As we turned into a road we saw the advice Range Rover and they took the lead. The advice team would put us on the target property. At this stage the speed decreases until the target property is in sight. When safe to do so the team will accelerate towards the property – every second counts because the element of surprise would be slipping.

Over the radio: 'ETA one minute.' The side doors of the van were pulled open and secured. The first team member out put his feet on the footplate. 'Standby, standby,' came over the radio. The Range Rover pulled up and with a sudden jolt, we were thrown forward and then settled back into place. 'Strike! Strike! Strike!' was shouted and we piled out of the van, sprinting towards the premises. It was the second time I had entered these premises.

I was virtually surrounded by wooden splinters as the MOE team smashed open the front door and immediately I was hurtling upstairs with my partner close up my arse. Into the master bedroom – the same shithole, worshipping the Nazis.

'Room clear!' I shouted and I could hear the other lads shouting, 'Room clear.' Dino declared the levels one and two safe and whispered to Leaky, 'Do the loft.' A loft entry is always a tricky time. Over the years we developed many options for a loft entry and practised continually, entering them playing the part of a suspect and the entry team. Once a premises was secured we would go quiet and listen for telltale noises from the loft. The hatch would be studied for signs of disturbance and then an entry made, similar to a room entry. We would always try to get a two-man team into a loft and search it the same as any other room but it had obvious dangers apart from a suspect. The light and the condition of its structure added to the problems.

On two occasions I have fallen through the floor of a loft after losing my balance and ended up with bollocks on either side of my neck. If I was tasked with searching a loft then I would always ensure it was safe.

During my early days on the team I had searched a loft in a property in Moss Side looking for Jason Bennett, an up-and-coming Gooch Close gang member, wanted for questioning. I declared the loft safe and we returned to Bootle Street. During the debrief we received a call from the local CID to say that while they were finishing off the evidential search, they had found Bennett in the loft. I was surprised and highly embarrassed by this fact – and somewhat dubious of the detective who informed us. He was a poisonous fucker who had been rejected by VO8. Nonetheless, I could have put officers' lives at risk and it was a lesson well learned.

Leaky and his partner cleared the loft and declared it safe. The premises were empty with no sign of Hughes. We were instructed to stand down at Bootle Street. Hughes was obviously elsewhere and while the police intelligence system started to locate him, there was nothing for us to do but go home.

* * *

On September 12, 1989, I was covering an evening shift at Bootle Street. It was our team's week for advice duties and I was working with Parker (not my favourite person) but I could make do. The crew room was quiet, the operational team had finished duty and were on their way home. I had just finished an hour's training in the gym while Parker covered the phones. He had nipped up to the canteen and I was sat contemplating how to fill the next five hours of duty when the phone next to me started to ring.

'Firearms, Andy Hailwood speaking.'

'Hi Andy, it's Dave Gough at the force intelligence office.'

I have known Dave for quite a while. He was a capable detective sergeant.

'What can I do for you, Dave?'

'I think we may have a job for your lads. I'll make my way to your office and brief you.'

Parker sauntered from downstairs into the office. I told him what was happening and waited for Dave to arrive. Dave and his partner wandered into our office and over a brew informed us that Anthony Hughes had been located in Didsbury. They had good intelligence that Hughes had shacked up with his gay lover in a bedsit. The Force Intelligence Unit was trying to establish OPs on the premises. Dave suggested that a joint recce would be appropriate. Obviously, once Hughes was housed, VO8 would arrest him. Like I said, Dave is an astute policeman and a recce together made sense.

Dave and I drove over to Didsbury and reccied the premises. It was a Victorian stone semi-detached property broken down into bedsits. Hughes's was on level two and accessed by a metal fire escape. The property was surrounded by a small courtyard area fenced in by a stone wall, with open access for vehicles.

As we walked past, I cheekily asked Dave where he was getting his intelligence from. He would either tell me to fuck off and mind my own business (nothing wrong with that – he was protecting his source) or reveal his cards. Dave surprisingly told me it was Hughes's lover. I took advantage of this and asked if Dave could get hold of a key for the premises. He didn't think this would be a problem and also said we would know when Hughes was housed because his motorcycle would be by the fire escape.

All this information was excellent. I could now put a plan together for the OPs team. My intention was to return to Bootle Street, sketch out the target property and points of entry, establish an RVP for the team and inform them that the intelligence unit was trying to procure a key for them and also, once their OPs were established, they would be able to confirm his presence by the position of his motorcycle and intelligence from his boyfriend.

I returned to Bootle Street confident that in the next day or so Hughes would be in custody. I walked into the crew room and was confronted by Keith, the OPs team sergeant, and Parker. Keith let on.

'Hi Andy, give us the plan.'

I looked at Keith confused. 'I have got the plan but the FIU are still firming it up,' I said.

It was Keith's turn to be confused. 'What do you mean?'

'We have the premises but he isn't housed yet, and why are you here?'

'I have been turned out by the senior detective in charge of the enquiry – we are going to bump the place later.'

'Fuckin' hell Keith, he isn't housed, there's no point,' I angrily replied.

'For fuck's sake Andy, I've no choice, the detective superintendent has ordered it.'

All three of us knew this was wrong. The FIU were working hard to house Hughes. Once he was housed then that was the time to go for him.

'Ring the fucker,' I snapped at Keith. 'Let him know it would be a waste of time.'

'And that he is going against tactical advice,' added Parker.

Keith is a private man and made his way to a phone out of hearing. Within minutes he returned looking downcast.

'He has ordered me to bump the address.'

I was livid. This would be a pointless exercise. I couldn't see any logic in us entering the address until Hughes was housed. It was just a waste of time and resources – and piss-poor policing. However, Keith had his orders and there was nothing we could do. I sketched out the premises and left Keith with all the relevant information. The OPs team would be parading at 03.30 for a

04.00 briefing. I wouldn't be back on duty until 14.00 on September 13.

At 14.00 the following day I was back and immediately consulted my colleagues on the 06.00–14.00 shift.

'How did Keith's job go on?'

'No result,' said Vinny. 'The fucker wasn't there.'

Surprise, surprise. For a couple of seconds I mentally questioned the superintendent's decision but my shift finished at 22.00 and we were replaced by the night team.

In the early hours of September 14, 1989, Inspector Ray Codling and Sergeant Jim Bowden from the P Division, Rochdale, received a radio message that the cashier of the petrol station at Birch Motorway Services on the M62 had contacted the police regarding a male acting in suspicious circumstances. Could an officer attend? Inspector Codling and Sergeant Bowden acknowledged the transmission and confirmed they would attend the scene.

Both officers made their way to the petrol station and then decided to search the area. At some stage they disturbed a man – one Anthony Hughes – trying to hide in a nearby grass verge. Without warning or provocation, Hughes indiscriminately opened fire on both officers.

Inspector Codling was killed. Sergeant Bowden was badly wounded. Hughes then fled, heading north towards Yorkshire.

A full-scale major crime incident procedure was immediately implemented. The firearms advice and OPs teams were turned out but Hughes had fled the force area.

Some hours later, Hughes was contained by a Yorkshire firearms team and he did the decent thing by shooting himself dead. His gun proved to be the weapon that killed Inspector Codling and wounded Sergeant Bowden and that had been discharged on the upstairs of the bus. It was the 9mm Tangfolio SLP that was stolen from Diggle Range. Intelligence from Hughes' boyfriend suggested that Hughes buried the SLP in his back garden before his initial arrest and recovered it once he was released from prison.

I am not a senior officer and at times not privy to the information they have available. However, I will always question the senior officer's decision to force Keith and his team to enter the property in Didsbury. I believe that decision was ill thought out and hasty. It put Hughes, a character of limited qualities, into a panic. It is believed that Hughes was at the petrol station to commit a robbery in an effort to fund an escape from Manchester to Cornwall.

Some years later I was informed that the detective superintendent took early retirement.

CHAPTER SIXTEEN

Moss Side Infiltrator

In the late 1980s and early 1990s, Greater Manchester's VO8 unit typically dealt with armed robbers. To a lesser extent the department dealt with 'domestics' when firearms had been produced, and anti-terrorist incidents. Times, however, were changing, and Manchester was on the cusp of an era of crime more shocking and violent than anything before. In particular, armed crime, gang-related murder and drug-dealing escalated in the Moss Side area of the city.

Moss Side had been pretty much left alone since the 1981 riots. Although Manchester didn't have no-go areas, this division was treated delicately. When I was on TAG we had clear instructions to stay away from the Moss in our dark blue vans and under no circumstances to activate our sirens if we had to go in. Moss Side appeared to be treated with kid gloves by the senior command. In my eyes, and perhaps with a touch of hindsight, this was a major mistake.

Don't get me wrong, the officers who worked the division were excellent and under trying circumstances produced fantastic results. But many of the people who lived in the area were mis-serviced by the authorities. I speak from experience: I worked in a plainclothes robbery team in Moss Side while on TAG and over the years entered the area on many occasions to arrest offenders. I spoke to many people who lived there, and most welcomed the intervention of the police.

During the economic climate of the late 1950s and early

1960s, Moss Side, along with various other inner-city areas such as Handsworth in Birmingham, St Paul's in Bristol and Brixton in London, saw an influx of West Indian immigrants. It might seem a cliché but many of these people were God-fearing and law-abiding – that was how they had been in the Caribbean. They were often housed in old terraced slums, but gradually these were demolished, to be replaced by 1960s and 70s developments such as the Alexandra Park Estate.

Most of the families housed there were hard-working but many produced offspring who were perhaps not similarly minded. Some of the second and third generations decided that perhaps there was an easier way of earning a living. It could be dishonest, but it could prove to be profitable, and a new era of drug supply started. If GMP had listened to officers in the late 1970s, they may have seen the writing on the wall.

A task force of officers was gathered and assigned to work in the Hulme, Moss Side and Rusholme areas. Their duties were to stop vehicles between the hours of 18.00 and 04.00 and question occupants in relation to the Yorkshire Ripper enquiry. Peter Sutcliffe – at that time unknown and undetected – had attacked a victim in Manchester. One of the spin-offs from this enquiry was information received about people travelling from other cities to buy drugs in Moss Side. In those days it was mainly cannabis, but 'powders' were on the increase. If this intelligence had been acted upon, history might have been different.

Moss Side sadly became synonymous with drugs and gangs. The powder of the day was heroin, an addictive substance craved by many. Its suppliers quickly realised the extent of profit available to them and small, structured gangs started to appear to sell the drug.

There are many theories on how the notorious Moss Side gangs developed, even research from universities. Perhaps a commonsense explanation is simply territorial boundaries. To study the area, visualise its geographical position. Locals talk of new Moss Side and old Moss Side, divided by the A5103 Princess Road, which runs south from the city centre. The east divide, old Moss Side, which had such landmarks as the Harp Lager Brewery and the Nile and Reno clubs, now long gone, is predominantly terraced properties with streets running west to east, such as Great Western Street, Claremont Road and Platt Lane. New Moss Side, built in the early 70s, is bordered by a park known as Alexandra Park, hence the Alexandra Park Estate. It has more modern properties and is a warren of roads and streets, including Quinney Crescent, Pepperhill Close and Doddington Close.

The Alex Estate is itself divided by Alexandra Road, another major arterial road running north to south. The area east of Alexandra Road, serviced by a club known as the Pepperhill, became the Pepperhill Boys' territory. The area west of Alexandra Road became the Gooch Close Gang's territory. Simply, if you were born or lived in one of those areas, you became affiliated to that zone. The Pepperhill Boys, who would later become the Doddington Gang, controlled the drugs supply and distribution within their area. Likewise the Gooch. The Gooch also had affiliations to an up-and-coming gang from the Cheetham Hill area of Manchester, due to blood ties: one of their leaders was the cousin of a top Cheetham Hill member.

The gangs started to bring in heroin from London, Liverpool and Birmingham. Manchester soon became infamous as the drug capital of the country. To control the ever-increasing demand and the high profits, command structures developed between the gangs, and certain key figures emerged. For example, the Doddington ranks included Ian McLeod, Delroy Brown and Winston Brownlow. For the next five years, these and other characters would become a familiar part of VO8's operational commitments, until many were arrested for serious crimes or killed by each other. Yet they represented only a small part of the manpower available to the gangs.

Inevitably, feuding started. Although these characters sometimes went to the same schools, they were affiliated by territorial
boundaries. The feuding increased in hostility after Delroy
Brown's girlfriend was messed around with by a Gooch member.
Brown was an up-and-coming Pepperhill boy, later to command
its offshoot, the Doddington Gang. In his own words, his
girlfriend was 'violated'. What this means is hard to guess, but it
led to an increase of hostilities.

At this stage in the development of the gangs, the police started
to take interest. However, they were limited in the way of
resources. The division had to allocate its own manpower in the
form of an operational support unit and a plainclothes department, tasked to collate active intelligence. One officer, who I will
refer to as Delta (the reason for this will become clear), had a
gift for targeting the gangs, in particular the head men. Delta is
one of my closest friends and a truly skilled detective. He can
only be described as tenacious once he decides to investigate a
criminal. He is highly intelligent and resourceful and has
inherited a gift for policing, perhaps from his father who policed
Moss Side in the mid to late 1960s. Although young, Delta had
no hesitancy in targeting the gang members. He made it his
business to know them and in turn be recognised by them. There
was a method to this type of policing. Delta believed that by
actively stopping and talking to gangsters, he might be able to
turn one of them into an informant.

It paid off. In early 1990 Delta, after receiving informant-
based information, raided a house behind Pepperhill Close, Moss
Side. He forced an entry and arrested a Jamaican yardie for the
possession of 12 ounces of crack cocaine. The yardie, a known
gangster who spoke in patois, was in the process of converting
cocaine into crack. This was a startling discovery, as until that
time Manchester had not seen crack on its streets.

In 1990 a kilo of cocaine was worth £30,000. There are 28.3
grams to the ounce and 15–16 ounces to the kilo. It doesn't take

a mathematical wizard to work out how much this find was worth. It also created a major problem for the command structure of GMP. The dilemma was to either reveal the find or keep it secret. In the end they decided to inform the *Manchester Evening News* and Piccadilly Radio of Manchester's latest drugs trend.

Delta would become a serious threat and deterrent to the gangs. By the 1990s, he was running two of GMP's major informants in the Gooch and Doddington hierarchy.

The majority of VO8's operational work sprang from intelligence from the CID or Squads. One of the best sources of intelligence comes from informants. The rules of running informants have drastically changed, but in the late 80s and early 90s they were an excellent way of gaining up-to-date and regular intelligence. Informants can have many reasons to pass on information: money, revenge, excitement, manipulation or self-preservation. I know that some of Manchester's major criminals were paid informants and so-called honour among thieves is absolute bollocks. The majority of 'hard men' I have come across would sell their own mothers down the road if it assisted them in their pursuit of self-centred activities.

By 1990, with the division's manpower stretched to its limit, Operation Takeover commenced. It was preceded by Operation Vixen, a task force of officers, including Delta, dedicated to investigating serious gang crime, including drugs and firearms. By the late 1980s two of the Doddington Gang's head men, Maurice McPherson and Ian McIntosh, had been arrested at Piccadilly Railway Station by VO8 for possession with the intent to supply. They had a large amount of heroin on them, which they had brought by train from London. This weakened the Doddington – and the Gooch Gang were aware of it.

A dangerous young Gooch Close member, who I shall call 'Psycho', shot Darren Samuels dead in Blackburn Bakery in Moss Side Precinct. Samuels was the best friend of Winston Brownlow, a Doddington dangerman.

With McIntosh and McPherson in prison, Brownlow and Delroy Brown now proceeded to head the Pepperhill/Doddington Gang. Over the next few months, Moss Side became a fury of firearms-related crimes. The Doddington's main shooter wanted revenge for the murder of Samuels and hunted Psycho. His weaponry included a sub-machine gun, which was used to spray a Spar off-licence in the hope of hitting Gooch Close members. But as the feud hotted up, it began to concern Delroy Brown, the de facto leader of the Doddington.

The Operation Vixen team was busy trying to investigate and prevent these shootings. Delta had attained two key informants, both highly placed in the Gooch and Doddington, feeding him up-to-date intelligence. It was particularly important that the main Doddington shooter was arrested, as he was becoming extremely reckless and it wouldn't be long before his actions would result in needless deaths. An unprecedented step by GMP's senior command was taken and the *Manchester Evening News* was approached. In the following day's edition, the man was identified as being wanted and highly dangerous.

Delta was approached by his main informant within the Doddington Gang: none other than Delroy Brown. He would give Delta information on the shooter's current residence. Brown had become Delta's informant over a period of time, and during these periods he had ascended the ranks of the Doddington and eventually assumed leadership. It was in Brown's interest to have the shooter arrested, as he was becoming a threat to his command and the cause of increased police activity in Moss Side, disturbing the smooth distribution of drugs.

★　★　★

It was January 1991, and the middle of a freezing and miserable night, when my team turned out to Platt Lane Police Station. The time was 03.30 and Delta briefed us as we sat around a quiet and undisturbed police canteen. He wasn't going to release his source of information but he was informing 14 of us, all fully kitted-up in dark blue overalls, heavyweight body armour, ballistic helmets by our sides, the majority armed with 9 mm Beretta SLPs and H&K MP5s with a full complement of ammunition (60 rounds), siege shields and door-opening kit placed on the canteen floor.

'At present our target is housed in a third floor flat on Barlow Moor Road, West Didsbury. As you are all aware he has been responsible for several shootings in the Moss recently. It is believed he is shacked up with his latest girlfriend and in possession of a sub-machine gun.'

Delta, in his practical and articulate way delivered the following message. 'I have the authority to turn you out. I know you will require a recce of the premises but this is an ideal opportunity to arrest. I am in possession of the relevant warrants. Any questions?'

'Is the place under observation?' asked Foz.

'Yes, front and back and there is no sign of movement but my source says he's definitely there.'

This was good enough for me. Delta was one of those rare officers whose source of information was generally bang-on.

Dino instructed two of the team to get down to the property and commence a quick recce. Two of the lads set off with two of the Operation Vixen team, which had also started to gather. Dino gave a quick IA briefing. We already had the intelligence, and if the recce team stated that the POE for the property could be quickly accessed – then we would quick-entry the place. Deployment duties were given and we got into the vans bound for West Didsbury.

The recce team met us at the designated RVP. By now a senior officer for the division had been dragged out of bed and informed of the operation taking place on his patch. He went to the RVP with other uniform call signs. At the RVP we met up with the recce team who efficiently briefed us.

'The target property is on the third floor of a set of flats in an old Edwardian detached house. Access is gained by a communal door. The door is knackered so we have clear access to the target's flat.'

'What's the target's door like?' enquired Joe.

'Wooden, piece of piss.'

'OK, get ready to make the FUP,' whispered Dino.

We got back into the vans and drove over half a mile to the FUP as per standard operating procedures. We silently debussed with the recce team taking up the scout positions with MP5s, shoulder mounted, indicating our direction of travel. It was bitterly cold with a clear sky and excellent natural lighting from the stars. Frost had started to appear on the pavement and surrounding street furniture. Sound travels in an environment like this so the team were moving in a deliberate and stealthy manner.

As soon as everyone was kneeling, we set off towards the target premises. I was number one on the entry team, and after the door had been smashed down I would be the first officer into the bedsit. Because we didn't have internal plans, I would have to quickly assess the interior and make my way to the sleeping area. At this time of day I would expect the suspect to be asleep, however, he was a creature of the night and a known drug dealer – his sleeping pattern would be all over the place. I also had to consider whether he was a user of his own illegal substances, making his behaviour pattern again contrary to the norm.

The recce team placed us on the target property and without a sound moved off to take positions of cover. I entered the communal door and went into the foyer. I indicated all clear and the rest of the team silently filtered in. To our right I spotted a set of stairs and moved towards them. As I moved my number two, Murf, was covering me.

I had known Murf since I was 17 and played rugby with him for the force league team. We had crossed paths through our careers but it wasn't until he came to firearms that I got to know him. He is one of the most capable and confident firearms officers I have come across. His skills were really untapped and for the time he was on firearms, I couldn't have had a better partner or friend. Unfortunately, some idiot during a training exercise discharged a blank round by the side of his face, rupturing his eardrum. This led to his loss of operational status – but assists somewhat when it's his turn to get the drinks in.

Silently we started to ascend the stairs covering and moving. I insisted all my team's kit was fully prepped, all loose items of equipment and clothing were covered in black tape. We couldn't afford the D-ring of an MP5 sling slapping into the magazine and the metallic noise compromising the whole operation. We were paid to be professional and I expected us to act like it. Sloppy kit wasn't acceptable and anyone found ill-prepared was fined a round of Stella Artois. We made our way on to the third floor. In front of us were two doors, obviously entrances to individual bedsits.

Delta had informed us the target premises had a shitty-brown coloured door. No mistaking it. Our eight-man team was now at our FAP. Joe and Foz, carrying the double-man wham ram, checked the POE and then with a nod from me, he smashed the wham into the door. Crash! On the second blow the door was in. I could hear Dino shouting, 'Strike! Strike! Strike!' over the air.

I moved into the premises in double time, not sprinting but not walking either. My body position would have reduced by three inches, the MP5 into my right shoulder and my left hand activating the 'surefire' torch mounted on the fore end of the weapon. I could see clearly ahead a living room; the TV was still on and casting shadows across the walls. To the left was a bathroom with an open door and to the right a closed door which appeared to lead into a bedroom. I now had to make a decision. Carry on to the living room or turn right and assault the bedroom. Murf is directly behind me and will follow wherever I go. Experience tells me to go through the tight corridor and into the living room. If I go for the bedroom maybe the door is obstructed – either bolted or a loose carpet rucks up and hinders its motion – I then have six of my team behind me with nowhere to go. Worst case scenario, if the target decides to retaliate, we are effectively stuck in a killing zone.

Without hesitation I moved aggressively through the small corridor and into the bedsit. I shouted 'Armed police!' and could hear the others shouting the same. I stepped into a poorly furnished shithole. Murf moved to the left. I was first into the room, therefore more dominant. I went firm and shouted 'Close!' I covered Murf as he searched towards the settee, we both clocked two people, one male, one female, huddled together under a dirty blanket on the settee. Murf tactically moved toward them and ripped away the blanket. He had to ensure we could see their hands. It looked like we had our target, a young man of skinny build, about 5ft 7ins tall, with close-cropped hair. He had a natural arrogance but was clearly shitting himself.

'Keep still,' instructed Murf.

The girl was close to tears and was trying to adopt a foetal position. I shouted 'Support!' and Foz and Joe moved into the room and without being told they handcuffed both occupants.

'Room clear! Room clear!' came the shouts from the team.

'Room clear!' I shouted back.

The bedsit was safe. Delta was summonsed over the radio. He entered the flat, positively identified the target and arrested him for attempted murder.

Later that morning, after a debrief, Delta contacted me and asked me to thank the lads for a job well done, but he was a little dismayed that a subsequent search of the flat didn't reveal a firearm.

* * *

Over the following months, I would meet with Delta many times. I went into Moss Side with him and his partner, usually engaged on recces and intelligence gathering operations. His knowledge of the area was formidable and his tentacles of intelligence impressive. On several occasions I saw local prostitutes approach him and divulge important information.

Although Delta and his colleagues were making progress, it was limited, and drug-related crimes were massively on the increase. At this period in GMP's history, an average of 90 reported firearms incidents – from reports of gunshots to actual murders – were the monthly crime figures for the force. In response, GMP formed the Major Armed Crime Unit (VO15). The unit was to be headed by a DCI and DI with two DSs and ten DCs. Its primary function was to proactively investigate major gangs within the force. Delta was transferred to this unit.

Over a period, with the assistance of his informants, Delta was responsible for recovering crossbows, Skorpion sub-machine guns, SLPs, six shotguns and parts of a Kalashnikov AK47 assault rifle, along with large quantities of ammunition and drugs. The majority of these weapons had been used in violent crimes. Delta was becoming a major thorn in the side of the gangs and his two main informants were working at considerable risk towards themselves.

Over the years, Delroy Brown would feed critical intelligence to Delta. At times it suited his agenda and allowed him to operate with an amount of clemency. Delta had to understand him and manipulate him and his intelligence to suit the requirements of whatever investigation Delta and his team were currently working on. Although Brown was a criminal, it was hard not to admire his tenacity and bravery.

On several occasions Brown was shot and wounded. He was once stabbed, and possibly even raped, by a leader of the

Cheetham Hill Gang. They surprised Brown in the PSV, commonly known as the Russell Club, in Hulme. He was held at gunpoint and buggered and his throat was slashed. Bleeding profusely, he managed to escape, grabbing a towel on his way out, which he used to bandage his wound. Brown then drove to hospital in Birmingham, fearing reprisals if he showed up at a Manchester hospital. This goes some way to show Brown's determination and resilience.

Within 12 months, the Doddington gunman we had arrested in the flat was free. The criminal proceedings against him had failed due to witness intimidation and the climate of fear that surrounded the Moss Side gangs. He soon took up where he had left off and before long had the Gooch Close Gang actively seeking retribution. In January 1993, in perhaps one of Manchester's most infamous murders, 14-year-old Benji Stanley, clad in a bubble coat and bandana, was brutally shotgunned to death at a fast food premises on Great Western Street, Moss Side. It is known that members of the Cheetham Hill Gang committed this atrocity on behalf of their 'brothers-in-arms', the Gooch. It was a tragic case of mistaken identity: their intended target was the Doddington gunman.

During 1992, VO8 increased again in strength and dropped the ad hoc system of armed response vehicles. The training team split from CID and went under the umbrella of the U Department (Training). They were therefore no longer part of our manpower. The majority of them were anyway out of touch regarding operational duties. VO8 was growing in experience, and the criminal climate of Manchester was changing drastically due to the increase of the drug trade. The only operational responsibility they retained was to supply an independent tactical adviser to senior command. The majority of the tactical advisers let the experienced VO8 lads plan and run the operation and, as long as the plan was safe, endorsed it. However, all good things come to an end and certain sergeants started to impose their amateur knowledge and inexperience onto operational planning. This created a general bad feeling among the two departments and the rift continues to this day.

UT9 (training department) tried to take over the training of the operational teams. Apart from classification shoots, VO8 resisted this and for years continued to train within the department. In my opinion, this was the right course of action, apart from several exceptions. UT9 personnel were often limited – either too old or inexperienced or rubbish. However, VO8 would fight a losing battle and eventually handed over the operational training to UT9.

VO8 increased to four teams of ten police constables and one sergeant. The teams covered the force over a 24-hour period with two response vehicles. Both were three-litre Range Rovers, and they also had an equipment vehicle and personnel carrier. The team had transport enough to escort them anywhere in the force. Instead of independent armed response vehicles running separately, the team now had two high-powered vehicles which, in theory, could get eight men quickly to any incident in the force. The teams were now self-contained and available for immediate deployment. This was possibly the best system I worked under. The teams had all the resources at hand to become competent in all tactics. There was no excuse not to physically and operationally train, they were not required by police divisions, they were the force's immediate response to any firearms incident within GMP. All they lacked was a hostage rescue capability.

Morale soared as the department recruited some skilled and professional officers from TAG and divisions. However, this system had one disadvantage: because the department was now 50 strong, officers didn't experience the same amount of jobs as I had in my initial years within the department. On average, I would say that I would be engaged on three operations a week, with at least one turnout from home. At times in the early stages of the Moss Side wars, Murf and I found ourselves turned out at least six times in one day. Because of the sheer volume of operations, an officer could not help but become experienced. As the department grew, officers obviously didn't attend the same amount of operations. The increase in manpower spread operations over a wider range within the department, therefore depleting experiential gains.

* * *

It was a Sunday morning and I was driving an unmarked Range Rover with Bert as my passenger. Bert had joined us from the TAG. He was a decent lad but possessed a strange thought process. We were screaming through the city centre towards Moss Side. Bert had picked up a phone call from the force control room and they had told us to monitor Channel 4 on the CK radio system (force coverage) for Moss Side and Hulme. Divisional officers were chasing a black adult male along Stretford Road from John Nash Crescent, one of the huge, semi-circular blocks of flats in Hulme. The man was holding officers off by pointing what appeared to be a handgun. He was also believed to have an 18-inch bayonet and had stabbed a man in the chest.

The sirens were activated and the emergency blue lights were flickering, causing the surrounding buildings to reflect the light in circular patterns across the brickwork. We had both been training in the gym and were dressed in shorts. The Range Rover, as per our team duties, had been loaded with our weapons and operational kit prior to training.

Bert was monitoring the radio and shouting above the noise of the sirens the latest developments on the chase. It appeared the man was running towards the heart of the Moss. I drove as fast as possible, negotiating the minimal Sunday morning traffic.

The sun was shining through the windscreen as I screwed up my eyes and looked ahead, conscious of traffic pulling out. The day was going to be another swelterer. My stomach churned as I tried to remain calm. I wanted to floor the accelerator to get there quicker and assist the divisional officers. Bert shouted, 'He's heading towards the precinct!' I accelerated along Princess Road towards Moss Lane West.

I turned into Moss Lane as Bert took out our Beretta SLPs from an internal safe in the vehicle. He placed the magazines into the grips of the weapons and racked both top slides, chambering a round in each weapon, and shouted, 'One in the spout.' I looked ahead and saw a convoy of divisional vehicles heading towards us. Between our vehicles and the divisional convoy were two people on foot and running. One was a black male, the other a uniformed police officer, obviously chasing. The gantry, which was part of the shopping precinct, was above us as I braked sharply. The black male cut left towards the precinct and the gantry's stairway. Bert passed me my Beretta and I jumped out. A couple of section officers were shouting that the suspect was armed with a pistol.

As I ran towards the stairs, I could see the white shirt of a police inspector disappear up the stairs. I was yards away and screaming at him to back off. He either chose to ignore me or couldn't hear me due to the excitement of the chase. I hit the first step, sprinting and covering with my arms extended in a semi-weaver shooting position, the Beretta held in a two-hand supported grip. Bert was behind me but not so close that we made a big target. I was still screaming at the departing inspector to back off. I needed him out of the way and safe. It was mine and Bert's job to deal with an armed man and the inspector knew this.

As I sprinted up the stairs covering my arcs of fire, I was thinking, I wish this inspector would fuck off. I arrived at the top of the stairs and stepped to my left to allow Bert room to gather on the gantry platform. I immediately took in the situation. I could see a black male, approximately 25 to 30 years of age, 6ft tall, well-built, shaven head. In his right hand was a .45 Colt SLP. Directly in front of him – and blocking my line of fire – was the inspector, who was literally pawing at the fucker with the weapon. The black male, who I later found out to be a gang associate called Jordan, raised the pistol from the hip. I started to take up the pressure on the trigger of the SLP. My thoughts were clear and concise, I intended to grab the shirt of the inspector and fling him away and at the same time shoot Jordan. Incredibly, the inspector again started to paw Jordan and virtually smothered him, preventing a clear shot.

Both Bert and I were shouting 'Armed police!' I was absolutely livid with the inspector. Fair enough if he decided to attack Jordan, then knock his head off in accordance with Section 3 of the Criminal Law Act 1967 (self-defence), but don't start pawing him as if he was a delicate piece of tissue. I grabbed the inspector and so did Bert and we flung him down the gantry. We had both been compromised.

As the inspector sailed down the gantry platform, we stepped towards Jordan. I would have no hesitation in pulling the trigger. Quick as a flash, he threw his weapon in the air. We had no option now but to kick him to the ground. Even at this stage the troublesome inspector returned, trying to get hold of Jordan and put him in some stupid WWF move, screaming at him that he was under arrest. Between Bert and me we handcuffed Jordan and handed him over to the inspector.

We recovered the Colt and made it safe. Throughout the chase Jordan must have depressed the magazine release catch and lost the magazine. When I made the weapon safe it was minus the magazine but had one round in the chamber. Jordan wasn't knowledgeable enough to load a weapon in this manner and a full TAG search was activated to find the magazine. Unfortunately neither the magazine nor the bayonet were recovered, but this didn't surprise me due to the area we were in and the climate of the time.

As Bert and I drove back to Bootle Street, we discussed the inspector's actions. We couldn't work out whether he was brave or stupid. I have made my decision and I will leave it to you to make yours.

Some months later Bert and I had to appear at Manchester Crown Court for the case. Jordan had pleaded not guilty to the stabbing and also the firearm-related offences. The assault victim decided to retract his evidence and failed to appear in court. It was believed he had been the victim of a 'taxing' (demanding money with menaces) and it was in his best interest to forget about the incident. The judge instructed that the case be withdrawn due to jury intimidation. Jordan and his cronies had somehow got to the jury and scared them enough to report it to the clerk of the court who, in turn, informed the judge.

Months later Bert and I found ourselves at Carlisle Crown Court, where the case had been sent to be re-tried. Neither of us gave evidence, but the jury delivered a verdict of not guilty. They believed an 'angelic' Jordan's defence. He stated he had found the firearm and was running towards Moss Side Police Station to hand it in when he was pounced upon by the police. The stabbing was inadmissible. At times you question the judicial system although on the whole I believe it is a decent system.

* * *

In the summer of 1993, Delta received frightening intelligence. The Gooch Gang were becoming more confident in their activities and were regularly moving between Leeds and Manchester in vehicle convoys. It was believed that the vehicles contained firearms. Delta had been told that they were preparing to make a show of strength. At the weekend the whole gang would drive from Leeds between the hours of 20.00 and 22.00.

They would attend a shebeen/blues club at Portman Close, Moss Side, and when a certain rap song was played the gang would discharge their arsenal of guns into the air.

If this intelligence was correct – and it came from Delta's main Gooch informant – then this would be an opportune time to arrest Gooch members for possession of firearms. I was summonsed to the VO15 office and asked to put together an operational order and plan for arresting the Gooch. This wasn't the first time – and wouldn't be the last – that I had planned an operation of this nature. I was and still am confident that a plan of this scale can be implemented. However, you need a senior officer with balls of steel to authorise it. Fortunately in those days GMP retained a smattering of CID officers who would give that type of authorisation.

I spent days with Delta planning for an ambush and arrest on the whole Gooch Gang. Once it was finalised we had to present it to the division's chief superintendent, Andy Glaister. Mr Glaister was a good boss and many times authorised my operations. Unfortunately on this occasion he decided to refuse. I harbour no grudges at all with this decision. Instead he told me to plan for a full operational firearms deployment from Friday to Sunday. He was going to deploy his full divisional resources into the area and wanted the appropriate protection for his officers. His intention was to 'hard police' the gangs, targeting them, stopping them, searching them and if possible arresting them. He wanted the public to see a high visual presence of armed and unarmed officers.

A statement as bold as this had never been undertaken in the history of Greater Manchester Police. Not so long before they had been frightened of the public seeing officers carrying firearms! I think Mr Glaister was sick and tired of the gangs and the abject misery they brought to decent people in Moss Side. Also Mr Glaister wasn't far from retirement and perhaps he didn't give a fuck who he upset.

Over that weekend period, VO8 turned out 30 operational officers, in full turnout kit. I broke them down into six- or four-men mobile units, with the simple task of supporting either divisional or VO15 officers who had spotted a known gang member and requested a vehicle stop.

The operation was a huge success in the sense of morale for the divisional officers. They could stop and question known gang members, knowing they had immediate armed back-up. What surprised me was the response from members of the public who came up to us while we were ensconced in armoured Land Rovers and Range Rovers and said it was about time the police took this sort of action. This came not just from the old but the young as well.

My team worked alongside Delta and were quickly stopping and dealing with Gooch members. We didn't fuck about with them and they weren't treated with kid gloves. We needed to make our own statement. Many of them would talk with us and accept the operation for what it was, others would work themselves up in to uncontrollable tempers, ranting and raving about how they would kill us or rape a policewoman. One jug-eared twat almost had a hernia and because he had unwittingly made us laugh so much he prevented himself from being arrested.

Over the weekend the division was buzzing, and the uniformed officers really got stuck in, questioning and arresting gang members. For once a real 'feelgood' factor appeared among the personnel. But, as usual, one senior officer decided that we were treating these unconvicted murderers and drug dealers too harshly. He had witnessed my team extract several Gooch members from a property. While questioning, we pointed our MP5s at them and lit them up with the surefire lights, causing them to blink severely and starring their vision for several minutes, a bit like when you stare at a lightbulb. He thought this was too aggressive and asked to see us at Longsight Police

Station. He instructed us to stop shining our torches at the Gooch. We all nodded as one, returned to the streets and took not a blind bit of notice of him. He's now an assistant chief constable.

Delta asked us to pull a known Doddington member, known to us as Lardy. He was shuffling along Claremont Road towards Princess Road wearing the usual bubble coat and curfew cap. His hands were in his pockets and his head was bent. Lardy was known to have possession of a sub-machine pistol. He was cute enough not to carry it, but made a young member of his gang carry it – one under the age of criminal responsibility.

Whenever we arrested a gang member, such as by a foot strike, I would always plan for a perimeter protection covering any of his associates, in particular the youngsters. This was thought by some members of VO8 and the firearms training wing to be extreme and gung ho. To me it made perfect sense. I listened to the intelligence Delta gave me and acted upon it. I didn't sit in an ivory tower and pontificate from the secure environment of a heated police station.

We pulled up alongside Lardy, who was alone. He snarled at us with disdain. He was spoken to and told to take off his coat while one of the lads covered him. Underneath his coat was lightweight body armour. I noticed that he had several indentations in the armour and told him to take it off. His upper torso was a mass of bruises. When I inspected the armour, I found several spent bullets stuck in the Kevlar. He had obviously been shot at, recently. He wouldn't say jack shit, and who could blame him? We gave him his body armour back and let him go on his way. Although we had reasonable intelligence, we really didn't know half of what was happening. The operation ran until Sunday and we were hoping it was going to run again on an irregular basis, but for reasons best known to high command it was never repeated.

During this period Delta was trying to track down an Ingram

Mac 10 sub-machine gun, a weapon that had appeared on the streets of Moss Side. It is small and concealable and fires .45 calibre rounds at a cyclic rate of 1,200 rounds a minute. It was developed for American special forces as an anti-ambush weapon, creating a tremendous field of fire. It isn't an accurate weapon but it is fearsome. The SAS used it for a while. The gangs were trying to get more of these guns; they gave great kudos, and were almost a fashion statement. They had several sources of supply: burglaries, smuggled products from former Eastern Bloc countries, deactivated weapons which could be legally bought and illegally reactivated by people with engineering knowledge and sold on the black market. DW, a prominent Gooch nutcase, was believed to be in possession of one. It had been used in an attempted murder at the Leeds carnival in Chapeltown and several serious incidents in Manchester.

Delta received information that DW and the weapon would be at Westerling Walk in the Moss. On an exceptionally cold morning in March of 1994, my team entered the property at 04.30. The door of the council maisonette had been reinforced but it didn't present a problem to the MOE team. Within 40 seconds the property was secured and a female occupant arrested. A quick search of the property revealed the Mac 10, ammunition and nine ounces of 83 per cent pure heroin, concealed in the airing cupboard. Unfortunately DW was not there. The evidence was seized and within days forensics had discovered DW's fingerprints all over it. This put him to flight and he went to London. It wasn't long before Delta and the Metropolitan Police's SO19 (the equivalent of Manchester's VO8) arrested him in a squat in a suburb.

Delta was no longer a thorn, he was more like a branch in the side of the Gooch, and from his prison cell DW, along with the young gunman Psycho, conspired to kill Delta. They hatched a plot to lure him to a disused property in Yarburgh Street near to the Alex Park Estate. Psycho would be waiting with a revolver, would kill Delta and would send the revolver back to a source in London. Psycho's clothes would be burnt and Delta's body left in the disused property. The method they would employ was simple. Delta made sure his paging unit's number was readily available to the criminal fraternity in case any of them decided to inform. Psycho would input a public phone box number to it. Delta would ring the number and Psycho's disguised voice would inform Delta that he would find a large amount of ammunition in a disused property on Yarburgh Street. This wasn't unusual for Delta – he had received similar information on many occasions, resulting in many successful recoveries of drugs or firearms. He would try to locate the ammunition quickly and generally go alone to the location, hence the trap would be set.

Fortunately for Delta, before the plan took fruition his highly placed source among the Gooch told him of the plot. Delta immediately contacted me and requested that I meet him and his DCI at the VO15 office as soon as possible. The DCI wanted to know whether I could look after Delta and the practicalities. I said we could run an overt and covert protection operation on Delta. I also informed him that I could plan to turn the tables on Psycho and arrest him once he had activated his plan. The DCI appeared to like these options and informed the senior command of Delta's predicament.

And that was when disaster struck.

I can honestly say I felt for Delta and the lack of support he was given. He was without doubt the most successful detective to ever infiltrate the gangs of Moss Side and Cheetham Hill. His results were outstanding and his informants' identities were known to certain high-ranking officers, who financed them – informants were often paid for their information. The higher-ups, however, decided to pull Delta out of Moss Side and ordered him not to set foot in the district. He was informed that a Home Office alarm would be fitted to his house and that he wasn't to worry. The decision not only compromised his informant, but also allowed the Gooch's plan to work: unwittingly, and without firing a shot, they had hamstrung Delta – he had become ineffective.

Delta is a proactive and lively individual and this was a massive blow to his morale. He had a right to expect more from GMP. His informant was also telling him that the threat to his life hadn't gone away but was growing. The Gooch knew something had happened because Delta's activity within the Moss had decreased. The command decided to relocate him and moved his family out of the area. Imagine the impact on his family. The threat hadn't been eliminated but in a sense Delta had. He was intensely frustrated. With the correct policing methods, Psycho could have been arrested and the real threat taken away.

Though he and his family were relocated, he wasn't given any protection in the way of an armed presence or response. Eventually his family had no option but to return to their home address and live under a cloak of fear and suspicion. Delta made a brave decision. He decided to arm himself with a family heirloom, an old pistol. He knew it was against the law but he had now become the hunted and had no option but to protect his family, who were desperate and extremely vulnerable.

His family life started to deteriorate due to the pressure of living under constant threat. Somehow certain police officers found out that he was in possession of a firearm and he was arrested. It was shameful, shabby behaviour towards a colleague. Within hours the *Manchester Evening News* had heard of this and quite sympathetically printed a headline story. Delta was suspended and, to his credit, didn't 'go sick'. For a long period he anxiously waited while the Director of Public Prosecutions studied his case.

Fortunately, the DPP saw sense and recommended 'no action'. It wasn't in the interests of the police service or public to prosecute the officer. Delta was exonerated and returned to CID duties elsewhere in the force, but not without damage to his family, and he and his wife divorced.

I believe Delta's successes within Moss Side and Cheetham Hill were some of the best pieces of detective work I have been privileged to work alongside. GMP did not support a loyal and hard-working officer but instead unwittingly assisted the gangs in eliminating the real and only police threat.

After Delta left Moss Side, I cannot remember one single successful operation when a firearm was discovered.

CHAPTER SEVENTEEN

Bank Job

In the early 1990s, GMP increased its firearms strength again. The 'advice' system – two men on eight-hour shifts who were responsible for turning out an operational team if need be – that had worked so well was terminated and a system of four teams, each with a sergeant and nine constables, was adopted to give the force permanent 24-hour cover. The days of standby duties were over.

GMP also tried to cobble together a system of armed response vehicles. Each force in the UK has a different way of manning their ARVs. A crew's strength could be either two, three or four firearms officers. The vehicles varied: Volvos, people carriers, Range Rovers. Some forces allowed officers to openly carry firearms, others made them conceal them in safes within the vehicles. GMP, for a period, ran with a four-man crew in Range Rovers but also had another six AFOs to create an operational team.

What this often meant in practice was that while four of the team were taken away to do the ARV, the other six were sat around doing little. Their numbers were too few to properly train together and team morale began to suffer. For me this was one of the worst periods of VO8's history. Teams were not allowed to self-generate training, and became stale and unmotivated.

At the same time, a gang of prolific armed robbers known as the McDonalds were using an unusual modus operandi. The McDonalds were from Salford and usually targeted banks around the city centre, generally old buildings near to or adjoining decrepit buildings in need of repair. Overnight the McDonald gang would break into parts of the bank and lie in wait for staff to open up. When they did, the gang would literally appear out of the walls and terrorise the staff at gunpoint. Most bank vaults open on a timelock and it was the intention of the gang to attack just before the vault was activated. They would force the staff to empty the vault and escape from the bank. Although this was an ingenious MO, the gang were violent thugs and many staff members had been hurt and seriously traumatised.

The Serious Crime Squad had set up an operation with the intention of capturing this gang. The SCS had purchased the latest in detection technology, a microwave detection system. I had received a briefing on this system some days earlier by a detective inspector from the SCS called Illing. He was a great boss but regarded affectionately as daft as a brush by some of the lads.

We were told that, by a process of elimination, the SCS had worked out which would be the likeliest banks to be robbed. Each of these banks would have the microwave system installed. It could only be activated by human presence. It could not be set off by animals, the weather or structural faults; it was meant to be foolproof. An intruder wouldn't know it had been activated but a transceiver would receive a warning tone of intrusion.

It wasn't long before we had an activation. Six of my team were downstairs in the armoury at Bootle Street. Jig, a likeable lad who had served in inner-city divisions, then Manchester Airport, before transferring to VO8, answered the phone and after a short conversation of affirmatives, put the receiver down and in his usual enthusiastic way said, 'Murf wants us at the NatWest Bank, Chapel Street, Salford.'

Murf was on the ARV and had been turned out to a microwave activation. He required a full team deployment and was containing the bank with three colleagues. It took us at least five minutes to reach the building on Chapel Street, near its junction with Trinity Way. As we arrived, I couldn't help noticing a gathering presence of SCS officers. Also divisional Chief Superintendent Frank Halligan had attended the scene. It was obvious that this incident would be of an overt nature.

I was the most senior and experienced AFO on the scene and was hastily summoned by the chief superintendent and DI Illing. They wanted quick options for an arrest. It was pretty obvious that we were going to have to close down the surrounding roads and create chaos in rush hour traffic.

I started to question Mr Illing:

'Have the staff arrived?'

'No.'

'Do you really think someone is in the bank?'

'The microwave is never wrong.'

'How long ago was it activated?'

'About two hours.'

'How long have you been here?'

'About half an hour.'

Mr Halligan had already started to instruct his officers to close down roads and divert traffic away from the incident and the press and TV had arrived. Murf had been prompt deploying his team and we had armed officers covering all four aspects.

Now this was a strange situation to be in. The bank was situated on the left of Chapel Street as you drive out of the city. It is a large stone block building with another more derelict building attached to it. If the gang was in there, it seemed obvious they were not about to come out. Therefore we had no choice but to break in. I told my team to start prepping shields, ladders, door-opening kit and search kit such as mirrors. Once we had gained entry, we would have to search to contact and I preferred to do it in a slow and defensive form. I went back to the DI and asked him if we could locate a key holder for the premises.

'I've tried, I can't get hold of anyone,' he informed me.

I took off with Murf, checking all four aspects of the bank to see if we could ascertain how the gang had gained entry. The black aspect and red aspects were surrounded by a 12-foot wall, the green aspect was a gable end without any sign of entry. The white aspect's windows were clearly barred with a large wooden double door securely shut.

We returned to the team and, from the equipment vehicle, grabbed a pair of assault ladders and – with the assistance of Jig – returned to the black aspect. We assembled the ladders and leaned them against the wall. I ascended and peered over the wall and into the yard. The ground level was completely different, there was about a 20-foot drop on the other side. I looked at the building and realised that due to its construction, it was going to be a nightmare to search. I was also looking for signs of entry. All the windows and doors were secure and barred as you'd expect for a bank. The only possible POE was the roof.

I descended the ladder and spoke to Murf and Jig.

'This is going to be hard, we are going to have to break in if they don't get a key holder.'

'Shit, break into a bank,' declared Jig.

'I can't think of any other options, can you?'

'What about the roof?' asked Murf. 'I know we can't take our team through, but it might reveal how the gang got in.'

I made a quick radio call to the rest of the team and told them to hold. I then informed the containment team to expect movement on the roof. So the three of us – not the most nimble or gifted of mountaineers – set about climbing onto the bank's roof. Using the assault ladders, we managed to gain access to the rear yard and then onto the roof.

For the next 30 minutes we scrambled all over the roof and the hidden nooks and crannies looking for an entry point. Eventually we spotted something that looked likely and also what appeared to be a secreted wooden pair of ladders. The area needed further investigation, but to get to it we needed to cross over a gap approximately ten feet wide and with a drop of at least 40 feet. The only other way was to cross over a particularly steep side of the roof covered in roofing tiles and none of us favoured that approach.

The other option was to bridge the gap with a section of the assault ladders. The ladders are designed for this type of work but it still appeared daunting crossing the gap. We quickly spanned the gap, laying the ladders flat. We had another problem – the stone composite on either side of the gap was uneven and the ladders wobbled fiercely. I noticed this and must have gone white – the same colour Murf was quickly turning. Jig was oblivious.

I made a tactical decision and, pushing Murf out of the way, said, 'You two hold the end of the ladder as tight as fuck, while I cross.'

Murf and Jig held the ladder to counterbalance it and I was quickly across. Murf knocked Jig out of the way and virtually threatened him to hold the ladder. Jig by now had realised what was happening and had matched our facial colour. I held one end of the ladder and Jig the other end as Murf hurried across, not daring to look down. In all situations like this, it's quite easy to see the funny side. Murf and I were safely across and Jig was stranded on his side. The ladder was raised about four inches on the right side.

'Fucking hurry up,' Murf shouted at him.

'Stop fucking about and get across,' I shouted.

Jig just looked at us with contempt as we nervously giggled. He got on the ladder on all fours and we started to piss ourselves.

'I fucking hate heights,' he declared.

'You were at the airport,' I said.

'What the fuck's that got to do with it?'

'Well you must like heights.' Murf and I were now belly-laughing.

'Just hold the ladder,' he snarled and continued to edge along. If the press had seen this it would have been: 'GMP's Crack Firearms Team Scale Bank Walls'. Instead we were more like the Keystone Cops. But then the ladder wobbled to one side and Murf and I couldn't prevent it. Jig grabbed the ladder, his knuckles white and his eyes firmly closed.

'I'm not moving,' he declared.

'Come on you twat.' We used our most sympathetic tones.

'No chance,' he firmly stated.

'Stop fucking about and hurry up.' We had lost patience and started throwing pebbles at him. Jig was so annoyed that he snapped and virtually sprinted the final three foot. I think that if we hadn't been on an operation, he would have punched us.

We moved over to a small window. It had signs of a forced entry and the presence of the ladders led us to believe it was the gang's entry point. There was no point going through the window, as there was a good chance the team was still inside. Murf radioed the black cover team and from his elevated position indicated to them the entry point we had found. It would be their job to cover this point, although they were on the ground some 40 feet away. We replaced the assault ladders and quickly descended.

I returned to the front of the building to an increased gathering of the usual crowds of senior and junior officers. I informed Mr Halligan of our findings and asked him if the key holder had been located. There was a negative response, and all we could presume was that the key holder had been diverted from the scene and was unable to get through the cordons. In a further consultation with Illing and Halligan, it was decided that we had no option but to enter the bank and search to clear it.

We were now faced with the problem of breaking into a bank. I returned to the team and informed them of our predicament.

Joe had studied the double doors of the bank. Joe had started to specialise in entry techniques and he believed we could force a way in by using a single man wham ram. I instructed a couple of the lads to assemble two large siege shields. The bank was a large building with at least three levels. We didn't have any interior plans and therefore once we were in, a slow progressive search using shields would be the best option. It would give us time to assess from an area of safety (behind the shields) and then slowly search ahead, clearing the building in a precise and progressive manner.

By now a few more of our colleagues had joined us. We looked a scruffy bunch, with officers dressed in different parts of uniform. Some of us were in operational turnout kit, others in ARV uniform and others in training overalls.

Like I said, this ad-hoc system of ARVs and part-teams had affected the professional way we approached jobs. Although one good thing had come out of this mish-mash of integration: the revolver had been replaced by the SLP and most of the team carried a Beretta 9mm pistol with two magazines of 15 rounds each.

As a unit we moved to the doors of the bank and proceeded to smash fuck out of them with the wham ram. The doors absorbed most of the ram's force and Joe was forced to increase his work rate. Although he was extremely fit, it wasn't long before he was knackered and another member of the team took over. Eventually, after swapping several times, they forced an entry.

The shields were brought through. Murf was my number one and I backed him up. Murf assessed the situation and relayed back to the rest of the team his proposed search pattern.

We had actually entered part of the bank which we would later find out was classed as a listed building. From the front doors the property opened up to a large foyer where customers would have stood. It was about the size of a tennis court, tiled with beautiful glazed floor tiles. Directly in front and approximately 25 yards away was a series of glass screens and partitions which the cashiers would stand behind. Behind the screens was the secure vault. To the left of the foyer was a set of winding stairs. Approximately 30 feet above us was a stained glass ceiling. Just looking into the whole area was like taking a step back in time to the 1940s.

Although all this registered, it took up a very small space in the corner of my mind. Once the doors had been forced, Murf started relaying instructions. He was the number one of the team and we were in competent hands. There was still a possibility that the gang was inside.

If they had remained inside, they would be pretty desperate now after the commotion we had caused. I was concentrating on my role, covering my arcs of fire and making sure I listened to Murf's instructions. The two of us, backed up by another pair, started to clear the foyer. The search was proving difficult because of the large open space. Angles quickly opened up, leaving us exposed.

Murf had started shouting challenges: 'Armed police, show yourselves!' No response. We listened for telltale signs. None. Murf continued to shout challenges as we continued clearing level one.

I shouted for a couple of lads to come through, find a position of cover and gain a foot on the ground for us. A slow search tactic is physically and mentally draining and within minutes we had started to sweat buckets. This was due to the heavyweight body armour we wore and also the demanding circumstances – someone just might want to blow your head off.

We had ballistic helmets, which are a great bit of kit but they are cumbersome at times. When I first joined VO8 I was issued a helmet made by Bristol Armour. It was equipped with a full-face visor. These helmets are similar to what the British Army wore in Northern Ireland in the 1970s, at the height of the Troubles. The visor was a real twat and would steam up, preventing clear vision. I took to wearing the helmet with the visor up.

On one quick entry, I was legging it up a set of stairs when I came to a sudden and violent halt. My neck felt like it had been compressed six inches into my shoulders and I couldn't progress any further. Jim, who was behind me, almost rammed his head up my arse, then realised that my visor had got stuck in the dust rail running along the wall of the stairs. The helmet has now improved in design and is much easier to wear. One thing I hate is officers wearing beanie caps to search. They are a dangerous bit of kit due to the amount of vision they restrict.

You may have noticed, when watching American cop movies, that officers from the NYPD at times wear their peaked caps back-to-front with the peak over the neck. This isn't to effect a nice pose; they are given special dispensation to wear them back-to-front while involved in a firearms incident. In the NYPD's history, two officers were killed pursuing an offender up a metal fire escape. The offender waited at the top and as the officers continued chase, they couldn't see the ambush because of the restricted vision caused by their peaks. After this tragic event, the NYPD issued the dispensation. Lesson learned.

We moved to the stairs. Murf called up to Jig, who had a midi shield. 'Clear the stairs mate,' he instructed. I covered Jig as he efficiently moved forward and searched the stairs. 'Clear,' Jig shouted and held at the top of the stairs. Murf picked up his shield and carted it to the top. Jig withdrew and Murf related the search pattern.

'We have a corridor, approximately twenty foot long, two doors to the left, two to the right all closed,' Murf whispered to me. 'This is going to be difficult, let's move a shield forward of each door and quick-entry the room.

This made sense and I agreed. The other shield team moved forward of the first door on the right and covered the corridor and rooms. Murf and I formed up on the door. I would be the number one and enter first. Murf was the number two and would go the opposite way to me. First rule of MOE: check the door handle – locked. Joe was brought up and instructions were quickly relayed. He was to force the door with the wham ram.

Joe moved through. Smash! The door – of egg box design – flew inwards.

I stepped in and to my right. 'Oh shit!' my mind screamed. In what appeared to be minutes, but were obviously seconds, my mind had assessed the situation and was warning me that I was in trouble. The floor of the room was layered with off-white fibre-glass insulation, and above the insulation were cylindered white ventilation pipes. I immediately knew why the insulation was there – it was covering the stained glass ceiling below.

I had my Beretta in my right hand, I was committed to the entry and couldn't backtrack. I was moving too fast. I made a decision to dive for the nearest pipe. I hit it with my left arm as the weight on my right side forced my leg through the glass. This motion yanked me back as I tried to tuck my right arm over the pipe, keeping hold of my weapon. My left leg shot forward, Crash! My full body was through the glass and I was hurtling towards the floor.

I can remember as clear as day what I was thinking as I plummeted towards the floor: Fuck, this is going to hurt. I sailed 30 feet and hit the glazed tiles. I tried to tuck my neck into my shoulders to avoid a head injury. My back, protected by my body armour, took the full force. My right hand slammed into the floor but I was determined to hold on to my pistol. Both heels smashed into the floor.

As I hit the deck, I sucked in air with shock and mouthed, 'Oh fuck.' It was not a clever move, as glass and insulation was showering down on me. I was choking on the amount I swallowed. I remember bouncing a couple of times and then shuffling into a corner. It didn't hurt immediately due to the endorphins kicking in – the body's natural painkillers.

I quickly assessed my injuries. I was breathing but struggling. I was bleeding and couldn't stand. Two of the team with me gave first field care. They managed to extract me from the bank and drove me to hospital rather than wait for an ambulance.

I was transported to Manchester North General Hospital. I was immediately admitted and treatment commenced straight away. I was X-rayed and treated for a broken right hand, two badly bruised and cut heels which required stitching and a damaged lower back. There was nothing they could do for my inhalation of glass and insulation but let nature take its course.

Later on I spoke to the lads and they informed me that the search had proved negative, although it was believed the gang had been in the premises at some time. The part of the bank where I had fallen had been closed down by the NatWest due to some protected building legislation.

Murf told me that he thought I was a goner when I fell through the ceiling and was surprised to see me scuttle off. I really believe that some of us get chances in life and I used all mine up on that fall.

I wouldn't know it at the time but this incident, in 1994, would cause a slow deterioration in my physical health and fitness.

CHAPTER EIGHTEEN

The Cali Cartel

In January 1994 I was sat in the crew room with most of my team. We had just finished a particularly violent game of Scrabble. We had taken to playing the word game in our downtime and as usual it had become a competitive battle. One of the lads, Macky, had accused Foz of cheating – possibly correctly – and the two of them had been rolling around the floor. Foz tried to apply his best wrestling submission moves and, with an agonising cry from Macky, succeeded in vindicating himself.

Mick, my sergeant, had been on the phone while the pair had been wrestling and with a smile on his face told them to quit.

'We have a job and it sounds a good one.'

We were all ears.

'Andy, you and me will go to Collyhurst nick, the rest of you standby.'

As we were driving to Collyhurst, Mick explained that the call had been from Antro and we were to meet him in the CID office at Collyhurst along with officers from Customs and Excise and the Covert Operations Unit.

The Covert Ops Unit are a highly secret unit used to infiltrate the criminal fraternity. When we arrived at Collyhurst I recognised a couple of their handlers and also their DCI, who was with Antro. Seated around the table were a couple of suits I hadn't seen before but were obviously customs officers. One of them introduced himself and, in a no-nonsense manner, related the following stunning facts.

Customs had managed to infiltrate Colombia's notorious Cali Cartel, the richest and most powerful criminal organisation in the world. A consignment of cocaine worth a million pounds was under surveillance at Schipol Airport in Holland. Very shortly this consignment would leave for Manchester airport. Once there, it would be taken to a secure warehouse in the Collyhurst area. At the warehouse it would be broken down, ready for sale on the open market in Manchester.

Customs, along with Covert Ops, hoped to entice two of the cartel's head men to Manchester. Following strict guidelines in relation to agents provocateurs, they would enter into a transaction with the men from Cali. The operation would be terminated once enough evidence of drug distribution had been collated and a successful prosecution could take place.

The two players were Gerardo Baron, number 16 in order of influence within the cartel, and Francisco Lopero, number six. The customs officer informed us that the majority of the operation was controlled. However it was believed that the Cali Cartel was connected to some of Manchester's drug gangs and both Baron and Lopera would be meeting with them.

I raised my hand, somewhat confused. 'Why do you require the assistance of firearms?' If the operation was so controlled, surely they could arrest both targets once the deal had been struck. The customs officer looked at the DCI from Covert Ops. It was one of those expressions that said, how much should we tell them? I hated this sort of need-to-know stuff. They had a duty to share their information with us. No matter what their rank, it would be me and my mates knee-deep in shit if anything went wrong.

Some years earlier, I had been summonsed to Chester House with four of my team. We were briefed by Customs and Excise and the Special Branch to arrest an Afghan drugs baron who was tying up a multi-million-pound deal with a London gang in the Hilton Hotel at Manchester airport. It was believed everyone was armed. Customs knew which room the deal would take place in and had taken the room next to it. Our job was to arrest everyone. We duly plotted up in our room and were given a key card for the target room. On the nod of Customs, we formed up outside the target room, all armed with pistols. One of our lads opened the door and we burst in, to be confronted by six suspects. We were outnumbered and poorly briefed. One of the suspects, dressed in full Middle Eastern garb, decided to attack us. The five of us, all ex-TAG lads, decided the best form of defence was attack and decimated the room. I ended up decking the one dressed as an Arab, who yelled, 'Take it easy, I'm Customs!' The idiot had attacked us to make his cover more realistic; he was lucky he got away with only a swollen pair of bollocks.

I didn't want that to happen again. 'It's important you give me a full threat assessment,' I said.

The customs officer relented a little and told us that the crucial part of the operation was at the warehouse in Manchester. Baron would hand over the consignment of cocaine to a full undercover team. This would be enough to arrest him. However, Baron and Lopero's movements in England would not be fully controlled. Customs could not confirm who Baron would arrive with at the warehouse or who the two would meet while in Manchester. They did know that both targets would be staying at the Dominion Hotel on Whitworth Street, in the city centre. Once the consignment was handed over, two Customs operatives would drive Baron and maybe Lopero back to the hotel. Then the armed team would arrest them.

By asking and sticking up for the team, I had gained useful information. On many occasions, I have suffered from limited information. I know at times that the investigating team are scared of divulging too much in case of leaks, but there comes a time to trust in order for the job to run smoothly and safely.

'When is the deal going to take place?' asked Mick.

'Tomorrow morning,' said one of the customs officers.

'What route will your team take back to the hotel?'

'I'm not sure,' said the officer, a little puzzled.

'Tell them to drive along Dantzic Street,' said Mick

'Can you give us descriptions?' I asked.

'Baron is extremely fat, the customs UC [undercover] is bald and the driver will be undercover.'

'What about Lopero?'

'Smart, about five–ten, Hispanic-looking.'

Antro pulled me and Mick over. 'Get back to Bootle Street and start planning. Give me a ring later.'

On the way back to Bootle Street, myself and Mick drove along Dantzic Street and found a suitable ambush site underneath a railway bridge. It had a service tunnel, which was a suitable lay-up point for the team.

Dantzic Street isn't an unusual area for VO8 to operate. I had planned two raids on a large travellers' site there. It was as large as two football pitches and the travelling fraternity were legally allowed to pitch caravans and reside without committing trespass. The travellers are usually big, hard people with Irish ancestry. Some of them make a living from petty crime and make little effort to pay taxes and local community charges. They are also fond of a drink, and once they have imbibed, they love a fight. It's not unusual for them to destroy the interior of a pub and to continue fighting with the law who will have been summoned to the disturbance. Many a police officer has had an unpleasant experience with the travellers.

The Manchester travellers are generally close-knit families. As with all families, feuds develop and can escalate into serious offences such as rioting, wounding and gunplay. During Christmas these feuds seem to increase in severity and families have taken to shooting each other. On two consecutive New Year periods I had been summoned to Collyhurst Police Station and, after consulting with CID Officers and divisional commanders, planned for large-scale raids on the Dantzic Street caravan sites.

This is no mean feat. At that time of the year the sites are particularly crowded and contain up to 30 caravans. The caravans need to be searched for firearms. On both occasions I have turned out a full team, along with the unit's armoured Land Rovers, and I have borrowed armoured Land Rovers from the airport. Using these vehicles we drove on to the site, and announced our presence through public address systems in the vehicles. We rounded up the occupants and corralled them into groups and observed them for any suspicious movements while teams searched the site and caravans for weaponry.

To the reader it might sound draconian to treat members of the public like this. However, travellers are not averse to violence and this includes females as well as males. They are also reluctant to comply with the police; it's almost part of their culture. The last thing we could afford was a large-scale violent affray while handling firearms. By using high intensity searchlights on the vehicles and a constant stream of orders announced over the public address systems, we were just able to physically dominate them into complying.

Once the travellers – men, women and children – were herded into groups, we alighted from the vehicles, covering them with our MP5s and announced our intention. On several occasions we had to make arrests of men who were suspected of shootings. The arrests were quick, aggressive and dynamic in order to extract the offender from the crowd, get them into a police van and off the site, so further enquiries could take place.

The sites are not pleasant places, generally poorly facilitated with poor hygiene standards. Old vehicles are scattered about the place, dogs are tethered on leads, the place stinks of diesel, human body waste and dogshit. Once a suspect is arrested it creates a real unease among the crowds, with several of the men becoming agitated and openly hostile. This has to be dealt with quickly, as travellers understand a show of strength, and anything less is something they will manipulate to their own end. We would move towards them shouting instructions, telling them to either stay where they were or move away to the left or right. I swear on several occasions I have heard the following reply: 'Which way is that sir?' in an Irish accent. At first I thought they were taking the piss, but soon realised they didn't actually know which was right or left. I used the barrel of my MP5 to indicate the direction of travel.

On both occasions, when the site was searched, we recovered at least six sawn-off shotguns and an assortment of nasty weapons including machetes, swords and knives. On the first occasion, we also discovered a crate of molotov cocktails, but amusingly they had been made with diesel instead of petrol (diesel is nowhere near as flammable). Unfortunately on both occasions, although weapons and explosives were recovered and suspects were arrested, none of those events led to criminal proceedings. Many travellers war amongst themselves, but are reluctant to inform on each other.

* * *

Back in the crew room the lads gathered round, eager to hear what the OP was. We quickly relayed the information and our concerns. Although there was an element of control, we didn't know anything about Baron's or Lopero's associates.

The lads on the team were becoming skilled operators and I took pride in the fact that I had trained many of them. Each displayed different qualities. Some had a few years of operational experience and were eager to offer opinions. Not one of them was happy about the uncontrolled element of the operation and they voiced concerns that it appeared those in command and control of the operation were making light of the fact that this was two of the top men in the Cali Cartel, an extremely ruthless drugs gang with tentacles all over Europe.

I outlined the proposed ambush option under the bridge at Dantzic Street. We would need an articulated lorry to block the road. Once the road was blocked, we would attack the target vehicle as per vehicle drills, assaulting all four doors and incapacitating the occupants by physical domination. Contingencies would be planned for such things as locked doors. A blocking vehicle would be driven behind the suspect one to prevent it reversing off. We had decided to treat the OP like any other.

There were a few unanswered what-ifs. What if Baron turned up with a criminal associate? What if Lopero wasn't in the car? What if the intelligence was wrong and they had guns?

Mick made a phone call to Antro telling him we needed to hire an articulated lorry.

'How much?' was Antro's reply.

'Fuck knows!' was Mick's.

'Who will drive it?'

'Leaky.'

'All right, get on with it but for fuck's sake don't bump it.'

Leaky had moved on to other duties but was quickly contacted and tasked. A briefing was planned for 06.00 the following morning. I had requested the assistance of the DSU and they were only too happy to provide three vehicles and drivers. Mick and I carried on with the operational order and prepared the crew room for a briefing at six.

I was in for 05.30, prepped my kit, loaded the magazines of my SLP and MP5. We had decided to make the OP a covert option. Most of the team were in about this time, busy sorting out kit. At 06.00 we commenced the briefing with Antro, customs and the DCI from Covert Ops present. I related the information and tasked duties including the DSU's duties.

I had built in a contingency phase in case we got tasked to

deal with Lopero. Once I had finished briefing, I asked the customs officer for an update. He informed us everything was running according to plan – the cocaine was in Manchester, en route to Collyhurst. He anticipated that his undercover team with Baron should arrive at our ambush site at approximately 09.30. I asked him if he could confirm the undercover vehicle. 'A dark blue Ford Mondeo,' was the reply from the Covert Ops DCI.

Leaky was due to collect a wagon from a hire company and would be on plot at 08.45. I had allowed an hour for rehearsals, and after a short drive to Openshaw Complex, we practised dry drills on assaulting a four door vehicle. We were all pretty familiar with this option but I would not allow complacency to creep in. I worked our team hard, I knew the attitude of some members of the other teams towards our training and operational ethos. Many of those individuals had about five minutes in the department and were typical of some bobbies – totally work shy. As long as I was operational and with influence, I would strive to be the best – and to stay alive – and would expect the same from those who worked with me.

After rehearsals we moved to our ambush site underneath the railway bridge on Dantzic Street. I deployed two of the team to a DSU vehicle and tasked them with a blocking role. They would also be our foot on the ground. We didn't have a radio link to the Customs operation. The blocking vehicle would position itself further along Dantzic Street towards the warehouse. They would be our comms link, and once the blue Mondeo drove past they would radio all relevant information to us at the ambush site. This would be limited due to the increase of criminals using scanners – at this time we didn't have a secure net.

The blocking team would covertly follow the Mondeo towards the ambush site and once the ambush was initiated it would contain the Mondeo. The two team members would provide covering arcs of fire if required. The rest of the team positioned themselves in the service tunnel, which was big enough to conceal the two DSU vehicles.

Leaky eventually turned up in an enormous articulated lorry. 'Right, where do you want this?' he shouted from the cab.

'Hide it for now,' I answered.

'Fucking hide it? It's massive.' He had a point.

'Well, park up, you miserable fucker.'

I could hear him mumbling 'miserable fucker' to himself as he attempted to park. I was wandering back to the team when my radio burst into transmission.

'Target en route, approximately twenty-five mph. Three on board, ETA four minutes.'

I ran back to Leaky. 'Stop fucking about and block the road!'

He looked at me and grinned, 'Fuck off.'

I ran back to my team under the bridge, knowing full well the road would be blocked. 'ETA three minutes,' the radio blurted. Leaky was moving the wagon into place.

'Condition Red,' I shouted at the team.

The majority threw off their civvy jackets, revealing body armour underneath. Pistols were taken out of holsters and MP5s shoulder mounted. A couple of lads put on the ridiculous beanie caps that identify you as an armed officer.

'ETA two minutes,' the radio informed me.

I looked about the team. They were all keyed up with determined looks on their faces, each focused on the task ahead of them.

'ETA one minute,' came from the radio.

'Stand by,' I shouted, 'stand by.'

Leaky had fully blocked the road, leaving enough of a gap for us to run through. He was getting out of his cab and climbing down. He placed his hands on his head and started to shake it as if he had a problem with his wagon.

The Mondeo was in sight with the blocking vehicle behind. It started to slow down and come to a halt.

'Strike! Strike! Strike!'

The two in the blocking vehicle, armed with H&K 53s jumped out of the vehicle, moved into position to prevent crossfire and provided a vital element of sniper lock. Leaky started to reach into the cab for a concealed MP5. The six-man assault team ran towards the Mondeo. Baron was sat in the front passenger seat. We hit the vehicle instantaneously.

'Armed police! Armed police!'

All four doors were ripped open. Within seconds the driver and the rear passenger were lying prone on the floor and handcuffed.

I was dealing with Baron. He looked like a big, fat, wide-eyed toad. His mouth was dangling open and his eyes couldn't comprehend what was happening. I ripped open his door and shouted, 'Armed police, get out.' He was trying to move but he was so fat he appeared stuck to his seat. 'Get out, you fat fuck,' I screamed. He was trying to, but wasn't making headway.

My next option was to shout, 'Locked doors.' This means I would get help. I knew I didn't have locked doors – I had a fat Colombian stuck in a car – but that would be difficult to shout in the heat of the moment. Foz ran over, weighed up the situation and yanked him out of his seat and onto the road. He was quickly cuffed. It was important that we kept up the charade for the sake of the UCs, so we continued roughing them up a little until transport arrived and Baron was taken away.

The first phase had gone well but where was Lopero? As Mick and I were pondering this, we were joined by the customs officer and the Covert Ops DCI.

'Great job,' they said. 'But we have a problem.'

We were still in the middle of Dantzic Street when they informed us that Lopero was at the Dominion Hotel. He was in possession of monetary documentation worth over a million pounds. It was believed he was going to bank this. Customs said this couldn't occur or it would be disastrous to the whole operation. They wanted us to arrest Lopero as soon as possible.

'Is he armed?' I asked.

'We honestly don't know.'

'Fair enough,' I said. 'Do you have him under surveillance?'

'It's limited. We have the room next to his and are monitoring his movements with the aid of technical.'

They had obviously held back quite a bit when Mick and I had met them at Collyhurst. Time was limited; we had to get to the Dominion Hotel, which was approximately five minutes away. We needed a quick recce and an immediate action plan within minutes. Without the interference of senior officers, the plan could run smoothly.

I requested a surveillance driver to take me to the hotel and I made myself as covert as possible. I told Mick to bring the team to the hotel in the rest of the vehicles and to hold outside. I would recce then brief. Foz and Rod jumped into my vehicle and the DSU driver sped towards the Dominion Hotel. My mind was racing with all sorts of options. Should we assault his room, ambush him on foot, contain and call him out?

In what appeared to be seconds we arrived at the hotel. I turned to Foz and Rod.

'Go into the lobby, locate the exits and wait for me to brief you.'

Both men are professionals, and without a word made their way into the hotel. We really were working with limited information.

As I entered the hotel it was like a scene from a third-rate spy film. The lobby was full of people with their faces buried in newspapers. The Covert Ops DCI had joined me and took me to the fifth floor. He led me to a room and gently tapped on the door. After a few seconds it was opened and we walked into a hive of technical activity. Tape recorders were rotating and two operatives were busy logging information.

The DCI introduced me. One of the operatives informed me that Lopero had just made a phone call and indicated he was about to leave his room. I asked if his room was the same as the one we were in. Exactly, came the reply, it's directly next door.

I was governed by time, but the option I was working towards was arresting him in his room. I left the room with the intention of making my way to Mick and briefing for a quick entry into his hotel room.

As I walked towards the lift, I passed Lopero's room. To my surprise the door was open and he was stood by his dressing room mirror. He was dressed in a smart grey suit and was adjusting his tie. It was obvious he was about to leave at any moment. The devil crept into my mind. I was armed, should I arrest him myself? Then sound tactical judgement took over. I carried on to the lift but bypassed the lift for the stairs and legged it hell for leather down until I reached the lobby. Both Foz and Rod had separated and were keeping an eye on each exit. I made my way to them and brought them up to date.

I made the decision for a 'hard hit' drill. There is no finesse with the hard hit – it is exactly how it sounds, a hard and violent arrest technique that gives the offender no time to react.

'As soon as he comes into the lobby, I will challenge him and the nearest of you will disable him,' I said.

Both of them nodded. I stood back and watched the lifts. The hard hit was the right option; there were all sorts of people in the lobby and there was no way of moving them without revealing our hand. We couldn't afford to follow onto the street – it wouldn't take him long to 'ping' us the way we were dressed.

It wasn't long before I watched the numbers of the lift indicate number five and then drop down again. The doors opened and out stepped Lopero, dressed like a million dollars. As he walked past me I drew my pistol, moved towards him and shouted 'Armed police.' Both Foz and Rod now knew their target. I was moving to his right, keeping an eye on his hands and making sure I had a good backstop, when the full force of Foz hit him. Lopero hit the deck with a resounding smack. Foz and Rod were on him like a rash and he was quickly handcuffed. From behind the newspapers about ten operatives revealed themselves and took Lopero into custody.

Some months later we were out as a team on the piss in Manchester when Macky mentioned a new fly-on-the-wall TV programme called *Undercover Customs* and how they had shown a re-enactment of Operation Begonia and the firearms arrest. He had our attention and continued to relay which actor had played me. 'You know that really famous actor, Reg Holdsworth from *Coronation Street*?' he blurted out, choking over his pint.

Begonia had been a good job for us as a team and for me in particular. I was approached by Covert Ops and offered a place on one of their courses.

CHAPTER NINETEEN

Corky's Return

For many years, the CID had been fighting hard to retain the Operational Firearms Department (VO8). In that time, changes occurred in the senior CID hierarchy. Experienced and seasoned commanders had completed 30 years or more policing and it was time for them to retire. These officers had held a tight grip on the CID and were reluctant to lose VO8. However, uniform operations, known as X Department, were battling, and in some ways justifying, a sideways move for the department. VO8 was a unique department. The majority of the personnel were X Department officers up to the rank of inspector, but the post of chief inspector had always been held by a senior detective.

The force had made the best use of VO8 by allowing commanders with CID experience to utilise it to its best attributes and abilities. X Department, on the other hand, was an unwieldy behemoth swallowing up one unit after another – it now included the Dog Section, Mounted Section, Contingency Planning, TASS and Air Support Unit – without necessarily having the skill levels on board to use all of these specialisms most efficiently.

Officers who had applied for TAG in the late 1970s and early 1980s and failed to get through the politically incorrect selection system had lain dormant. Many had passed exams and been promoted through the ranks. As the X Department grew in strength, so did TAG. These officers and others of a similar ilk were quickly swallowed up in positions of responsibility. By the mid-1990s the name Tactical Aid Group had been replaced by the Tactical Aid Unit and the department had trebled in size. In my opinion, it had become a toothless tiger. I echo the words of many of my colleagues when I state the ethos of TAG had been ruined.

The department still attracted some excellent officers. However, they were working under a limited and less than dynamic command. The leadership of the Tactical Aid Unit was, in my opinion, poor. However, politically they were becoming powerful within GMP, and were trying covertly to capture the reins of VO8, where Antro was now the chief inspector. His immediate supervisor was a superintendent called Roberts who had recently come from the airport. He had limited experience of firearms operations. Antro had been with either the Special Branch or firearms for most of his service, therefore his experience and skills spoke for themselves. Both officers were due for retirement.

Antro was aware of the undercurrents regarding an X Department takeover. He realised there was little he could do about it but he clearly stated the lack of benefit to the force. Antro was also faced with another dilemma. He had a list of officers on his desk who were subject to tenure of office. I was on that list. Tenure is the most stupid and illogical system I have ever come across. It states that once an officer has completed a certain amount of time in a specialised department, he or she must return to mainstream policing duties. I had nine years' experience on VO8 and four years on the TAG: thirteen years of specialised policing, twelve of them in firearms-related operations. The force had spent many thousands of pounds on my equipment and training, which would now go out of the window.

In 1984 the Home Office had introduced the Police and Criminal Evidence Act (PACE). This altered a great field of policing that I hadn't been trained in. I had been told to concentrate on arresting armed criminals. I had received only five days' training on PACE. Probationers, on the other hand, received weeks of theoretical and practical training on PACE.

Antro was tasked with depleting his operational strength and sending those officers on the list back to divisions with no training whatsoever. Antro spoke to me about tenure and said he had no intention of implementing it while he was in post and would file it in the 'too hard to do' basket. But I would have to realise that once he was replaced, his successor may not think the same.

I respected Antro enormously for this decision, but it left a cloud of uncertainty over me and some of my colleagues. Could you imagine tenure being implemented in industry, such as the building trade? A young labourer graduates from sweeping floors and mixing cement to hod-carrying bricks. From hod-carrying he learns to set out the foundation of a property and then lay a damp course and then a course of bricks that may tower into the sky. The labourer may have many years of experience, at a cost to himself and his employers in courses attended to reach this high standard. Now he is told to go back to sweeping floors to make room for someone else. Can you imagine the attack on his morale, his own feeling of value from his employers? The absolute nonsense of this system angers and upsets me. I think taxpayers have a right to see value for their money. Tenure just wastes that money. It is idiotic.

Inevitably Antro retired and was replaced by a new chief inspector. The CID lost its fight and the X Department took over the Firearms Department, renaming it X42. Subtle changes crept in. ARVs were resurrected and the force had two covering the north and south of the city. At this time the ARVs were part of the team, so it made little difference to our operating procedures. The only real difference was the response vehicles were liveried, termed ARVs, and we had to wear a uniform while in them.

It wasn't long before the new chief inspector started to make changes. I knew him from my TAG days; he had been a sergeant on Three Group at Longsight. Although a bit mard and excitable, he was OK – or so I thought.

He called me over to his office, which was in a new police complex known as Clayton Brook in Openshaw, sat me down and asked my opinions on the operational workings of the department. I gave him my honest views. He wanted to know how to improve it and I again gave him my ideas. He then went on to deliver one of the most impactful pieces of misinformation I ever suffered at the hands of a senior officer, and to this day one I feel bitter about.

He told me that I didn't have to worry regarding tenure of office. 'A good manager doesn't get rid of his best troops, particularly when their work reflects so well on him,' were his words. He then mentioned a few of the operations I had planned and told me to continue in that vein. I left feeling confident in my future in the Firearms Department.

* * *

Four pagers bleep shrilly and almost in rhythm: Mick's, Joe's, Macky's and mine. Each had the crew room's number on it, suffixed by a 'U' for urgent. We had been jogging along the banks of the River Irwell and the canal systems that wind through the city centre, but now we were required back in the office as soon as possible. We turned and ran back to Bootle Street. We had about two miles to cover and made it back within 15 minutes.

As we bounded in to the crew room, Mick turned to Foz, who was near to the phones, and out of breath enquired, 'What's the job?'

'Corky has been pinged by the DSU. They're surveilling him around Salford. Three vehicles are en route to us.'

Armed robber Parvo Corkovic (see Chapter One) was still wanted by GMP, even more so since we had failed to arrest him in Irlam. He had access to firearms, including pistols and an AK47 assault rifle. GMP command had classified him as highly dangerous and he wasn't to be approached unless the Firearms Department were present.

We threw off our sweaty training kit and dressed for a covert option. The rest of our team were arriving and quickly grasped what was occurring. Mick turned to me.

'Andy, will you deploy and brief the lads?'

'No problem.'

I made my way over to the dry-wipe briefing boards and wrote down the lads' duties and deployment to Alpha, Bravo and Charlie vehicles. The first phase of the plan was a vehicle drill option. I would make sure we had enough kit in the vehicles in case it turned into a building entry option. All the team had been part of the previous week's assault on Corky's gang, and had much intelligence and information on the target.

The crew room doors opened and three surveillance officers walked in with grins from ear to ear. I knew all three well. All were excellent operators and skilled at driving the firearms team about.

'We'd better hurry,' one of them said, 'Corky is driving a white Ford Sierra. He has dropped a bird and kid off in Salford and is making his way towards Broughton.'

MP5s and SLPs were loaded and we made our way to the enclosed yard. In no time I was running a radio check with the lads as they took up position in the vehicles. I was Alpha one, Macky was Alpha two. Mick, Foz and Bob were in the Bravo vehicle. Joe and the rest of the team were in the Charlie vehicle.

The three-car convoy sped out of the city towards the surveillance and made fast and aggressive progress as the drivers undertook and overtook and negotiated the lunchtime traffic. It didn't take long before we had tagged onto the rear of the surveillance. I asked my driver for a sit rep (situation report).

'Corky is approximately ten cars ahead, he is definitely in a white Sierra and alone, we think he is heading towards Mocha Parade.'

The driver had gleaned all this from the numbers being transmitted over his radio net. He acknowledged another transmission and turned to me.

'The eyeball is requesting a firearms arrest.'

The eyeball was right; a vehicle strike would be ideal. In my earpiece I heard Mick confirm to me that we had authority. He must have been on the mobile phone to command. I turned to the driver.

'Start to make progress through the surveillance.' Into my radio microphone I transmitted, 'Condition Amber, all teams acknowledge.'

'Bravo received.'

'Charlie received.'

My team would be making final preparations. They knew we were hunting for an arrest on the target. I could feel the excitement building. I had to concentrate hard not to give way to nerves by making hasty and jittery commands over the radio net. Brevity is the key; keep everything simple.

I looked around and realised we were on Blackfriars Road heading towards Clowes Street, Salford. Our three-car convoy was accelerating through the surveillance, trying to get sight of the white Sierra, when my driver shouted, 'Oh fuck!'

'What?'

'Corky's pinged the surveillance. He's turned right into Sandford.'

The surveillance team were now going through their SOPs regarding a compromise and trying to get new operators to the scene. My driver was asking for a sit rep from his team. Things appeared to be getting confusing and we turned into Sandford.

'Oh shit, no vehicle cover,' my driver cried, alarmed.

I could see the Sierra some 200 yards ahead. Our convoy had turned into Sandford and Corkovic had three vehicles with 12 men on board directly behind him. If he hadn't already clocked the surveillance, he would now. There wasn't another vehicle on the street.

'What now?' asked my driver, looking at me.

'Condition Red,' I transmitted over the air. 'Nothing for it, we'll strike on him.'

Corkovic accelerated; we had lost the element of surprise. He turned right into Leaky Street virtually on two wheels. Fortunately for us, this area of Broughton has numerous speed bumps and concrete posts to prevent joyriders hurtling around the streets. I could see ahead that Leaky Street was blocked by a series of concrete posts and our driver had seen this too. We accelerated towards Corkovic and tried to get on his off-side.

Smash! He drove his vehicle into us. Our driver braked and accelerated again onto his near-side.

Smash! We collided with him. We were being thrown about the vehicle and tried to hold onto anything to prevent it.

Smash! We hit him again. My head thumped into the passenger door window.

Corkovic was still accelerating. He hit the concrete posts and appeared to bed the underneath of his vehicle on them. The wheels of his car were racing but he appeared firmly stuck on the bollards. There was a smell of burning rubber and a cloud of black debris from his exhaust and tyres.

I got out of the front passenger side, followed by Macky from the rear of the vehicle. I ran towards the Sierra with an MP5 shoulder mounted, screaming, 'Armed police, get out of the car.' At the same instant, the Sierra gained some leverage and started to move. It hit me on my right side and knocked me into our surveillance vehicle.

'Fuck, that hurt.'

My right little finger felt as though it was broken. I had trapped it on the trigger guard of my MP5.

All sorts of shit was coming from the Sierra as Corkovic tried to drive away. His wheels screamed and black smoke enveloped his vehicle. Macky was trying to smash the windows of his car when Corkovic got out of the driver's door and started to sprint away. By now other team members had joined us and were trying to get into the Sierra.

Corkovic's initial 100 yards was astonishing – he moved like Linford Christie with a pack of lions on his heels. Macky and I gave chase. I had the edge on Macky and took the lead with him behind shouting, 'Andy!' While sprinting I wondered why he was shouting my name – then I heard him yell, 'Magazine.' I checked my MP5; it was minus its magazine. I must have depressed the release catch when the Sierra hit me. I had only one round in the MP5 and I didn't have a sling on it – if I had, I could have thrown it over my shoulder and relied on my Beretta.

I didn't appear to be making headway on Corkovic either; in fact he was leaving me behind. He knew the area and ran through narrow alleys, heading towards Bridgewater Street. I knew he was desperate and a cunning and ruthless individual. He didn't have any qualms about using firearms. If he was armed, all he had to do was wait for me as I ran round a corner and pop me as I ran towards him. So every time I turned a corner, I had my MP5 mounted ready to fire the one round I had.

The rest of the lads had used their nous and were back in the vehicles following my progress from the main road. I wasn't going to give up; there was no way Corkovic was going to outrun me. I resigned myself to settling into a comfortable pace and wearing him down. I could see him 100 yards away and he was starting to slow. The vehicles spotted this and managed to get in front of him. Corkovic realised he was trapped, slowed to a walk and put his arms in the air.

Foz, Bob and Mick were running towards him. Corkovic turned towards me and smiled as Foz and Bob took him to the floor. He was quickly cuffed and searched, and within minutes a divisional van was taking him from the scene. We had eventually arrested Parvo Corkovic.

I'm not in the habit of admiring villains, but Corkovic certainly had a pair of balls. He and his gang were subsequently sentenced to a total of 143 years in prison. Corkovic received 23 years and each of his accomplices from what was known as Operation Dalkeith received 15 years apiece.

* * *

At this stage of X42's development, hostage rescue training had at last been recognised as much needed. GMP decided that a force of its size should have this option and in 1995 ran its first hostage rescue/rapid intervention course. One of our sergeants from the training team attended a similar course in the West Midlands. He was instructed to train the department in its use, but before any officer could attend the four-week course, it was decided that a strict fitness and shooting selection process should be undertaken.

The majority of the department started to concentrate on their fitness, while the officers who were on the tenure were informed that they wouldn't be eligible for the course. I found this suspicious after what the chief inspector had said to me, but I was sidetracked somewhat because I was asked to put together the test shoot for the selection course. With my usual enthusiasm, I set about creating a realistic scenario for a hostage rescue shooting, using MP5s converted for use with paint rounds.

The fitness selection was held in the gym at Sedgley Park. Each candidate wore full kit, including respirator, and carried an MP5 and a Beretta. They had to negotiate an assault course at speed. This included climbing ropes, ladders, crawling, jumping spaces and crossing beams. Once they had completed this, they carried on into an enclosed room and engaged in a threat-or-no-threat scenario with paper targets as hostages and hostage takers. The room was full of smoke, with blue lights flashing and simulated bangs.

It took two weeks to put the whole department through the selection. As expected, the usual competent lads passed it but the high percentage of failures meant there were not enough people to participate in a full four-week course. So officers on the tenure list were allowed to take the selection. Both Pete and I passed, and I subsequently attended the four-week course.

The sergeant instructing it expected everything to be done by the book. I wouldn't let him dictate stupid and impracticable options and fell out with him more than once. It annoyed me and I didn't want to have to justify myself, but my experience – along with that of some of my colleagues – was overriden.

During my time on the team, I had trained with the Special Air Service, the Special Boat Squadron and had input from Russian Special Forces. Aside from that, I had nine years' operational experience. I had planned and participated in many house entries, a rapid intervention (Operation Dalkeith) and a hostage rescue in Wigan. It was hard to listen to someone with much less experience. I also believe that he was teaching the tactics adopted by the SAS at the Iranian Embassy. These tactics were a phenomenal success for the regiment but they were designed for large buildings such as embassies. The architecture of Manchester is not suitable.

The type of tactic we were taught hinged on four-man teams. Each team would be designated a part of a target property. Two teams were tasked to assault a stronghold. In theory, 20 fully armed officers could end up assaulting a two-up two-down terrace property. This was too many men; experience told me it would lead to fuck-ups. Of course we should have been taught four-man teams, but also three- and two-man teams. Manchester had a massive advantage – their dynamic entry had already been taught. Hostage rescue should have been an add-on to that.

After winding my neck in, I successfully completed the course. I ended up attending the second course in Manchester – and planned and instructed on a third.

CHAPTER TWENTY

White House Farm

I found myself as the lead scout as we ploughed through a boggy field. It was the early hours of a bitterly cold morning. It had just finished pissing down and if it hadn't been for our Goretex kit, the 15 of us would have been soaked to the skin. I indicated by hand signal that we had reached the JOP.

Riggers, 6ft 4ins and 17 stone, was carrying an empty rucksack. We all settled down in a defensive formation, quietly took off our foul-weather kit and handed it to Riggers, who placed it in his Bergen. It was imperative we maintain silence. The property we were creeping towards was protected by sensors hidden in the ground that indicated human movement.

Some days earlier, Foz and I had reccied this route and, at the same time of the morning, had reached the fencing around the target property and waited for a while. We wanted to see if we disturbed the occupants and also if the local division was informed of intruders. I hadn't come across movement sensors before and I was keen to see how effective they were.

We intended to make a forced entry into a detached farmhouse in a semi-rural location near Hazel Grove, Stockport. The occupants were a family involved in the fashion business. The father was believed to be heavily involved in the supply and distribution of drugs, including Ecstasy tablets. He was also believed to have corrupt police officers from Stockport on the payroll.

Foz had picked the job up from the Serious Crime Squad. He

had received the usual briefing from the detective chief inspector that on no account were we to recce the farm. The SCS had been involved in a protracted investigation of this family for many months and couldn't afford a heavy-handed firearms team stepping all over the property and blowing the investigation. Instead the squad handed Foz a VHS tape, taken by the force helicopter, of the premises. Foz viewed the tape and concluded it was next to useless. As usual, he nodded to the DCI and promised he wouldn't go near the property until we were told to arrest the occupants.

The squads can be pretty disrespectful towards the Firearms Department and have no knowledge of certain officers' talents. I have forgotten the amount of times I have been told not to recce a premises, then disregarded the instruction. A close target reconnaissance (CTR) is a skilled tactic, but for a competent operative it shouldn't present a problem. Recces are so important; they ensure the job runs smoothly. An operative can use many guises to complete his recce. A quick drive past the property can sometimes be enough, walking a dog, jogging, dressing as a member of the Gas Board or even strolling by in full police uniform can all do the job.

A recce is generally done in pairs (two heads are better than one). Routes and timings are noted, identification points recorded, notes are made of the presence of dogs, CCTV and security lighting. Points of entry are scrutinised to ensure the correct entry equipment is used. The structure of the property and the layout of the floors are considered. As much detail as possible must be recorded. In my early days of reconnaissance, I relied on memorising everything until I could get to a safe place and sketch it down. Later on, with the introduction of camcorders and other technical kit, information could be pinpoint precise.

Foz and I spent vital hours reconnoitring White House Farm. At one stage we even blagged some telecom engineers' equipment and vehicle and spent time at the top of a telegraph pole observing the front aspect of the property. The squad had informed Foz that an ideal entry point was the large wooden door at the rear. We spent some time in the fields observing this aperture and, when it was safe to do so, got a lot closer, only to find it was protected by steel mesh. The property was a large detached farm in its own grounds. It had three levels and approximately 15 rooms. Several detached stone and wooden barns flanked the farm and appeared to be occupied. From our recce, we decided that the most suitable entry point would have to be the front door.

My thoughts were broken by the sound of a loud fart. I looked around and although I already suspected the culprit, Riggers whispered that he had wind. The rest of the lads were giggling quietly. I looked at Riggers and scowled.

'Keep fucking quiet.'

I indicated for the team to move off and we continued moving through the field towards the black aspect. I would lead the team to the rear of the property. Once they were in the grounds they would split up and contain the outbuildings, while five of us would assist with entry. Fortunately I had taken this route several times over the last couple of days. I estimated we had another 15 minutes to go before we reached the farm.

Ahead of me I spotted movement and screwed my eyes in the low light, trying to identify what I could see. As I moved on, the movement ahead became more noticeable and I dropped to one knee, covering with my MP5. The rest of the lads dropped into a kneeling stance and started to cover alternative fields of fire.

'What is it?' Riggers whispered into my ear.

'Fuck knows, but it's coming closer.'

'It's a herd of cows,' exclaimed Riggers.

He had correctly identified a herd of cows making their way towards us. The majority of us had been trained for policing in an urban environment, and although we had rural training, none of us knew how to handle a mass of bovines.

I stood up and made the sign for moving off. I had decided to walk right through the cattle, which were blocking our route. I hoped they would move. As I approached, however, I'm not sure whether it was my imagination or not but they appeared to bunch up even closer and continued towards us. Within seconds the 15 of us were surrounded by the cows and they started to close in on us. We obviously couldn't shout to scare them off, so we pushed them. Riggers also tried a unique farming trick of gobbing on them. Surprisingly this didn't work either.

I can't say I was frightened but I was certainly concerned when they started to almost herd us and even worse started to gently crush us. I hit one of the creatures in the centre of its head with the muzzle of my MP5 barrel hoping to startle it away but it wasn't fazed and just stared at me. I noticed a barbed wire fence to our right and indicated to the team to head there. Eventually we extricated ourselves from the cows and climbed over the fence.

It was obvious we couldn't get past the cows, so we would have to detour. This would throw our timings out. I had reccied the field on a couple of occasions and each time there had been no evidence of cows. Sod's Law had stepped in and we were now behind time. I indicated we would quicken the pace and off we set, moving quicker than I really wanted.

'Hello Andy, this is Foz. Hello Andy, this is Foz.'

'Go ahead Foz.'

'ETA to FAP.'

Foz was leading the rest of the team, including AFOs from the airport who had been requested to supplement our numbers due to the large area that needed to be contained. Foz was entering the front aspect of the property on a different route to us. It was important that we all arrive at the same time. I could now just make out the silhouette of the farm in the grey light.

'Four minutes,' I gasped and quickened the pace.

It was hard going, running through fields over uneven ground in poor light. Our FAP was the meshed wire fencing around the farm. Before reaching the fence, I indicated a stop. The lads knew what to do and we dropped into the prone position and crawled the last 75 yards towards the fence. I smelled something sweet and sticky and realised we were crawling through recently deposited cowpats.

'Hello Foz, this is Andy.'

'Go ahead.'

'FAP and ready.'

My team were at the mesh fencing. Because it was almost eight foot high, we had decided to cut through it with industrial bolt croppers. If the property had listening spikes, this would probably be the time we would activate them. It was crucial that Foz and his team were in place to respond in case we alerted the suspects. Foz had held off from his FAP, the front door, until he knew we were in place. We now waited until he deployed the rest of his team and made his FAP. It took several minutes before I started to hear the following reports.

'Red team FAP and ready.'

'Green team FAP and ready.'

'White team FAP and ready.'

All teams were in position.

'All teams standby,' Foz relayed. 'Strike! Strike! Strike!'

A couple of the lads off my team started to cut through the steel fence. It was like a knife through butter. Holes were quickly kicked into the fence and the rest of the team fanned out and supplemented other containment teams. They would search outbuildings and barns after the farm had been searched. Four of my team and I legged it round to the front of the property at the precise moment the MOE men shattered the front door.

Ian had been brought out of retirement from UT9 for this job and was number one on the search team. In his usual effective way he had gained ground immediately and was requesting ballistic shields. I joined the entry team, who were not too pleased with my smell, and saw that Ian had moved into the farmhouse. He faced a large set of stairs and two corridors, left and right, leading to further rooms. His experienced assessment dictated that ballistic shields were required to cover areas of fire. The lads were forcing shields into the property and effectively plugging holes.

'Stand still – armed police,' I heard Ian scream. 'Stand still – armed police.'

A man and woman, both in dressing gowns and in their late forties, were at the top of the stairs. The man, with the woman in front of him, was shouting, 'It's all right lads, it's all right.' He was clutching something in his right hand. As I looked more closely it appeared to be banknotes.

'Keep your hands where I can see them and make your way towards me,' Ian shouted.

The man, preceded by the woman, made his way down towards us. 'It's OK lads, look.' It was clear he was trying to bribe us. He was clutching a wad of £50 notes in his right hand. One of the team grabbed the woman and she was ferried to the rear of the team and dealt with. The man, who by now looked very worried, was grabbed. He screamed and fell, releasing the notes in a cloud of paper. It was clearly more than a month's salary of the whole entry team put together.

Ian stepped over him and continued with the ascent of the stairs. He held upstairs while I took a team and cleared downstairs. Foz continued to coordinate the search by the use of radio, deploying teams to enter and clear when he deemed necessary.

It took about an hour to effectively search and neutralise the property of any threat, before evidential search teams could continue with their duties. We had managed to arrest one of the suspects and the two sons were arrested later that day at their work premises. This had turned out to be a good job, particularly for Foz, who had spent a great deal of time and effort in planning it.

Although successful, the job had a sour side. When the search teams had finished, they found a great amount of evidence in relation to certain police officers from Stockport who were apparently being paid by the suspect and his associates for vital information on police activities and movements.

* * *

Some days later, I was sat in the crew room with a few of the lads when I took a phone call.

'Oh, I'm glad it's you that's answered,' said the voice on the other end.

'Who's that?'

It was one of the new inspectors who had joined the department from TAG, a man I neither liked nor respected.

'Do you want to come and see me?' he said.

'What about?'

'Your transfer back to division.'

At first I thought he was joking but he didn't have a sense of humour.

'Say that again.'

'You are being transferred back to division in November.'

I put the phone down on him and tried to digest what he had said. It was the end of September and I had been informed I was returning to division in four weeks. Mick looked across and asked what was up. I smiled and told him. He looked as stunned as me.

'That's not right,' he said. He had also been told by the chief inspector that I wasn't going to be tenured.

I rang Clayton Brook and asked to speak to the chief inspector. They said he was on leave for two weeks. I requested a meeting with any of the inspectors, and it was arranged for the following day. Mick and I met the inspector who had been on the phone and another I had known for years and who I felt was more suited for community contact than firearms. Some would say he was a nice bloke; I had actually seen Ian take his revolver off him and load it for him because he was so nervous on a job.

They informed me that it was the chief inspector's decision and I was going to be transferred back to Ashton-under-Lyne, the G Division, on November 27. I started to protest and tell them what the chief inspector had said. I soon realised that I was wasting my time. I lost my temper and in no uncertain terms told them what I thought of them. The pair of them were crapping themselves. I asked for one thing, a request to see the chief inspector before I was transferred. I was truly gutted. For the last nine years I had given the department 200 per cent effort.

It may sound conceited, but I had made a difference, at times on my own. I had developed new tactics and, with my colleagues, had arrested some of Manchester's most notorious criminals. Even with my worst injuries, I hardly ever went sick. OK, I didn't suffer fools gladly, but firearms isn't a place for those type of people.

I felt betrayed. If the chief inspector had said, 'Listen, I have no option but to tenure you,' I wouldn't have been happy but I would have accepted it. What I found hard to accept was this deceitful way of invoking tenure.

CHAPTER TWENTY-ONE

Gory Detail

On November 27, 1995, I returned to Ashton-under-Lyne and stood in the parade room where some 15 years before I had started my first day as a police officer. I felt like a fish out of water. I knew how to arrest armed criminals but I didn't have a clue about mainstream policing.

I had requested a course on PACE but had been refused. I had requested a course on how to use the new computer systems on recording crime but had been refused. I had been in the middle of an argument between the G Division and the X Department over who was going to finance the supply of my uniform. I was extremely pissed off.

Fortunately my section at Ashton was a good young crew and nearly all keen police officers. My inspector and patrol sergeants were excellent and helped me settle in. But no matter how smooth they made my transition, there was still no easy way to learn. All the paperwork and procedures had changed and it took me hours just to book in a prisoner. I was unhappy and frustrated. One minute I was locking up hardcore criminals, the next I was outside a shop in the pissing rain waiting for a key holder to attend because the alarm was ringing. I had done this all before. Now, because I hadn't taken a promotional exam but had tried to further myself in a specialised department, I felt as though I was being punished.

Because I had retained a hostage rescue status, I was still regularly attending firearms training at the range complex at

Clayton Brook. I still had to qualify in the SLP – now the Glock 17 – the MP5, the Remington tactical shotgun and the H&K 53. This created another problem for the division, who were reluctant to release me. Eventually an assistant chief constable's order put paid to the division's objections. I was also not fit. I hadn't wanted to admit it, but the fall at the NatWest Bank in Salford over a year earlier had hurt me more than I let on. I was having problems with mobility, particularly in my lower back. If I reached out or strode out, a shooting pain would hit me in the centre of the back and travel down towards my heels. It was excruciating. I should have gone sick and sought medical advice but I felt it would be a cop out. My pride said I had to conquer my time on division.

To be able to re-apply for specialised duties, I had to complete 12 months on a division. I was determined to do this without going on the sick. Eventually I started to settle down and stop sulking. I was working with an excellent young officer on the divisional van, Roger, a credit to the service. He was fit, keen and motivated. He wanted to become a dog-handler and had just completed an advanced driving course. If he was driving and we got an emergency shout, he didn't need any encouragement to put the blues and sirens on and rip shit about the division, scaring me to death.

One Tuesday morning in April we were working the van together. We had just had yet another report of a serial flasher in Ashton bus station. I was pretty sure who was exposing himself to schoolgirls. The cunning cop in me thought that if I drove to this scrote's flat and he was not there, the chances are he would be in the town centre. If the description fitted, then I had him. Roger good-naturedly went along with this complex theory. My best skills of policing were rubbished – the scrote was home and it looked like he had been there since the previous day.

Roger smiled and said, 'We have just had a radio message to ring comms.'

We jumped into the van and I drove to a public phone box. Roger radioed in the number and soon received a call.

'What was it?' I asked as Roger got in and shut the door.

'We have to go to 88 Stockport Road, park outside the front and wait for some woman to identify herself. She's collecting some furniture from the property. She used to live there with her ex-husband but they are splitting up.'

'So our role is to prevent a breach of the peace if the husband gets nasty?'

'That's it,' said Roger.

We arrived there at about 09.30. It was a shitty-looking shop with grilles on the ground window and a dirty old door signed Jeff's Video and TV Repair Shop. It was a terraced property in the centre of a row of shops, all in need of a lick of paint and a clean-up.

Roger and I were chatting away when we saw a male, wearing a horrible lime green shirt and with a mop of curly black hair, sprint out of a junction 50 yards in front of us. He slid to a halt, saw our police van and ran towards us. His face was ashen and his eyes bulging. He stuck his head through my window, which fortunately was open, and started babbling.

'It's horrible, it's horrible, come quick, please come quick!'

Then he ran off in the direction he had come from. I started the van and followed. He ran to the rear of 88 Stockport Road, towards a light blue Transit box van. There was another man beside it looking equally shocked. There was also a small grey hatchback with both its doors open. As we got out and walked over to the scene, a smart young Asian lad ran up to me.

'It's fuckin' horrible man, there was loads of screams and now it's gone quiet.' He was obviously very shaken.

'Calm down and try to tell me what happened.'

The two lads from the box van ran over and between the three of them, Roger and I worked out what had happened. The grey hatchback belonged to two sisters, one of whom was married to the occupant of 88 Stockport Road, Jeff Gough. The other sister was disabled and walked with the aid of crutches. The two lads with the van were the furniture removal men. The Asian lad was a neighbour and had witnessed what had happened.

The two ladies and the removal men had turned up at the rear of the property and decided not to wait for the police. Liz Thorn, wife of Gough, knocked on the back door, accompanied by the removal men. Gough had come to the door and let Liz in but told the men to wait. Liz's sister Clementine, walking on crutches, then hammered on the door, telling the removal men she shouldn't be in there on her own. Gough opened the door and allowed her in. Then the witnesses heard horrendous screaming.

I went to the back door and started knocking. Roger clocked a male figure in the upstairs window, watching us, and shouted for him to come down and open up. The door was locked. I top-and-tailed the door, stepped back and kicked it. It was poorly constructed and the lock casement soon splintered and the door swung open. Out bolted two large Alsatian dogs, almost making me fall backwards. Their ears were pinned back and their tails were between their legs. Something had terrified them.

I took out my side-handle baton and stepped inside. Automatically I resorted to my firearms training and stepped left – and did the splits. My left leg shot out, sending a shooting pain into my back and arse; I had slipped in a pool of blood. I took in the scene. Both Roger and I had stepped into the kitchen. It was pretty unhygienic, but to make matters worse it was like a butcher's shop. Blood was splattered over the walls and dripping from the ceiling. Directly in front of me in the right-hand corner of the room lay a woman, on her back with crutches by her side. Roger made his way to her.

'She's dead, Andy.'

It was pretty obvious; she had almost been decapitated. Her head was connected to her neck by a sliver of sinew and she was leaking blood all over the kitchen lino. I made a quick decision.

'Roger, get back to the van and get the shields.'

Most police vans are now equipped with round plastic riot shields. I checked the kitchen while I waited for Roger, but I was concerned about the other woman. I moved to the stairway opposite the dead body and examined them. Blood was splattered across the walls and stairs.

I looked up the stairs and saw Gough at the top, holding a machete in his right hand. He was silhouetted against the back wall.

'Get down here,' I shouted.

He stared at me.

'Get the fuck down here!'

My pounding heart was almost breaking my chest. All I had was a bit of plastic tubing. Six months ago, I would have had an arsenal of weaponry to rely on; now I had a PR24 baton. Fuck it. I made my decision and started to sprint up the stairs. I had a duty to try to help Liz but already had a bad feeling about her.

Gough stood his ground. I raised my PR24 and slowly he walked away from the top of the stairs. For a second I lost sight of him and then I hit the top of the stairs and turned right. I had stepped into a living area, furnished with a green settee, a television in the corner and cupboards in the other corners. The place was a charnel house. Blood dripped from the walls. To add to the macabre scene, a pet parrot had somehow escaped from its cage and was flying around the room. Liz lay on the settee, facing upwards. I grabbed Gough and struck him once with the PR24; he dropped the machete. I placed him on his knees and cuffed his hands behind his back.

I heard Roger legging it up the stairs.

'No point, mate,' I shouted. 'Can you secure downstairs?'

There was no need for Roger to step into the crime scene upstairs. I checked Liz on the settee. She was in the same condition as Clementine, virtually decapitated.

Within minutes my supervision had turned up and shouted did I require anything.

'Just Phoraid,' I shouted back. Phoraid is a strong disinfectant; I was covered from head to toe with blood and gore.

I went over to Gough and examined his wrists. He had a large wound on one of them with sinews poking out. I told him he was being arrested on suspicion of murder and cautioned him.

Eventually the paramedics arrived and pronounced both women dead. At the same time the CID turned up. The DI in charge was Stan Egerton, who later dealt with the Harold Shipman enquiry. He was obviously as vague as me in regard to PACE, as he handed me a piece of A4 paper and told me to write down anything Gough said. In accordance with PACE, I was not supposed to interview Gough once I had cautioned him. If I did, it would start what is known as the 'PACE clock', and was contrary to good practice. I didn't know this and rambled on with Gough about why he had killed them, jotting down his replies. Eventually the scene was secured and Gough was transported to Ashton Police Station.

Some weeks later, Roger and I were summoned to see the chief superintendent in charge of the division. This would be an ideal time for me to apply for a specialist post. A position on firearms training had become available and also a position with the Special Branch surveillance team. I decided to apply for both but I needed the chief superintendent's endorsement.

He thanked me for a job well done and I cheekily asked him to endorse my application. 'No problem,' was his reply. Within ten months I had left G Division for a second time. In August 1996 I transferred to UT9, the force's Firearms Training Unit, as an instructor.

At about the same time, Roger and I were summoned to Manchester Crown Court. Gough had decided to plead not guilty. After a confusing day of legal argument, he changed his plea to guilty and was sentenced to life imprisonment.

As Roger and I listened to the judge summing up, Roger leant over to me and whispered, 'I bet we will get a judge's commendation for this.' I wasn't so sure but nodded. My suspicions were confirmed when the DCI in charge of the case was called to the judge's chambers. After half an hour he returned with a sheepish look and walked over to me.

'The judge would like you bollocked, and also Mr Egerton, for your lack of legal knowledge in relation to PACE,' he said. I looked at the DCI hard but he just shrugged.

Fuck it, I thought. I will just add that bollocking to one of my many in the police service. Roger wasn't as philosophical and felt cheated but I suppose the judge had a point. If Gough's guilt had not been so clear I could have cocked things up with my lack of procedure and maybe the suspect would have escaped justice through a technical error. It shows you how fickle the system can be.

* * *

This was not the happiest period of my career. I was stationed at Clayton Brook, a superb, indoor, 100-metre shooting range with eight lanes. It also has a 180 degree range with a turning target system as well as computer enhanced training rooms and enough teaching areas to facilitate the force's AFOs.

At the same period as my transfer, GMP implemented a full ARV system with four vehicles covering the force 24 hours a day. This increased the Firearms Department by another 60 officers.

The majority of these officers had to be put through basic firearms courses before MP5 courses and then an ARV course. I was shocked at the standards. Fitness wasn't a requirement and classification shoots were made easier by lowering them to a 70 per cent pass rate. Eventually you had to be blind to fail a shoot and I really don't think this would have prevented some of them becoming AFOs.

Standards were lowered to allow for the massive increase within the department. Some who came through the system would, with time, become good firearms officers. Others were diabolical. It was such a shame that after all the years my colleagues and I had striven for excellence, we had to watch this slow erosion of good standards. I saw experienced team members become increasingly frustrated by the supplementation of teams with sub-standard AFOs.

I was given the remit to create a ten-day ARV course. It was to include tactics for vehicle stops and foot drills and I was to create tactical shoots for the officers. I spent four months delivering these courses. Eventually most of the ARV officers were trained and I was given the tactical training for the operational teams.

During this period I attended West Mercia National Firearms School and passed their instructors' hostage rescue course. This allowed me to teach at national level. I spent many months with the tactical teams, creating shoots and operational exercises. It was a very frustrating period. I was starting to see officers on the teams who had joined the department only 12 months earlier and was having to teach them advanced tactics that were beyond their comprehension. Many failed either tactics or shoots or both.

In time some of the new members may have been OK but they lacked a critical element of what makes a good firearms officer – experience. Some were keen to learn, others were arrogant buffoons who should never have carried a firearm. It saddened me greatly to watch the erosion of hard-fought-for standards.

In the spring of 1999, I ran a four-week hostage rescue course with some very experienced instructors. The course was for 16 officers and was pass or fail. After an intensive four weeks of tactics and shoots, only two managed to pass. Yet it was no more difficult than any of the three courses I undertook. The majority of those officers are now on GMP's tactical teams.

As this book goes to print, God help anyone who is taken hostage in GMP. They do not have an effective response, though with the assistance of certain disillusioned PCs and sergeants, the force would manage to cobble together at least an attempt at a rescue. Although I believe an abseil option for entry for extraction purposes should be part of the hostage rescue team criteria, I shudder at GMP's option. They are taught rope access tactics ideal for mountain rescue but pure bollocks for an operational team. It frightens me to see the extent to which the teams' standards have dropped. I believe much of this is due to senior officers from the X Department who have little experience in live firearms operations.

* * *

On a lighter note, one of my more patriotic moments came when I gave a shooting display in front of the Queen. The Clayton Brook complex was officially opened by Her Majesty and Prince Philip. It was a great day of splendour and pageant. The extinct police band was brought out of mothballs and every senior officer who could arrived at the range. My great moment came when the Queen and Prince Philip observed me from a secure area demonstrating my sense-of-direction shooting skills on multiple turning targets. 'One hundred per cent and *marvellous* shooting,' said Her Majesty – I wish! It should have been marvellous too, as I spent hours practising.

I served for 22 years in the Greater Manchester Police Force. Apart from my last couple of years, I enjoyed every moment. I was excited about going to work. I was privileged to work with some fantastic officers and to be involved in some of GMP's major operations.

It's a pity the service attracts officers with a different motivation and work ethic. Who knows, perhaps I'm wrong and my passion was misdirected. I have only touched the surface on what I experienced and I am not unique within officers in GMP and around the country. I have tried to write about my experiences from my own honest viewpoint. Unfortunately my injuries caught up with me. I found it impossible to operate physically at my previous level, and began to see myself as a liability. So in June 2000, I retired from the police service.

After leaving, I was offered a partnership in a company that had started to venture into private security. It was owned by two former colleagues, one I had served with in the Firearms Department and the other a senior officer. Although at times my injuries have hindered me, through struggle, research and hard work we have built a business that already had solid foundations into a reputable and ever-growing company advancing personal safety and security in the work place. I have also worked protecting certain celebrities, given tactical advice to film companies and taught many organisations in personal safety techniques.

On one occasion we applied for an important local authority contract and our background was investigated by a private agency to assess if we were suitable. After researching my CV, they expressed strong scepticism that a former officer could have taken part in so many courses and operations in a police career. Well, I was not unique. Any officer who served in GMP or another large urban force during the same period and who was attached to any of the various operational departments will have a similar, if not more extensive, CV. Yes, I did it all, and a lot more besides.

It was a great time and I have no regrets.